THE

BOOK

OF

TAPAS

THE

**SIMONE
& INÉS
ORTEGA**

BOOK
OF
TAPAS

WHAT

JOSÉ

IS

ANDRÉS

TAPAS?

When I was asked to write the preface for *The Book of Tapas*, I didn't hesitate. To be associated with Simone and Inés Ortega is a huge honor for me. I can't over-emphasize the importance of the Ortegas' books in Spain, and their cultural significance. When I was growing up in Barcelona it seemed that just about everyone had a copy of *1080 Recetas* (published by Phaidon in English as *1080 Recipes*) in their kitchen. It was the equivalent of *The Joy of Cooking* or *Il cucchiaio d'argento (The Silver Spoon)* for Spain. New brides received one when they married, and the well-thumbed books were given pride of place in the kitchen.

That is not to say that *1080 Recetas* was simply a bestseller. It arrived at a key moment when Spanish cooking began to be about more than subsistence and survival, when people no longer had to stretch their food as far as they could. At the moment *1080 Recetas* was published, things were becoming more prosperous, people had more economic optimism, and one of the ways they expressed this was in their kitchen. People were beginning to look at food as something pleasurable, as a way to entertain, or as a hobby, and the Ortegas' book helped them make this transition.

In this new book we explore the world of tapas, those little plates of this and that, which are enjoyed in bars all over Spain and have become a craze around the world, and which you can now make easily at home. Along with paella and sangria, tapas are perhaps Spain's best-known contribution to the world of food and cooking.

I probably should explain at the beginning that I am not a hard-liner when it comes to tapas. I define tapas more as a style of eating than as particular recipes. They are an informal way of sharing small dishes. With that in mind, almost anything could be a tapa as long as the portion is small. Garbanzo beans (chickpeas) with spinach served in big bowls is not a tapa. But put those garbanzos on a small plate and it is a tapa. A large traditional *tortilla de patatas*, or potato tortilla, is not a tapa. But if you cut it into small squares or even make a smaller one, the tortilla can be a tapa.

The main appeal of tapas, I think, is that they offer such an informal, fun and social style of eating. You meet your friends. You chat. You have a glass of wine and order a few little plates. You share and you sample a little of everything. Maybe you don't even sit down, but lean against the bar instead. If you are not terribly hungry you order one or two items. If you are hungry, you order more. The point is that you are not locked into a formal meal structure with a large entrée (main course). You get a chance to tailor the meal to your appetite. If you can't make up your mind, you get a chance to sample a lot of different dishes, which is great when you want to be adventurous and try something new. There is very little commitment involved in sampling a new tapa. You don't like the snails? Well, just don't order them next time.

People have embraced the charming style of eating that tapas offer, and today you find tapas-style restaurants in cities all over the world. Although this was not always the case—when my partners and I opened Jaleo restaurant nearly twenty years ago in Washington, DC I must confess I was a little skeptical about its potential for success. My limited experience in America had shown me that most diners were unfamiliar with Spain and its gastronomy. And perhaps it was my accent, but when I told people I was a chef at a tapas bar, they always thought I meant a topless bar! It certainly created some interesting misunderstandings. Almost two decades later I am happy to report that I was wrong. Diners enthusiastically embraced tapas and a whole generation of Washingtonians has grown up eating *croquetas* (croquettes), *patatas bravas* (potatoes with spicy sauce) and *pan con tomate* (bread with tomato).

In this book you will find a wealth of tapas recipes, some very traditional and some more modern. My advice to you is take this book and look at it as you would a guidebook when you travel. You are about to take a journey into the world of tapas. Build yourself a menu of lots of different flavors, some hot and some cold, look for a balance, pour some good Spanish wine, or maybe make a sangria, and invite your friends over for a tapas party.

TAPAS
IN
SPAIN

INÉS

ORTEGA

Tapas originated in Andalusia, southern Spain, but they are now common all over the country. Originally, a small, free tapa was served with drinks in bars, and it was often a piece of sliced cold meat such as cured ham or chorizo, or a piece of cheese. According to culinary legend, these tapas were used to cover wine glasses to keep the aroma in and to keep the flies and insects out. The word *tapa* originally meant "cover," a reference to this practice. Nowadays, however, tapas can also be small portions of any of the dishes that make up Spain's wide and varied cuisine. For example, it is common to find paella being served in small portions as a tapa.

It is difficult to define tapas precisely: they can be hot or cold, eaten with the fingers or served with a fork and a piece of bread. Even Spaniards are not all in agreement: in the Basque Country, tapas are known as *pinxtos*. In other parts of Spain, *pinchos* are a type of tapas consisting of small pieces of bread on which different toppings are held in place with a toothpick (cocktail stick). They are eaten without cutlery, in the same way as Serrano ham, olives or fried squid, while other tapas such as stuffed peppers or small cuttlefish are eaten with a fork. Deep-fried dishes—and it has to be acknowledged that the Spanish do them better than anyone, especially in Andalusia—homemade rice dishes, stews, braised meat dishes such as delicious *albóndigas* (meatballs), chopped meat and vegetables, fish, eggs, kidneys: all of these can be served as tapas. And nothing goes better with a glass of good wine, or a nice cold beer.

The bars in which tapas are served also vary widely, from the simplest taverns to the most fashionable and sophisticated venues. Many bars have the tapas and *pinchos* displayed on the counter, so customers can easily see what is on offer. Alternatively, the waiter may recite a list of what is available, almost like a poem, or will bring a menu.

In Spain we like to eat late, so it is no wonder that a custom has developed for having an aperitif with a snack alongside it to keep hunger at bay. In addition, going to a bar for a glass of wine and some tapas is a social ritual that gives people an opportunity for conversation with others. The time period for eating tapas can begin at midday and go on until 3:00 pm, and in the evening it typically starts at 7:00 pm and lasts until 10:00 pm. Often people do not stay in just one place, but move from bar to bar enjoying the specialties served in each one. On vacations and special occasions, this ritual can take place over an even longer period, with each person buying a round of drinks in turn.

Tapas are not only common in bars—at home, when guests arrive, it is common to serve a small homemade tapa or something to nibble before sitting down to the meal, even if it is something as simple as marinated olives or potato chips (crisps). This book shows how easy tapas are to prepare at home.

What we Spaniards love about tapas is the philosophy of life they represent. I believe our climate, the sun, our wine and our character help to elevate the ritual of tapas into a moment of pure delight. It is an unhurried, enjoyable and sociable time, and involves being in good company and catching up with friends, discussing business or even politics. This leaves us ready to go home with a much happier heart, and often ready for a siesta if the tapas have been plentiful.

When you taste tapas in other countries, as I have done many times on my travels abroad, you will constantly be reminded of one of the most appetizing aspects of Spanish life. It is wonderful to see the number of tapas bars that are opening all over the world.

I wholeheartedly recommend that you try the recipes in *The Book of Tapas,* and take inspiration from Spanish tapas culture. You will be thankful for the advice!

ABOCADO A wine from Jerez in southern Spain, which contains a mixture of sweet and dry wines.

ACEITUNA An olive, which can be green, black or purple. There are many varieties, such as the *manzanilla* or Spanish olive, which is small, the *corval* or large olive, which is longer, and the *zorraleña*, which is small and round.

ADOBAR To marinate, pickle or cure by placing food into a liquid preparation to preserve or flavor it.

AJILLO A method for preparing certain dishes such as shrimp (prawns), clams and elvers, in which chopped garlic is fried in olive oil for a few minutes with parsley, pepper and salt, and sometimes chile.

ALBÓNDIGAS Balls of finely chopped meat or fish bound with egg, spices and bread crumbs. Once the balls are formed they are coated in flour, fried, and then served in a sauce or with fried parsley and sometimes mustard. In Andalusia they are also called *almóndigas* or *almondiguillas*.

ALIÑAR To dress or to season food so that it has more flavor.

BOQUERONES The name given to anchovies when they are prepared to be tinned or conserved in brine. Those from the towns of Santoña, La Escala and La Victoria are particularly famous.

AÑADA The year of the grape harvest used to make wine. Wines from Jerez do not have a vintage as the wine is produced using the solera system, in which wines from different vintages are blended together.

AÑEJO Wine which is more than two years old and has been aged in a barrel or bottle.

ANGULAS Elvers, or young eels, highly valued in gastronomy. They are particularly popular in the Basque Country.

APERITIVO The drinks served before a meal, including sherry, port or vermouth, and the little snacks served with them, such as olives, potato chips (crisps), and so on.

BANDERILLAS Snacks speared onto toothpicks (cocktail sticks) and served as appetizers. The name comes from a spear used in bullfighting.

BOCADITOS Savory preparations served as appetizers, such as croquettes, or tiny fried fish.

BRINDAR To drink a toast to the health of others.

BUTIFARRA A sausage made from chopped pork seasoned with several ingredients and spices. In Spain, those produced in Catalonia are famous, and they are eaten raw, baked or fried. There are several different varieties.

CABRALES A blue cheese from the northern Spanish principality of Asturias. It is most often made with cow's milk, but may also be made with sheep's or goat's milk. Roquefort cheese is a good substitute.

CAÑA A type of narrow glass which holds the equivalent of a small wine glass or sherry glass. They are typical in Andalusia, especially in Seville and Cádiz. The name is also used for beer on tap.

CATAVINOS A special sampling ladle used for testing wines from the barrel or from large earthenware jars.

CAZUELA A wide, shallow dish used for cooking and serving, which can be earthenware, aluminum or steel. The name is also given to the dishes served in this receptacle.

CHANQUETE Whitebait, a small fish which resembles a small anchovy. Those from Málaga are the most famous. Often fried in olive oil.

CHIPIRONES Small cuttlefish which are usually served in their ink, fried, in sauce or stuffed.

CHIQUITO A small quantity of wine, and also the name given to special small wine glasses.

CHISTORRA A spicy sausage originally produced in Navarra and the Basque Country, although today it can be found almost anywhere. It is usually served fried as an appetizer or as an accompaniment with eggs, stews or vegetables.

CHOPITOS Young squid, which are generally fried and eaten whole.

COPA A special receptacle for drinking, made from crystal, glass or metal. There are Champagne glasses for Cava, balloon glasses for liqueurs, Martini glasses, and so on, and they come in different sizes. The expression "Let's go out for a *copa*" is used when going out for some drinks.

EMPANADA A pasty or pie made from a filling covered in bread dough, pastry or puff pastry and cooked in the oven. They originate in the regions of Galicia and Asturias.

EMPANADILLA Little pastries or pies, similar to empanadas, which can be filled with meat, tuna, hard-boiled eggs, and so on.

ESCABECHAR To pickle food in a mixture comprising vegetables, aromatic herbs, spices, and wine or vinegar. The method can be used for fowl, game and fish. Pickling food keeps it edible for longer.

FINO A type of dry sherry, golden in color, between 15 and 17% proof. It is suitable to serve as an aperitif as it does not affect the palate before a meal.

FRITADA A collection of fried foods.

GARRAFA A vessel or demijohn for storing wine or cool drinks. Sometimes a drink such as whiskey or gin is said to be from a *garrafa* when it is suspected that it has been adulterated.

GUINDILLA A small, very hot chile pepper, used to season dishes such as garlic shrimp (prawns) or elvers.

IDIAZÁBAL A hard Spanish cheese made from sheep's milk. It has a slightly smoky flavor. Manchego or other full-flavored hard cheeses can be substituted.

MAJAR To crush or break down food in a mortar.

MORCILLA A type of blood sausage (black pudding) typical of Asturias in northern Spain. There are several different varieties with different flavorings, such as onion or paprika.

PADRÓN PEPPERS Small, green hot bell peppers from the town of Padrón in Galicia, northwest Spain. They are a typical tapa when fried in olive oil and sprinkled with salt.

PALILLO A small wooden toothpick (cocktail stick) used to hold the ingredients on a piece of bread in place, to attach them to each other, or to spear food.

PELEÓN Meaning "rough" or "cheap", this term is used to refer to an average-quality wine that has been adulterated, sometimes by the addition of water.

PEPITO A steak sandwich made from warm bread with a fried fillet of beef inside.

PIJOTA Young hake, generally served fried or sometimes in sauce.

PINCHOS Little brochettes or skewers, a type of bar snack or appetizer and another word for tapas.

PISCOLABIS A light snack or meal, which could be a selection of *pinchos*.

RACIÓN A small quantity of food served on a plate or in an individual casserole dish.

REVUELTO Eggs scrambled with other ingredients such as bell peppers or sausages.

SALPICÓN A dish made from chopped meat, fish or vegetables with oil, vinegar, onion, salt and sometimes green bell peppers and tomatoes.

SANGRÍA A refreshing drink made from red wine with brandy or rum and pieces of fresh fruit, lemon and sugar.

TORREZNO A piece of fried bacon sometimes served as an appetizer.

A–Z
OF
SPANISH
INGREDIENTS

ACEITUNAS NEGRAS
BLACK OLIVES

AJO
GARLIC

ALCACHOFAS
ARTICHOKES

ALMEJAS
CLAMS

AZAFRÁN
SAFFRON

ANCHOAS
ANCHOVIES

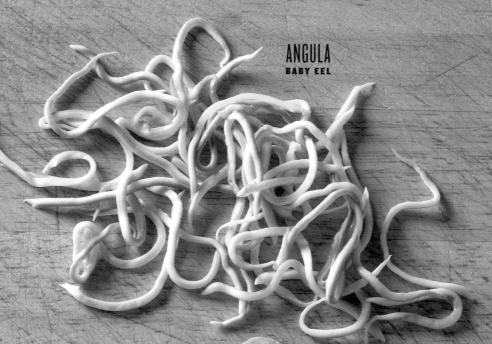

ANGULA
BABY EEL

ATÚN
TUNA

ARROZ
RICE

BOGAVANTE
LOBSTER

BACALAO
SALT COD

BERENJENAS
**EGGPLANTS
(AUBERGINES)**

CALABICINES
ZUCCHINI
(COURGETTES)

BONITO
BONITO

CALABAZA
PUMPKIN

CANGREJO DE RIO
CRAYFISH

CARACOLES
SNAILS

CEBOLLINO
CHIVES

CHAMPIÑONES
MUSHROOMS

CEBOLLAS
ONIONS

CHORIZO
CHORIZO

CIGALA
NORWEGIAN LOBSTER
(LANGOUSTINE)

ESPARRAGOS BLANCOS
WHITE ASPARAGUS

COLIFLOR
CAULIFLOWER

CHIPIRONES
BABY SQUID

CONEJO
RABBIT

GARBANZOS
**GARBANZO BEANS
(CHICKPEAS)**

HABAS
**FAVA (BROAD)
BEANS**

ESPINACAS
SPINACH

GUISANTES
PEAS

GAMBAS
**SHRIMP
(PRAWNS)**

ESPARRAGOS VERDES
GREEN ASPARAGUS

JAMÓN SERRANO
SERRANO HAM

HIGOS
FIGS

HUEVOS DE CODORNIZ
QUAILS' EGGS

JEREZ
SHERRY

JUDÍAS BLANCAS
NAVY (HARICOT)
BEANS

HUEVOS
EGGS

LECHUGAS
LETTUCE

JUDÍAS VERDES
GREEN BEANS

LIMÓN
LEMON

LANGOSTINOS
JUMBO SHRIMP
(KING PRAWNS)

MEJILLONES
MUSSELS

MELÓN
MELON

MORCILLA
BLOOD SAUSAGE
(BLACK PUDDING)

MENTA
MINT

MIEL
HONEY

NARANJAS
ORANGES

PATATAS
POTATOES

MERLUZA
HAKE

PEREJIL
PARSLEY

PEPILLINOS
**DILL PICKLES
(GHERKINS)**

PIMIENTOS DE PADRÓN
PADRÓN PEPPERS

PEPINO
CUCUMBER

PIMIENTO ROJO
RED BELL PEPPER

PIMENTÓN
PAPRIKA

QUESO CABRALES
CABRALES CHEESE

QUESO IDIAZÁBAL
IDIAZÁBAL CHEESE

PULPO
OCTOPUS

PIMIENTOS VERDES
GREEN PEPPERS

PUERROS
LEEKS

PIÑONES
PINE NUTS

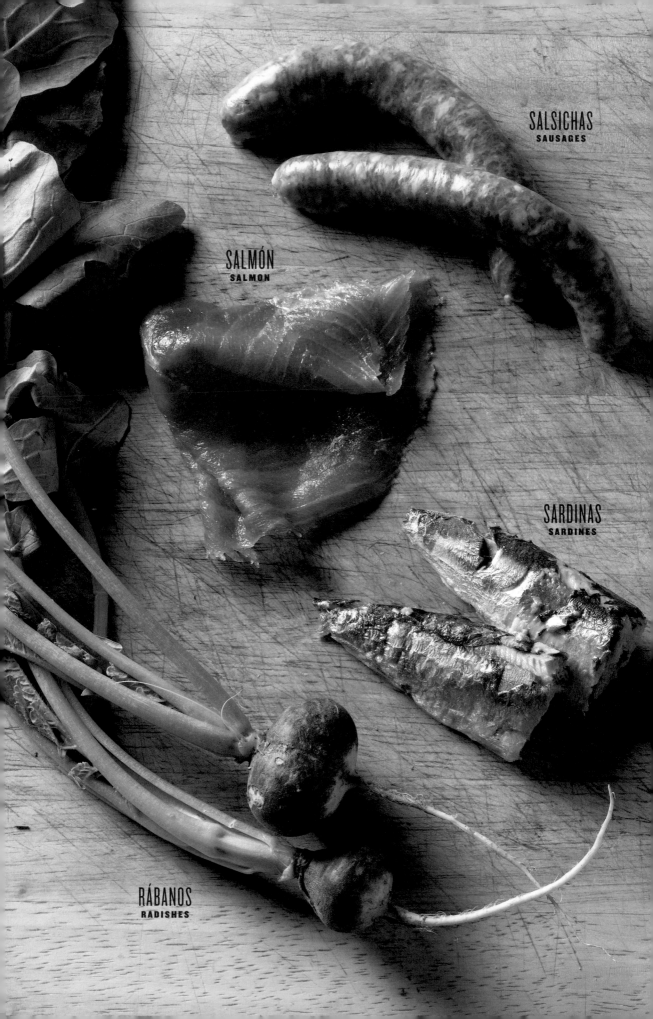

SALSICHAS
SAUSAGES

SALMÓN
SALMON

SARDINAS
SARDINES

RÁBANOS
RADISHES

REQUESÓN
CREAM CHEESE

SETAS
WILD MUSHROOMS

SOBRASADA
SOBRASADA

TOMATES
TOMATOES

TOMILLO
THYME

ZANAHORIAS
CARROTS

VEGETABLE TAPAS

COLD

GARLIC MAYONNAISE

INGREDIENTS

- 3 cloves garlic
- 1–2 egg yolks
- generous 2 cups
  (500 ml/18 fl oz)
  sunflower or olive oil,
  or a combination
- 2 tablespoons white-wine
  vinegar or lemon juice
  Serves 8

Crush the garlic with a little salt to a paste in a mortar. Transfer to a bowl and add the egg yolks. Stir lightly with a whisk and then gradually whisk in the oil, 1–2 teaspoons at a time, until about a quarter has been added. Whisk in the remaining oil in a slow, steady stream to create a thick mayonnaise. Finally, add the vinegar or lemon juice and 1–2 tablespoons warm water, then serve. This garlic mayonnaise can be served with all kinds of cold meat. It also makes a good accompaniment to poached salt cod or a dish of potatoes and vegetables such as artichokes, leeks, turnips or carrots.

WAYS TO DRESS OLIVES

INGREDIENTS

- 1–2 cups (120–240 g/4–8 oz)
  cured black and green olives
- 1 clove garlic, unpeeled
- 1 sprig winter savory
- 1 piece pared lemon zest
- salt
  Serves 6–8

Rinse the olives thoroughly and then pour oil over them to cover. Season with salt to taste, add the garlic, winter savory and lemon zest and leave for a few days until they are ready for eating.

Note: Black olives can be removed from the marinade and eaten as they are or dressed with oil, paprika and finely chopped onion. For an alternative marinade, combine 1–2 cups olives with very finely chopped garlic, a small pinch of cumin, chili powder to taste, ½ teaspoon dried parsley, ½ teaspoon dried thyme, the zest of half a lemon, the zest of half an orange and 2 teaspoons sherry vinegar.

OLIVE CAVIAR

INGREDIENTS

- 1¼ cups (150 g/5 oz) black olives, pitted (stoned)
- 4 canned anchovy fillets in oil, drained
- 1½ tablespoons capers, rinsed
- 2 tablespoons olive oil
- toast or savory crackers, to serve
  Serves 8

Put half the olives, anchovies and capers into a blender or food processor and blend until they form a paste, then remove and set aside. Repeat with the remaining ingredients. Combine both portions of the paste in a bowl, then slowly beat in the oil. Cover with plastic wrap (clingfilm) and store in the refrigerator until ready to use. Serve spread on toast or savory crackers.

Note: This cream will keep for up to a week when stored covered in the refrigerator.

PHOTOGRAPH PAGE 105

OLIVE AND ALMOND TAPA

INGREDIENTS

- 1½ tablespoons (20 g/¾ oz) butter, softened, for spreading
- 1 teaspoon red chili flakes
- 12 black olives, pitted (stoned)
- 12 blanched almonds
- 2 oz (50 g) canned anchovy fillets in oil, drained and halved lengthwise
- 3 slices of bread, each cut into quarters
- finely chopped parsley, to garnish
  Makes 12

Put the butter in a bowl and beat in the chili flakes. Fill the cavity of each olive with an almond, then cut each in half horizontally. Wrap each olive half with an anchovy fillet. Spread the pieces of bread with the butter. Place an olive half in the center of each square of bread. Sprinkle parsley over each tapa.

Note: Cookie cutters in various shapes, such as stars, trees and so on, can also be used to cut the bread.

RICE AND OLIVE SALAD

INGREDIENTS

- generous ¾ cup (200 g/7 oz) dried currants
- 1¾ cups (300 g/11 oz) leftover cooked rice
- generous ¾ cup (100 g/3½ oz) black olives, pitted (stoned) and halved
- generous ¾ cup (100 g/3½ oz) pine nuts
- 2 red tomatoes, peeled, seeded and diced
- 2 cloves garlic, finely chopped
- 1 onion, finely chopped
- 1 roasted or bottled red bell pepper, drained, if necessary, and diced
- 1 tablespoon chopped parsley

FOR THE VINAIGRETTE:

- 2 tablespoons white-wine vinegar
- 6 tablespoons olive oil
- salt

Serves 8

Put the currants in a bowl with water to cover and let soak for 10 minutes. Put the rice into a salad bowl, and add the olives, pine nuts, tomatoes, garlic, onion, and bell pepper. Drain the currants and add them, then toss everything together. Set aside.

To make the vinaigrette, dissolve a pinch of salt in a bowl with the vinegar, then add the oil, whisking until all the ingredients are amalgamated. Pour the vinaigrette over the salad, then let stand in a cool place for 30 minutes. Sprinkle with the parsley just before serving.

ARTICHOKE SALAD WITH ANCHOVY DRESSING

INGREDIENTS
- 1 lemon, halved
- 12 artichokes
- salt and pepper
- 1 tablespoon chopped parsley, to garnish (optional)

FOR THE ANCHOVY VINAIGRETTE:
- 12 canned anchovy fillets, drained, plus a few extra for garnish
- 3 tablespoons red-wine vinegar
- juice of 1½ lemons, strained
- 9 tablespoons olive oil
Serves 8

Fill a bowl with water and squeeze in the juice from one half of the lemon. Cut the stems off the artichokes, trim off the tips of the leaves and remove the hard external leaves, then cut them into quarters lengthwise and scrape out the central hairy choke, if necessary, rubbing each cut side with the remaining lemon half and dropping it into the bowl of water as it is prepared.

Meanwhile, bring a large pan of salted water to a boil. Add the artichokes and when the water returns to a boil, reduce the heat to low, cover the pan and let simmer for 35 minutes, or until tender. Test by pulling off one leaf, which should come off without any resistance. Drain the artichokes well, shaking off any water, then arrange them on a serving platter with the cut sides uppermost.

Meanwhile, to make the vinaigrette, puree the anchovies in a small food processor or blender. Add the vinegar and lemon juice and blend again, then slowly pour in the oil. Pour this over the artichokes and garnish with extra anchovy fillets. Add a sprinkling of parsley, if desired. Serve at room temperature.

PHOTOGRAPH PAGE 106

EGGPLANT (AUBERGINE) SALAD

INGREDIENTS

- 3 eggplants (aubergines), peeled and chopped into large pieces
- 4 tablespoons extra-virgin olive oil
- 1 clove garlic, very finely chopped
- 1 tablespoon chopped fresh oregano, or ½ tablespoon dried
- 1 tablespoon chopped parsley
- juice of 1 lemon, strained
- ½ teaspoon Tabasco sauce, or to taste
- 2 large tomatoes, cut into wedges
- salt and pepper
- black olives, to garnish

Serves 8–10

Bring a pan of salted water to a boil. Add the eggplants and cook for 14 minutes, or until they are tender but not overcooked and falling apart. Drain well and pat dry with a clean dish towel.

Meanwhile, beat the oil, garlic, herbs, lemon juice and Tabasco sauce together in a large serving bowl with a fork, then season with salt and pepper. Add the eggplants and tomatoes and mix everything together so the vegetables are covered with the dressing. Cover and chill until required. Garnish with black olives just before serving.

Note: This dish should be prepared well in advance so it can be served chilled.

EGGPLANT (AUBERGINE) CAVIAR

INGREDIENTS

- 1 lb 2 oz (500 g) eggplants (aubergines)
- olive oil, for brushing
- 1 lb 2 oz (500 g) tomatoes, seeded and finely diced
- 4 canned anchovy fillets in oil, drained and finely chopped
- 1 small onion, finely chopped
- 1 tablespoon chopped parsley
- 1 tablespoon chopped chives
- generous ½ cup (100 ml/ 3½ fl oz) single (light) cream
- salt and pepper
- bread slices, quartered and toasted, to serve

Serves 8–10

Preheat the oven to 425°F (220°C/GAS MARK 7). With the exception of the eggplants, keep all the ingredients in the coldest part of the refrigerator so they are well chilled and almost frozen, when needed. Cut the eggplants in half lengthwise and brush them with oil, then cook them in the oven for 20–30 minutes, or until the flesh can easily be removed with a spoon.

Remove them from the oven and, when they are cool enough to handle, cut the flesh into little cubes. Put the eggplants in a large bowl, then add the tomatoes, anchovies, onion, parsley and chives. Return the mixture to the refrigerator.

When you are ready to serve, lightly whip the cream and stir it into the eggplant mixture. Season with salt and pepper and serve with small pieces of toast.

CARDOON SALAD

INGREDIENTS

- 1 cardoon
- ½ lemon
- ½ cup (120 ml/4 fl oz) dry white wine
- 1 onion, studded with 1 clove
- 1 sprig parsley
- 1 tablespoon tomato paste (puree)
- generous 1 cup (250 g/9 oz) mayonnaise, homemade (see page 62) or ready-made
- salt
- chopped parsley, to garnish

Serves 8

Bring a pan of salted water to a boil. Meanwhile, prepare the cardoon. Trim the base and remove and discard the hard outer stems, then pull off the inedible strings. Remove the inner stems, one at a time, rub with the lemon and cut into pieces about 1½ inches (4 cm) long. Put the cardoon in the boiling water and boil it for about 3 minutes. Drain the cardoon and immediately place it a bowl of cold water to stop it cooking.

Put the wine, onion and parsley into a pan over medium heat, then add the cardoon and enough water to cover it. Season with salt and pepper. Let cook slowly until tender, then drain and let cool.

Once the cardoon is cool, place it in a dish. Stir the tomato paste into the mayonnaise, then add to the salad and mix together. Sprinkle with chopped parsley and serve.

CARDOON IN VINAIGRETTE

INGREDIENTS
- 1 cardoon
- 1 lemon, halved
- 1 tablespoon all-purpose (plain) flour
- 1 sprig parsley, finely chopped
- 1 hard-boiled egg, chopped (optional)
- salt

FOR THE VINAIGRETTE:
- salt
- 3 tablespoons white or red-wine vinegar
- 9 tablespoons extra-virgin olive oil
  Serves 6–8

First, prepare and blanch the cardoon. Trim the base and remove and discard the hard outer stems. Pull off the inedible strings. Remove the inner stems, one at a time, rub with half of the lemon and cut into pieces about 1½ inches (4 cm) long. Cut the heart into quarters. Put the pieces of cardoon into a large bowl of water and squeeze in the remaining half lemon. Put the flour into a bowl and mix into a paste with a little water. Tip this into a pan, pour in plenty of water (enough to cover the cardoon once it has been added to the pan) and add a pinch of salt. Partially cover the pan and bring to a boil. Add the cardoon and cook over medium heat for 1–1½ hours, or until tender. Drain well and put into a deep dish or bowl.

To make the vinaigrette, dissolve a pinch of salt in the vinegar in a bowl, then add the oil, whisking well until all the ingredients are amalgamated. Pour the vinaigrette over the cardoon. Sprinkle the parsley and the hard-boiled egg, if using, over the cardoon. Serve immediately.

Notes: This dish can be served hot but it is also very good cold. The vinaigrette can be varied in many ways, such as adding mustard, a little finely chopped onion, parsley or chopped capers.

PHOTOGRAPH PAGE 107

ONION AND MUSHROOM SALAD

INGREDIENTS
- 9 oz (250 g) mushrooms
- ½ lemon
- 2 tablespoons olive oil
- 3 carrots, peeled and sliced
- 9 oz (250 g) small onions, peeled but left whole
- 1½ cups (350 ml/12 fl oz) white wine
- 3 tablespoons tomato paste (puree)
- salt and pepper

Serves 8

Wash the mushrooms in a bowl of water with a few drops of lemon juice. Remove the mushrooms and set aside on paper towels. Heat the oil in a skillet or frying pan, add the carrots and lightly pan-fry over medium heat. When they begin to soften, add the onions, mushrooms, white wine and tomato paste, then season with salt and pepper and stir.

Bring to a boil, then turn the heat to low and simmer for 15 minutes. Remove the skillet from the heat and let cool completely, then transfer the mixture to a bowl and put in the refrigerator until required. Serve chilled.

MUSHROOM AND OLIVE SALAD

INGREDIENTS
- 1 lb 2 oz (500 g) large mushrooms
- juice of 1 lemon
- 2 tablespoons olive oil
- ½ red or green bell pepper, seeded and thinly sliced
- generous 2 cups (500 ml/18 fl oz) tomato sauce, bottled or homemade (see page 181)
- generous ¾ cups (100 g/3½ oz) black olives, pitted (stoned)
- cloves garlic, very finely chopped
- salt and pepper

Serves 6

Wash the mushrooms in cold water with a dash of lemon juice. Remove them from the water, pat dry and trim the stems so that they are all the same size.

Heat the oil in a skillet or frying pan over medium heat. Add the bell pepper and mushrooms and pan-fry, stirring occasionally. As they begin to soften, stir in the tomato sauce, the olives and the garlic. Season with salt and pepper. Bring to a boil, then turn the heat to low and simmer for 10 minutes. Remove the skillet from the heat and serve warm or let cool completely and serve cold.

PHOTOGRAPH PAGE 106

CIRUELAS RELLENAS
DE ROQUEFORT, PASAS
Y PIÑONES

PRUNES WITH ROQUEFORT, RAISINS AND PINE NUTS

INGREDIENTS

- 3½ oz (100 g) Roquefort cheese
- 1 oz (25 g) pine nuts
- ¼ cup (40 g/1½ oz) raisins
- 1 tablespoon Malaga wine or sweet sherry
- 4 tablespoons light (single) cream
- 12 ready-to-eat prunes
  Makes 12

Crumble the Roquefort into a bowl and mash lightly with a fork. Add the pine nuts, raisins, wine or sherry and cream and mix to a paste. Remove the pits (stones) from the prunes and fill the cavities with the Roquefort paste. Close the prunes and secure with a wooden toothpick (cocktail stick). Put the prunes on a plate, cover and chill in the refrigerator for at least 2 hours before serving.

Note: To use standard prunes, soak them in warm water to rehydrate them, following the directions on the package, then remove the pits.

PHOTOGRAPH PAGE 109

TAPA DE COLIFLOR

CAULIFLOWER TAPA

INGREDIENTS

- 1 cauliflower, separated into small florets
- 2 oz (50 g) canned anchovy fillets in oil, drained

FOR THE SAUCE:

- scant ½ cup (100 g/3½ oz) cream cheese
- scant ½ cup (100 ml/3½ fl oz) light (single) cream
- ¾ cup (100 g/3½ oz) crumbled Roquefort cheese
- salt and pepper
  Serves 6

First, make the sauce by combining all the ingredients to create a smooth mixture. Transfer to a bowl and place on a serving plate. Rinse the cauliflower florets and dry thoroughly. Wrap each one in an anchovy fillet and hold it in place with a toothpick (cocktail stick), which will make the florets easier to pick up and dip into the sauce. Serve with the dip surrounded by the florets.

Note: For an alternative sauce, flavor homemade mayonnaise (see page 62) with 1 tablespoon tomato paste (puree) and a dash of cognac.

CAULIFLOWER AND SHRIMP (PRAWN) SALAD

INGREDIENTS

- 1 cucumber, peeled and sliced
- 1 tablespoon white-wine vinegar
- 3 tablespoons extra-virgin olive oil
- 1 small cauliflower, broken into florets
- 2 cooked potatoes, peeled
- 5 oz (150 g) cooked large shrimp (prawns), peeled
- 3 tablespoons mayonnaise, homemade (see page 62) or ready-made
- 2 hard-boiled eggs, shelled and cut into wedges
- salt
- 1 tablespoon chopped parsley, to garnish

Serves 8

Put the cucumber in a bowl, sprinkle with salt and set aside for 30 minutes. In a salad bowl, beat the vinegar and oil together with a pinch of salt using a fork.

Meanwhile, bring a large pan of salted water to a boil. Add the cauliflower florets and boil for 10 minutes, or until they are just tender but still firm to the bite. Drain them well and pat dry.

Rinse the cucumber slices and pat dry with paper towels. Add the cucumber, cauliflower florets, potatoes and shrimp into a bowl and gently mix together. Add the mayonnaise and mix together again. Arrange the hard-boiled egg wedges around the salad, garnish with parsley and serve.

PHOTOGRAPH PAGE 108

LETTUCE HEART SALAD

INGREDIENTS

- 2 lettuce hearts, halved, rinsed and patted dry
- 4 tablespoons light (single) cream
- 1 tablespoon Dijon mustard
- 1 tablespoon hazelnuts, toasted and chopped

FOR THE VINAIGRETTE:

- 1 tablespoon white-wine vinegar
- 3 tablespoons extra-virgin olive oil
- salt
Serves 6

To make the vinaigrette, beat the vinegar with a pinch of salt in a bowl with a fork, then beat in the oil. Put the lettuce hearts in a deep dish and pour the vinaigrette over them. Let marinate for about an hour, turning them from time to time.

Before serving, drain off the vinaigrette and place a halved lettuce heart onto each plate. Mix the cream, straight from the refrigerator, with a little mustard to taste, then pour it over the lettuce. Sprinkle with the hazelnuts and serve.

Note: As a variation, prepare as above, but instead of using cream, cover the lettuce hearts with semiliquid mayonnaise mixed with canned anchovy fillets crushed in a mortar. This version can also be served with chopped hazelnuts on top.

PHOTOGRAPH PAGE 110

ESCALIBADA

ROASTED MIXED VEGETABLES

INGREDIENTS
- 2 large green bell peppers
- 1 large red bell pepper
- 3 eggplants (aubergines), about 1¾ lb (800 g) total weight
- 1 large onion
- 4 potatoes, about 1¾ lb (800 g) total weight
- 1½ cups (350 ml/12 fl oz) olive oil
- 2 tomatoes
- 6 tablespoons white-wine vinegar
- 1 clove garlic, finely chopped
- salt and pepper

Serves 8

Preheat the oven to 400°F (200°C/GAS MARK 6). Put the bell peppers, eggplants, onion and potatoes (unpeeled) into a roasting pan. Pour in half the oil and toss to coat. Roast for 25 minutes. Stir gently, add the tomatoes and roast for another 20 minutes. Remove the roasting pan from the oven and set the vegetables aside until cool enough to handle.

Peel, halve and seed the bell peppers, then cut them into strips. Peel the eggplants and cut them into strips. Cut the onion into wedges. Peel the tomatoes and cut them into pieces. In a bowl, whisk together the remaining oil and the vinegar to make a vinaigrette. Season each vegetable with salt and pepper and sprinkle with half the vinaigrette. Cut the potatoes in half and scoop out the flesh with a teaspoon, taking care not to break the skins. Chop the flesh, season with salt and pepper and return it to the potato skins.

The roasted mixed vegetables may be served in 1 large dish or 4 individual dishes. Put the potatoes in the center of the dish and arrange the other vegetables around them. Stir the garlic into the remaining vinaigrette and pour it over the vegetables.

PHOTOGRAPH PAGE 111

ASPARAGUS, HAM AND MAYONNAISE TAPA

INGREDIENTS

- 24 bottled or fresh
  asparagus tips
- 12 slices cooked or cured ham
- 24 slices French baguette
- ¾ cup (175 g/6 oz) mayonnaise,
  homemade (see page 62),
  or ready-made
- 2 canned or bottled red
  bell peppers, drained and
  thinly sliced
  Makes 24

Preheat the broiler (grill) to high. If using bottled asparagus tips, rinse them well, then pat dry. If using fresh tips, steam them for 3–5 minutes, or until tender, then let them cool completely before assembling the tapas.

Using decorative cookie cutters, cut out 24 shapes from the ham slices. Toast the bread for 2 minutes on each side, or until golden brown. Use the same cutters to cut out 24 shapes from the toast, and spread each shape with a little mayonnaise. Top the toast shapes with the pieces of ham, then put an asparagus tip in the center of each. Add a bell pepper slice or two to each tapa. Serve immediately or the toast will become soggy.

PHOTOGRAPH PAGE 112

ASPARAGUS AND ANCHOVY FILLETS WITH SAUCE

INGREDIENTS

- 4½ lb (2 kg) white or green
  asparagus, trimmed
- 1 egg, at room temperature
- juice of ½ lemon, strained
- mustard, to taste
- 1 cup (250 ml/8 fl oz) olive oil
- 1 egg white
- 2 x 2-oz (50-g) cans anchovy
  fillets in oil, drained
- 2 hard-boiled eggs, chopped
  Serves 6

Bring a pan of salted water to a boil, add the asparagus and cook for 5–8 minutes, until tender. Drain and keep warm. Meanwhile, put the egg, lemon juice, mustard and a dash of oil into a blender. The ingredients should not cover the blades. Stir with a spatula, then blend for 20 seconds. Pour in the rest of the oil and stir, then blend for another 35 seconds. Add salt, extra lemon juice and mustard to taste. Transfer to a bowl. In another bowl, beat the egg white to stiff peaks and fold it through the egg and oil mixture.

Arrange alternate rows of asparagus and anchovies on a warm serving dish. Sprinkle with the chopped hard-boiled egg and spoon the sauce over the top.

ASPARAGUS, HAM AND MAYONNAISE SALAD

INGREDIENTS

- 1 bunch fresh white asparagus or 14 oz (400 g) canned white asparagus
- 3 firm tomatoes
- 1 cucumber
- 3 hard-boiled eggs
- 7 oz (200 g) York or other dry-cured ham, diced
- 1 tablespoon chopped onion
- 1 tablespoon chopped parsley
- salt

FOR THE MAYONNAISE:

- 1 egg
- 1 tablespoon white-wine vinegar or lemon juice
- 1¼ cups (300 ml/½ pint) olive oil
- salt

Serves 6

First, prepare the mayonnaise. Put the egg yolk in a bowl with ½ teaspoon of the vinegar or lemon juice and a small pinch of salt. Stir lightly with a whisk or fork and then gradually whisk in the oil, 1–2 teaspoons at a time, until about a quarter has been added. Whisk in the remaining oil in a slow, steady stream. Add the remaining vinegar or lemon juice, then taste and adjust the seasoning. It is a good idea to make the mayonnaise in a cool place and it should be stored in the refrigerator.

If using fresh asparagus, trim, peel and cook it (see below). Drain the cooked (or canned) asparagus well and place on a clean dish towel to dry. Dice the tomatoes, put them in a colander, sprinkle with a little salt and let drain. Peel and dice the cucumber, put it in another colander, sprinkle with salt and let drain. Rinse both ingredients and pat dry. Cut the asparagus spears into 1-inch (2.5-cm) lengths. Chop half of the hard-boiled eggs and slice the remaining eggs. Mix together the asparagus, tomato, cucumber, chopped eggs, ham, onion and half the parsley in a bowl. Stir in the mayonnaise, cover and chill in the refrigerator for 1 hour. To serve, garnish the salad with the sliced eggs and sprinkle with the remaining parsley.

To prepare and cook asparagus, allow 3¼–4½ lb (1.5–2 kg) to serve four. Try to buy asparagus spears that are all the same thickness. Peel them from the tip to the base, if necessary, then cut them all to the same length (about 10 inches/25 cm). Cut off the woody ends and put them into cold water immediately. Bring a large pan of salted water to a boil. Add the asparagus, submerging the spears completely, with all the tips pointing in the same direction so that they will not break when lifted out. Cover the pan, bring back to a boil and cook for about 8 minutes, for medium asparagus, or 15 minutes for fat asparagus. In both cases, check that the spears are cooked by piercing one with the point of a sharp knife. You can also buy a special asparagus pan which is tall enough to allow the spears to stand up, so that the stems cook in water while the tips are gently steamed.

NAVY (HARICOT) BEAN SALAD WITH SAGE AND THYME

INGREDIENTS

- 2¾ cups (500 g/1 lb 2 oz)
  dried navy (haricot) beans,
  soaked overnight in water
  to cover and drained
- 3 cloves garlic
- 1 carrot, scraped
- 1 small onion, halved
- 1 celery stalk
- 1 bay leaf
- 1 sprig fresh sage
- 1 small sprig thyme
- ½ cup (120 ml/4 fl oz)
  extra-virgin olive oil
- 1 teaspoon dried thyme
- fine sea salt and pepper
  Serves 6

Put the beans into a bowl, cover with boiling water and leave for 1 hour, then pour off and discard the water. Put the drained beans in a pan with cold water to cover and add the garlic, carrot, onion, celery, bay leaf, sage, thyme and 2 tablespoons of oil. Bring to a boil, then reduce the heat to low and let simmer, uncovered, for 30 minutes. Add salt and cook for another 20 minutes, or until the beans are tender but not overcooked (the time will depend on the type of bean used). If necessary, add more water during cooking to ensure the beans are always covered.

When cooked, drain the beans and put them into a large bowl. While they are still hot, add the rest of the oil, sprinkle in the dried thyme and pepper to taste. Serve hot, warm or at room temperature. Seasoned like this, the salad can be kept for up to 3 days in the refrigerator.

Note: This dish is extremely aromatic. Cubes of tomato may also be added. It can also be made using fresh beans, in which case there is no need to soak them first. Simply put all the ingredients except the dried thyme in a pan and simmer for 20 minutes, or until the beans are tender.

PHOTOGRAPH PAGE 112

LENTIL SALAD

INGREDIENTS
- 1 small onion
- 2 cloves
- 2⅔ cups (600 g/1 lb 5 oz) Puy lentils
- 1 bay leaf
- 1 carrot, cut into 4 pieces
- 2 cloves garlic, unpeeled
- 12 small sausages
- olive oil, to taste
- white-wine vinegar, to taste
- salt

Serves 6–8

Stud the onion with the cloves. Put the lentils into a pan, add the onion, bay leaf, carrot, garlic and sausage and pour in water to cover generously. Cover and bring to a boil, then lower the heat and simmer for 1–1½ hours, until the lentils are tender. When the lentils are cooked, drain them and remove the bay leaf, onion, garlic and carrot. Put the lentils into a glass or china salad bowl and dress with olive oil, vinegar and a pinch of salt. Mix the salad well and serve warm or cold.

Note: The lentils can also be mixed with mayonnaise and garnished with drained, canned anchovy fillets and sliced tomatoes.

ORANGE, FENNEL AND ONION SALAD

INGREDIENTS
- 1 lb 5 oz (600 g) fennel, peeled and cut in half lengthwise
- 3 large oranges
- 5 tablespoons olive oil
- 2 tablespoons lemon juice
- 1 small onion, thinly sliced
- handful of black olives, pitted (stoned) and sliced
- mint leaves, to garnish (optional)
- salt and pepper

Serves 6–8

Bring a pan of salted water to a boil. Add the fennel, bring back to a boil and cook for 2 minutes, then drain. Peel the oranges, removing any traces of white pith, and thinly slice crosswise, reserving any juices. When the fennel is cool enough to handle, thickly slice it and set aside. To make the dressing, beat the olive oil, lemon juice and reserved orange juice together in a large bowl with a fork. Season with salt and pepper.

Combine the fennel, oranges, onion and olives in the bowl, gently tossing together. Pour the dressing over the salad and toss gently just before serving. The salad can be garnished with mint leaves, if desired.

PHOTOGRAPH PAGE 113

POTATO SALAD WITH TUNA AND HARD-BOILED EGG

INGREDIENTS

- 2½ lb (1.2 kg)
  potatoes, unpeeled
- 2 tablespoons milk
- 8 oz (225 g) canned tuna in oil,
  drained and broken into chunks
- 3 hard-boiled eggs, sliced
- 3 tablespoons
  white-wine vinegar
- 6 tablespoons sunflower oil
- 1 scallion (spring onion),
  finely chopped
- 1 teaspoon chopped parsley
- salt
  Serves 8

Put the potatoes into a large pan of cold water and add the milk and a generous pinch of salt. Make sure that the liquid covers them completely. Bring to a boil, then lower the heat to medium and cook for 20–30 minutes, until tender but not falling apart, then drain well, peel and cut into slices. Put the slices into a bowl, alternating with the tuna and hard-boiled eggs. Whisk the vinegar with a little salt using a fork, then pour over the salad, then pour the oil over the top and add the scallion and parsley. Mix lightly to avoid breaking up the potatoes or eggs and leave until almost cold before serving.

RED BELL PEPPER, EGG AND ANCHOVY SALAD

INGREDIENTS

- 2 red bell peppers
- 1 lb 8½ oz (700 g) tomatoes, peeled, seeded and quartered
- 4 hard-boiled eggs, shelled and quartered
- 1⅔ cups (200 g/7 oz) black olives, pitted (stoned)
- 6 canned anchovy fillets, drained

FOR THE DRESSING:

- 3 canned anchovy fillets, drained and chopped
- 4 tablespoons extra-virgin olive oil
- 1 tablespoon lemon juice
- pepper

Serves 6–8

Preheat the broiler (grill) to medium. Broil (grill) the bell pepper for about 20 minutes, turning them regularly, until they are softened and charred all over. Place them on a cutting (chopping) board and cover with a cloth while they cool.

Meanwhile, to make the dressing, crush the anchovies in a mortar with a pestle then add the oil, lemon juice and pepper to taste and mix together. Set aside.

When the bell peppers are cool enough to handle, peel them, then cut in half, remove the cores and seeds and slice them. Put the bell peppers, tomatoes, hard-boiled eggs and olives in a salad bowl. Mix the dressing again, pour it over the salad and gently mix together. Garnish with the extra anchovy fillets and serve.

PHOTOGRAPH PAGE 115

RUSSIAN SALAD

INGREDIENTS

- 9 oz (250 g) potatoes, diced and blanched
- 1 lb 2 oz (500 g) carrots, diced and blanched
- 2¼ lb (1 kg) fresh peas, blanched
- breadsticks, to serve

FOR THE MAYONNAISE:

- 1 egg yolk, at room temperature
- 1 tablespoon white-wine vinegar or lemon juice, strained
- generous 1 cup (250 ml/9 fl oz) sunflower oil
- salt

Serves 6–8

First, prepare the mayonnaise. Put the egg yolk in a bowl with 1½ teaspoons of the vinegar or lemon juice and a small pinch of salt. Stir lightly with a whisk or fork and then gradually whisk in the oil, 1–2 teaspoons at a time, until about a quarter has been added. Whisk in the remaining oil in a slow, steady stream. Add the remaining vinegar or lemon juice, then taste and adjust the seasoning. It is a good idea to make the mayonnaise in a cool place and store it in the refrigerator.

Drain the vegetables, transfer to a bowl and let cool. Add the mayonnaise and toss to combine thoroughly. Refrigerate until ready to serve. Before serving, stick a few breadsticks into the salad.

Note: This is the classic version of Russian salad. Delicious variations include adding pieces of tart dessert apple, walnut or celery to the vegetables. Cooked, peeled shrimp (prawns) may also be added, which add an exquisite flavor to a simple Russian salad.

PHOTOGRAPH PAGE 116

RADISH
SALAD

INGREDIENTS

- 11 oz (300 g) mixed salad greens (leaves), such as lettuce, arugula (rocket), chicory and radicchio, well rinsed and patted dry
- ½ bunch radishes, thinly sliced

FOR THE DRESSING:

- ⅔ cup (150 g/5 oz) plain yogurt
- 1 tablespoon chopped scallions (spring onions)
- 1 tablespoon lemon juice
- salt and pepper
  Serves 6

To make the dressing, beat the yogurt, scallions and lemon juice in a bowl and season with salt and pepper. Cover and chill until required. Mix the salad greens and radishes together in a salad bowl, pour the dressing over it and serve.

Note: When washing the mixed greens, do not let them to soak for too long or they will start to lose their nutritional value. Green salad should always be seasoned at the last minute, but radishes should be seasoned when they are sliced. You can give this salad a personal touch by adding various herbs, such as parsley, mint, basil or chives. Cubes of apple are also delicious. A little mustard or some chopped herbs can also be added to the dressing.

PHOTOGRAPH PAGE 114

BREAD WITH
TOMATO

INGREDIENTS

- 4 slices bread from a large loaf
- 1 large clove garlic, halved (optional)
- 1 large juicy tomato, halved
- extra-virgin olive oil, to drizzle
- 4 slices Serrano ham, halved
- 8 canned anchovies in oil, drained
- salt
  Serves 8

Preheat the broiler (grill) to high. Toast the bread on both sides for 2 minutes, or until golden and crisp. Rub the toast with the garlic clove, if you like, then rub the cut sides of the tomato halves over the pieces of toast, pressing down, until only the skins remain. Drizzle some oil over each slice and sprinkle with a pinch of salt. Cut each slice of toast in half, and top each half with a piece of ham and an anchovy fillet. Serve immediately or the toast will become soggy.

PHOTOGRAPH PAGE 117

TOMATO AND MUSHROOM TAPA

INGREDIENTS

- 2¼ lb (1 kg) ripe, juicy tomatoes, peeled, seeded and chopped
- juice of 1 lemon, strained
- 9 oz (250 g) small mushrooms, trimmed and thinly sliced
- 2 tablespoons olive oil
- ⅔ cup (150 g/5 oz) butter, softened, for spreading
- 18 slices French baguette
- 4 tablespoons mayonnaise
- salt and pepper
Makes 18

Put the tomatoes in a nonmetallic bowl and season them with salt and pepper. Sprinkle with half the lemon juice and let marinate for 1 hour. Meanwhile, put the mushrooms in a separate nonmetallic bowl. Sprinkle with a little of the remaining lemon juice and let marinate for 1 hour. Drain the liquid from the tomatoes, then gently crush them with a fork. Stir in the olive oil and season with pepper. Butter one side of each slice of bread and spread the tomatoes over the buttered sides, then arrange mushroom slices on top. If desired, ½ teaspoon mayonnaise can also be put on top of the mushrooms. Serve immediately or the bread will become soggy.

TOMATOES FILLED WITH SARDINES

INGREDIENTS

- 12 tomatoes
- 3 tablespoons olive oil
- 2 green bell peppers, diced
- 1 tablespoon white-wine vinegar
- 3 tablespoons sunflower oil
- ½ teaspoon mustard
- 1 teaspoon chopped parsley
- 9 large canned sardines in oil, drained
- 3½ oz (100 g) pimiento-stuffed olives, halved
- lettuce leaves, to serve
- salt
Serves 6

Prepare the tomatoes as described in Tomatoes Filled with Tuna Cream (opposite). Heat the oil in a skillet or frying pan. Add the bell peppers, cover and cook over low heat, shaking the skillet occasionally, for 10 minutes. Just before the peppers have finished, lightly season with salt. Meanwhile, make the vinaigrette: dissolve a little salt in the vinegar in a bowl, then add the oil and mustard, whisking well with a fork until all the ingredients are amalgamated. Stir in the parsley. Remove the skin and bones from the sardines and flake the flesh into a bowl with a fork. Add the vinaigrette, mix well and divide the mixture among the tomatoes. Chill in the refrigerator for 2 hours, then top with the olives, garnish with the lettuce leaves and serve.

PHOTOGRAPH PAGE 119

TOMATES RELLENOS
CON ESPUMA DE VENTRESCA

TOMATOES FILLED WITH TUNA CREAM

INGREDIENTS

- 4 large tomatoes
- 7 oz (200 g) good quality canned tuna or bonito in oil, drained and chopped
- generous 1 cup (250 g/9 oz) mayonnaise, homemade (see page 62) or ready-made
- 5 tablespoons heavy (double) cream, whipped
- salt and pepper
  Serves 4

Cut out the stems and cores of the tomatoes with the point of a knife and scoop out the seeds and some of the flesh with a teaspoon. Cut a very thin slice off the bottom of each one so that they sit easily, and won't fall over when you serve them. Sprinkle a little salt in their cavities and let the tomatoes drain, upside down, for about 1 hour.

Meanwhile, put the tuna or bonito in a bowl with the mayonnaise and whipped cream, season with salt and pepper and gently stir together. Fill the tomatoes with this mixture and chill in the refrigerator for at least 1 hour. Serve cold.

SALSA VERDE

GREEN SAUCE

INGREDIENTS

- 1¾ oz (50 g) watercress sprigs
- 1¾ oz (50 g) spinach leaves
- 1 bunch parsley
- 1 bunch chervil
- scant 2¼ cups (500 g/1 lb 2 oz) mayonnaise, homemade (see page 62) or ready-made
- salt and pepper
  Makes about 1 lb 4 oz (550 g)

Bring a large pan of salted water to a boil. Add the watercress, spinach and herbs and cook for 3 minutes. Drain and immediately run the greens under cold running water, to stop them cooking and preserve their color. Drain again and dry the greens by putting them in a clean cloth and wringing dry.

Use a wooden spoon to work the greens through a fine strainer, set over a bowl. Stir in the mayonnaise, then season with salt and pepper. Cover and chill until required. This sauce can be served with cooked fish or potatoes, or served as a dip with bread or raw vegetables.

PHOTOGRAPH PAGE 118

SALAD WITH YOGURT DRESSING

INGREDIENTS

- ⅔ cup (150 ml/¼ pint)
  plain yogurt
- juice of ½ lemon, strained
- 1 head lettuce,
  cored and trimmed
- 1 tart dessert apple
- ⅓ cup (50 g/1¾ oz) hazelnuts,
  coarsely chopped
- 1 tablespoon chopped parsley
- salt and pepper
  Serves 4

Mix together the yogurt and lemon juice in a small bowl and season to taste with salt and pepper. Line a salad bowl with the lettuce. Core the apple, cut into very thin slices and add to the bowl. Sprinkle the hazelnuts over the top. Pour the dressing over the salad and toss lightly. Sprinkle with the parsley before serving.

Note: When in season, green asparagus may be added to this recipe. It should be cooked in a pan of salted boiling water for 5–8 minutes or until tender, cooled and cut into 2-inch (5-cm) lengths.

CARROT SALAD WITH ORANGE

INGREDIENTS

- 2 oranges
- 1 lb 2 oz (500 g) carrots,
  roughly grated

FOR THE DRESSING:

- juice of 1 lemon, strained
- 1 tablespoon orange
  blossom water
- 1 tablespoon confectioners'
  (icing) sugar
- salt
  Serves 4

Peel the oranges, then carefully remove the pith and slice the fruit. Put them into a bowl with the carrots. To make the dressing, beat the lemon juice, orange blossom water and confectioners' sugar with the salt. Pour over the oranges and carrots, then cover and chill until required. Serve chilled.

PHOTOGRAPH PAGE 118

COLD RICE WITH VEGETABLES AND VINAIGRETTE

INGREDIENTS
- 2 cups (400 g/14 oz) long-grain rice
- 1 lb 10 oz (750 g) green beans, cut into short lengths, or 3¼ lb (1.5 kg) peas, shelled
- 1 pinch baking soda (bicarbonate of soda), optional
- salt

FOR THE VINAIGRETTE:
- 2 tablespoons white-wine vinegar
- 6 tablespoons olive oil
- 1 teaspoon chopped parsley
- 1 hard-boiled egg, fincly chopped
- salt

FOR THE GARNISH:
- iceberg lettuce leaves
- 1 lb 2 oz (500 g) ripe tomatoes, sliced
- 3 hard boiled eggs, cut into segments
Serves 8

Bring a pan of water to a boil. Add the rice, stir well to prevent the grains from clumping together and cook over high heat for 12–15 minutes, until tender. (The cooking time depends on the type of rice.) Drain well and season with salt while it is still in the colander. Spoon the rice into 8 individual molds and set aside.

To make the vinaigrette, dissolve the salt in the vinegar in a bowl, then add the oil, whisking well with a fork until amalgamated. Stir in the parsley and chopped egg, then pour into a sauceboat and set aside. If using the green beans, cook them in a large pan of salted boiling water for 5–10 minutes, until tender. (The cooking time will depend on the type and freshness of the beans.) If you like, add a pinch of baking soda to the water to make the beans greener. Drain the beans and let cool. If using the peas, cook them in a large pan of salted boiling water for 5–8 minutes. (The cooking time will depend on the size and freshness of the peas.) Drain well and let cool.

Turn out each rice mold onto a plate. Spoon the green beans or peas on top of the rice. Arrange lettuce leaves and tomato slices alternately around the outside of the rice. Garnish with the hard-boiled egg segments and serve, offering the vinaigrette separately.

Note: The dish may be kept in the refrigerator for up to 1 hour before serving.

HOT

RICE WITH SWISS CHARD AND NAVY (HARICOT) BEANS

INGREDIENTS

- generous 1 cup (200 g/7 oz) dried navy (haricot) beans, soaked overnight in water to cover and drained
- 3 tablespoons olive oil
- 1 onion, finely chopped
- 2 tablespoons tomato paste (puree)
- 1 clove garlic
- 1 sprig parsley, finely chopped
- 1 bay leaf
- ½ teaspoon paprika
- 1 lb 2 oz (500 g) Swiss chard, rinsed and chopped
- 1 lb 2 oz (500 g) cooked snails (optional)
- 1¼ cups (250 g/9 oz) long-grain rice
- salt
  Serves 4–6

Put the beans in a large pan with water to cover. Cover and bring to a boil, then drain. Return the beans to the pan with fresh water to cover and cook over medium heat for 1 hour, skimming any scum from the surface as necessary.

Meanwhile, heat the oil in a large skillet or frying pan with a tight-fitting lid over low heat. Add the onion and pan-fry, stirring occasionally, for about 6 minutes until softened but not colored. Add the tomato paste, garlic, parsley and bay leaf and stir for about 3 minutes. Remove the skillet from the heat and stir in the paprika. Set aside.

After the beans have cooked for 1 hour, stir in the Swiss chard and the onion mixture and season with salt. Continue simmering for 30 minutes, or until the beans are tender. Strain and reserve the liquid, then return the solid ingredients to the pan. Stir in the rice and 3 cups (750 ml/25 fl oz) of the reserved liquid and season with salt. Return the liquid to a boil and stir, then reduce the heat to low, cover the pan and let simmer for 20 minutes, or until the rice is tender. The texture should be quite liquid, but not so much so that it needs to be eaten with a spoon. Remove the pan from the heat, garnish the rice with the snails and replace the lid, then let sit for 4 or 5 minutes before serving.

Note: To cook the snails yourself, put them into a large pan and pour in just enough lukewarm water to cover. Heat gently until the snails emerge from their shells, then increase the heat to high and cook for 30 minutes. Drain well and discard the shells.

PHOTOGRAPH PAGE 121

ALCACHOFAS
REHOGADAS

FRIED ARTICHOKES

INGREDIENTS

- 1 lemon, halved
- 3¼–4½lb (1.5–2kg) small young globe artichokes
- 2 tablespoons (25g/1oz) lard (optional)
- 2–4 tablespoons olive oil
- 5oz (150g) Serrano ham, diced
- 1 tablespoon chopped parsley
- salt

Serves 6

Squeeze the juice from one lemon half and add it to a large bowl of water. Break off the artichoke stems and remove the coarse outer leaves. Cut off the tips of the remaining leaves. Cut the artichokes in half lengthwise and remove and discard the chokes. Rub the artichokes with the remaining lemon half and place them in the acidulated water.

Bring a large pan of salted water to a boil. Add the artichokes and bring back to a boil, then lower the heat, cover and simmer for about 25 minutes, until tender. (Test by gently pulling a leaf; it should come away easily.)

Drain the artichokes well, turning them upside down and pressing gently. Melt the lard, if using, with 2 tablespoons of the oil in a pan. If not using lard, add 2 tablespoons more oil and heat. Add the ham and artichokes and cook gently, stirring occasionally, for 8 minutes. Sprinkle with the parsley and serve immediately.

PHOTOGRAPH PAGE 120

ENSALADA TEMPLADA DE BERENJENAS Y ANCHOAS

WARM EGGPLANT (AUBERGINE) AND ANCHOVY SALAD

INGREDIENTS

- 3 eggplants (aubergines)
- 1 cup (250 ml/8 fl oz) olive oil
- 1 clove garlic, chopped
- 1 tablespoon chopped parsley
- 3 anchovy fillets in oil, drained and crushed
- juice of 1 lemon, strained
- salt and pepper

Serves 4–6

Peel the eggplants – although this dish is also delicious if they are not peeled – then cut them into slices about ¾ inch (2 cm) thick, sprinkle with salt, and place in a colander. Leave for 1 hour to draw out the juices, then rinse off the salt and pat dry.

Heat the oil in 1 or 2 skillets or frying pans over low heat and arrange the eggplant slices in a single layer so they have plenty of room. Cover and cook, turning once, for 20 minutes, or until the eggplants are tender and softened. Drain off nearly all the oil, leaving just enough to prevent the slices from sticking. Sprinkle the garlic, parsley and salt over them.

Mix the anchovies with the lemon juice and season with a little pepper. Pour this over the eggplants, covering them evenly, and serve.

EGGPLANT (AUBERGINE) APPETIZER

INGREDIENTS

- 1 lb 10 oz (750 g) eggplants (aubergines) (see Note)
- generous 2 cups (500 ml/18 fl oz) sunflower oil
- 1 clove garlic, finely chopped
- 1 tablespoon finely chopped parsley
- salt
  Serves 4–6

Cut the eggplants into ¾-inch (2-cm) slices, sprinkle with a little salt and put into a colander for about 1 hour to draw out their juices. Rinse well and pat dry. Heat the oil in 1 or 2 large skillets or frying pans. Add the eggplant slices in a single layer. Cover and cook over low heat for 20 minutes, or until soft. Pour off all but just enough oil to prevent the slices sticking to the pans. Sprinkle with the garlic, parsley and season with salt to taste. Cover the pan and cook over high heat, shaking the pan occasionally, until golden brown. Serve immediately.

Note: It is worth the effort to try and find the variety of eggplants with speckled skin, as they are usually seedless.

FRIED COATED ZUCCHINI (COURGETTES)

INGREDIENTS

- 3¼ lb (1.5 kg) fairly large zucchini (courgettes), peeled and thinly sliced
- ½ cup (50 g/2 oz) all-purpose (plain) flour
- 4 eggs
- sunflower oil, for deep-frying
- 1 teaspoon chopped parsley
- salt
  Serves 6

Put the zucchini slices in a colander, sprinkling each layer with salt, and let stand for at least 1 hour to draw out some of their juices.

Rinse thoroughly and pat dry. Spread out the flour in a shallow dish. Lightly beat the eggs in another shallow dish. Heat the oil in a deep-fryer or pan to oven to 350–375°F (180–190°C), or until a cube of bread browns in 30 seconds. Dip the zucchini slices first in the flour, shaking off any excess, then the beaten egg. Carefully add to the hot oil, in batches, and cook until golden brown. Remove with a slotted spoon and drain well, then keep warm while cooking the remaining batches. Serve immediately, sprinkled with the parsley.

FRIED PUMPKIN

INGREDIENTS

- 4 leeks, cut into 1-inch (2.5-cm) lengths, and rinsed well
- 3¼ lb (1.5 kg) pumpkin, peeled, seeded and cubed
- 1 cup (250 ml/8 fl oz) olive oil
- 3–4 slices of bread, crusts removed, cubed
- 3 cloves garlic, lightly crushed
- salt

Serves 4

Bring a pan of salted water to a boil. Add the leek and cook over medium heat for 20 minutes. Add the pumpkin and cook for about 25 minutes, until the pumpkin is tender (test by piercing with a fork). Drain off the water, cover the pan and set aside.

Heat the oil in a large skillet or frying pan. Add the bread and cook, stirring frequently, until evenly browned. Remove with a slotted spoon and drain on paper towels. Pour off most of the oil, leaving just enough to cover the bottom of the pan, and return the pan to the heat. Add the garlic and cook for a few minutes until well browned, then remove and discard. Add the pumpkin, leeks and croutons to the pan and cook over low heat for 5 minutes. Serve immediately.

PHOTOGRAPH PAGE 123

RICE WITH MUSHROOMS AND SHERRY SAUCE

INGREDIENTS

- 2½ cups (500 g/1 lb 2 oz) long-grain rice
- 1 lb 10 oz (750 g) mushrooms, trimmed
- juice of 1 lemon, strained
- 4 tablespoons (50 g/1¾ oz) butter
- 3 tablespoons olive oil
- 3 tablespoons all-purpose (plain) flour
- ¾ cup (175 ml/6 fl oz) good-quality dry sherry
- salt and pepper

Serves 6

Bring 4 cups (1 litre/1¾ pints) unsalted water to a boil. Add the rice, stir with a wooden spoon to prevent the grains clumping together and cook over high heat for 12–15 minutes, until tender. Drain the rice in a large colander and rinse well under cold running water, stirring to ensure it is well washed. Leave the rice standing in the colander until required.

Wash the mushrooms with half the lemon juice and water, then drain well and chop the caps and stems. Melt half the butter in a large skillet or frying pan over low heat. Add the mushrooms and the remaining lemon juice and pan-fry, stirring occasionally, for about 6 minutes. Set aside.

Melt the remaining butter in another skillet with 1 tablespoon of the oil. Gradually add the flour, stirring constantly, then slowly stir in the sherry and 1½ cups (350 ml/12 fl oz) water. Let cook and thicken, then season with salt and pepper. Add the mushrooms with all their juices, stir well, reduce the heat to very low and simmer for 5 minutes.

Meanwhile, melt the remaining oil in a large pan over high heat. Add the rice, season with salt and stir until it is hot and coated in oil. To serve, spoon the rice into 6 individual molds, then turn each mold out onto a warm plate. Spoon the mushrooms around the rice. Alternatively, serve the mushrooms with the rice on the side.

PHOTOGRAPH PAGE 122

MUSHROOMS WITH OLIVES

INGREDIENTS

- 1 lb 2 oz (500 g) large mushrooms
- 1 lemon, halved
- 2 tablespoons olive oil
- ½ red bell pepper, seeded and thinly sliced
- generous 2 cups (500 ml/ 18 fl oz) tomato sauce, bottled or homemade (see page 181)
- 3 cloves garlic, fincly chopped
- generous ¾ cup (100 g/3½ oz) black olives, pitted (stoned)
- salt and pepper

Serves 4

Wash the mushrooms in cold water with a squeeze of lemon juice, then drain, pat dry and trim the stems so they are all the same size. Heat the oil in a skillet or frying pan over medium heat. Add the bell pepper and mushrooms and cook, stirring frequently. Add the tomato sauce, the garlic, the olives and the juice of half a lemon. Cook for 10 minutes, stirring occasionally, then take the pan off the heat. Season to taste with salt and pepper. Serve warm or cold.

GARLIC MUSHROOMS

INGREDIENTS

- 9 tablespoons olive oil
- 3¼ lb (1.5 kg) white mushrooms
- 3 cloves garlic, chopped
- 2 tablespoons chopped parsley
- salt

Serves 6

Preheat the oven to 350°F (180°C/GAS MARK 4). Divide the oil and mushrooms among 6 flameproof earthenware ramekins or other individual cooking dishes. (If you do not have individual dishes, just cook the ingredients all together in a skillet or frying pan and divide between 6 serving dishes or ramekins to serve.) Season each dish with salt and add the garlic, then cook in the oven for 5 minutes. Increase the temperature to 425°F (220°C/GAS MARK 7) and cook, shaking the dishes occasionally, for another 5 minutes. Sprinkle the parsley over the mushrooms and serve immediately.

STUFFED MUSHROOMS

INGREDIENTS

- 4 large Portobello mushrooms, wiped clean
- 2 tablespoons olive oil
- 2 shallots, chopped
- juice of ½ lemon, strained
- salt

Serves 4

Preheat the oven to 350°F (180°C/GAS MARK 4). Separate the mushroom caps and stems, and chop the stems. Heat the oil in a small skillet or frying pan. Add the mushroom stems and shallots and cook over low heat, stirring occasionally, for about 5 minutes. Season with salt, stir in a few drops of the lemon juice and cook for another 5–8 minutes. Put the mushroom caps on a baking sheet and divide the filling among them, then bake for 5 minutes. Increase the temperature to 425°F (220°C/GAS MARK 7) and bake, shaking the tray occasionally, for another 5 minutes.

PHOTOGRAPH PAGE 125

BUÑUELOS
DE COLIFLOR

CAULIFLOWER FRITTERS

INGREDIENTS

- 1 cauliflower, about 3¼ lb (1.5 kg), separated into florets
- juice of ½ lemon, strained
- a little milk, for cooking
- sunflower oil, for deep-frying
- lemon slices and sprigs of parsley, to garnish
- salt

FOR THE BATTER:

- 2¼ cups (250 g/9 oz) all-purpose (plain) flour
- 3 tablespoons white wine
- 3 tablespoons sunflower oil
- generous ¾ cup (200 ml/ 7 fl oz) milk
- 1 teaspoon baking powder
- salt

FOR THE TOMATO SAUCE (OPTIONAL):

- 3 tablespoons olive oil
- 1 onion, chopped (optional)
- 2¼ lb (1 kg) ripe tomatoes, seeded and chopped
- 1 teaspoon sugar
- salt

Serves 6

Separate the cauliflower into florets and peel the stems a little so that they become tender when cooked. Rinse the florets in cold water mixed with the lemon juice. Bring a large pan of salted water to a boil. Add the florets and a little milk and cook, uncovered, for about 20 minutes, until tender. Drain well, taking care not to break up the florets.

Meanwhile, make the batter. Sift the flour with a pinch of salt into a bowl and make a well in the center. Pour the wine and oil into the well and stir in the flour. Gradually stir in the milk, a little at a time. When the batter is smooth, cover and let stand for 30 minutes.

To make the tomato sauce, if using, heat the oil in a skillet or frying pan. Add the onion, if using, and cook over low heat, stirring occasionally, for about 5 minutes, until softened but not browned. (If you are not using the onion, add the tomato immediately.) Add the tomato and cook over low heat, breaking the flesh up with the edge of a skimmer or slotted spoon, for about 15 minutes. Allow the mixture to cool slightly, then transfer to a food processor and process. Add the sugar, season to taste with salt and process briefly again.

When ready to cook the fritters, stir the baking powder into the batter. Heat the oil in a deep-fryer or pan to 350–375°F (180 –190°C) or until a cube of bread browns in 30 seconds. One at a time, dip the florets into the batter, carefully add to the hot oil and cook for about 5 minutes, until golden brown. Do not add too many at a time. Remove with a slotted spoon, drain well and keep warm. When all the florets have been fried, pile them into the middle of a round dish and garnish with the lemon slices and parsley. Serve the fritters immediately, with the tomato sauce, if using.

PHOTOGRAPH PAGE 124

ASPARAGUS ON TOAST

INGREDIENTS

- 9 oz (250 g) canned or fresh white asparagus tips
- 2 tablespoons (25 g/1 oz) butter
- 1 tablespoon olive oil
- 1 tablespoon all-purpose (plain) flour
- 1 cup (250 ml/8 fl oz) milk
- ½ cup (50 g/2 oz) grated Gruyère cheese
- 6 slices bread
- 6 pieces cooked ham, trimmed to the same size as the bread
- salt and pepper
- chopped parsley, to garnish

Serves 8

Preheat the broiler (grill) to high. Drain and rinse the asparagus, if using canned. If using fresh asparagus, bring a large pan of salted water to a boil, add the asparagus, cover and cook for 5–8 minutes, until tender but not falling apart. Drain well.

Melt the butter with the oil in a pan. Stir in the flour and cook, stirring constantly, for 2 minutes. Remove the pan from the heat and gradually stir in the milk, a little at a time. Return the pan to the heat and cook, stirring frequently, for 5 minutes, adding the cheese when the sauce has thickened slightly. Season to taste with salt and pepper.

Meanwhile, toast the bread on both sides. Place a slice of ham on each piece of toast. Put the asparagus tips on top of the ham and cover with the sauce. Place under the broiler until they are golden brown. Sprinkle with chopped parsley just before serving.

ESPÁRRAGOS VERDES
REHOGADOS CON AJO,
VINAGRE Y PIMENTÓN

FRIED GREEN ASPARAGUS WITH GARLIC, VINEGAR AND PAPRIKA

INGREDIENTS

- 4½ lb (2 kg) green asparagus, trimmed
- 6 tablespoons olive oil
- 3 slices bread, crusts removed
- 2 cloves garlic
- ½ teaspoon paprika
- 3 tablespoons white-wine vinegar
- 1 teaspoon chopped parsley
- salt

Serves 6

Cut the asparagus into 1½-inch (4-cm) lengths. Heat the oil in a skillet or frying pan. Add the bread and cook over medium heat, turning occasionally, for a few minutes, until golden brown on both sides. Remove from the pan and set aside. Add the garlic to the pan and cook, stirring frequently, for a few minutes, until golden brown. Transfer the garlic to a mortar, add the fried bread and pound with a pestle.

Pour the oil from the skillet into a pan and heat it. Add the asparagus and cook for 2–3 minutes. Remove the pan from the heat and stir in the paprika, then pour in 2 cups (450 ml/¾ pint) hot water. Return the pan to a medium heat, cover and cook, shaking the pan occasionally, for 15 minutes, or until the asparagus spears are just tender.

To finish, add the vinegar and a little of the asparagus cooking liquid to the mixture in the mortar and stir well, then stir into the pan containing the asparagus. Season with a little salt and cook for another 5 minutes. Sprinkle with the parsley and serve immediately.

PHOTOGRAPH PAGE 126

ASPARAGUS WITH SALMON ROE

INGREDIENTS

- 2¼ lb (1 kg) white asparagus
- 6 tablespoons light (single) cream
- 4 tablespoons chopped parsley, or a mixture of parsley and chives
- juice of 1 lemon, strained
- grated zest of ½ lemon
- 6 tablespoons salmon roe (keta)
- salt and pepper

Serves 4–6

Peel the asparagus from the tip to the base, if necessary, then cut all the spears to the same size (about 10 inches/25 cm). Cut off any woody ends. As they are cut, put them into cold water. Bring a large pan of salted water to a boil. Add the asparagus, submerging it completely and with all the tips pointing in the same direction so that they will not break when lifted out. Cover the pan, bring back to a boil and cook for 8–10 minutes, until tender. Check that the spears are cooked by piercing one with the point of a sharp knife.

Meanwhile, mix the cream with the parsley and lemon juice and zest and season with salt and pepper. Drain the asparagus well. Place the spears on an elongated serving dish. Pour the cream over the tips and arrange the salmon roe on top. Serve warm or cold.

**ENSALADA DE
GARBANZOS**

GARBANZO BEAN (CHICKPEA) SALAD

INGREDIENTS

– generous 3 cups (700 g/1 lb
  8½ oz) dried garbanzo beans
  (chickpeas)
– 1 pinch baking soda
  (bicarbonate of soda)
– 2 leeks, trimmed
– 1 ham hock
– 1 carrot, scraped
– 2 hard-boiled eggs, chopped
– salt

FOR THE DRESSING:

– 3 tablespoons
  white-wine vinegar
– 9 tablespoons extra-virgin
  olive oil
– 1 teaspoon chopped parsley
– 1 teaspoon chopped onion
– salt

Serves 4–6

Soak the garbanzo beans overnight in warm water with a pinch of baking soda and another of salt, then drain and rinse them thoroughly. Put them into a pan of hot, but not boiling, salted water, with the leeks, the ham hock and the carrot. Let simmer for a couple of hours, skimming the surface as necessary, until the garbanzo beans are tender. Strain the garbanzo beans, reserving 2 tablespoons of the liquid for the dressing and shaking off any excess liquid.

Beat together all the dressing ingredients, including the reserved cooking liquid, with a fork in a serving bowl. Season with salt and pepper. Stir in the garbanzo beans, then add the hard-boiled eggs, gently mixing together. Serve warm or cold.

Note: To save time, this recipe can be prepared with well-rinsed bottled or canned garbanzo beans. If using dried garbanzo beans, do not throw away the cooking liquid because it can be used to cook rice or to make soup. Just remember it might be salty because of the ham hock.

PHOTOGRAPH PAGE 127

GARBANZO BEANS (CHICKPEAS) WITH SPINACH

INGREDIENTS

- 1½ cups (250 g/9 oz) dried garbanzo beans (chickpeas)
- 1 pinch baking soda (bicarbonate of soda), optional
- 4 tablespoons olive oil
- 3½ oz (100 g) lean bacon, chopped
- 2 onions, chopped
- 1 large tomato, peeled and chopped
- 1 lb 10 oz (750 g) spinach, coarse stems removed and well rinsed
- salt and pepper
- 2 hard-boiled eggs, sliced, to garnish

Serves 4

Put the garbanzo beans in a bowl, pour in warm water to cover and add the baking soda, if using, and a pinch of salt. Let soak for at least 12 hours, then drain and rinse well. Bring a pan of salted water to just below boiling point. Add the garbanzo beans, cover the pan and cook over medium heat for about 2 hours, until tender but not falling apart. (The time depends on the type and age of the garbanzo beans and the softness of the water.) Drain and set aside.

Meanwhile, heat the oil in a skillet or frying pan. Add the bacon and onions and cook over low heat, stirring occasionally, for about 8 minutes, until the onions begin to brown. Add the tomato, the spinach leaves and 1 cup (250 ml/8 fl oz) water. Season with salt and pepper to taste, cover and cook for 30 minutes. Stir in the garbanzo beans and continue to cook over low heat for another 30 minutes. Serve garnished with the hard-boiled eggs.

GARBANZOS FRITOS
CON CEBOLLA

FRIED GARBANZO BEANS (CHICKPEAS) WITH ONION

INGREDIENTS

- 6 tablespoons olive oil
- 3 large onions, finely chopped
- 3 cups (500 g/1 lb 2 oz) cooked garbanzo beans (chickpeas)
- salt

Serves 6

Heat the oil in a large skillet or frying pan. Add the onions and cook over low heat, stirring occasionally, for about 10 minutes, until starting to brown. Add the garbanzo beans and cook over high heat, stirring constantly, for 5 minutes, until hot. Season to taste with salt. Serve immediately.

HABAS CON MENTA

FAVA (BROAD) BEANS WITH MINT

INGREDIENTS

- 4½ lb (2 kg) fava (broad) beans, shelled
- ¾ cup (175 ml/6 fl oz) olive oil
- 1 onion, chopped
- 1 bunch mint, tied together
- 1 cup (250 ml/8 fl oz) white wine
- 1 tablespoon eau-de-vie
- 9 oz (250 g) lean bacon, rinds removed if necessary, and thinly sliced
- 3½ oz (100 g) chorizo, casing removed and thinly sliced
- salt and pepper

Serves 6–8

Pop the fava beans out of their skins by squeezing them between your thumb and index finger. Bring a large pan of salted water to a boil. Add the beans and cook, uncovered, for about 5–10 minutes, until tender. Half way through cooking, remove some of the water, leaving just enough to cover the beans.

Heat the oil in another pan over low heat. Add the onion and mint, season with salt and pepper and pan-fry for a few minutes. Stir in the wine and eau-de-vie, then tip everything into the pan with the beans, along with the bacon and the chorizo. Cover the pan and cook on low heat for 30 minutes. Stir well, then remove the mint and serve.

FAVA (BROAD) BEAN RAGOÛT

INGREDIENTS

- 8¾ lb (4 kg) fresh fava (broad) beans, shelled
- 1 tablespoon lard
- 4 oz (120 g) bacon, diced
- 5 shallots, chopped
- 3 carrots, chopped
- 2 cloves garlic, finely chopped
- 1 bouquet garni
- 1 teaspoon sugar
- salt and pepper
  Serves 6

Pop the fava beans out of their skins by squeezing them between your thumb and index finger. Melt the lard in a large skillet or frying pan, add the beans and bacon and pan-fry, stirring lightly, over medium heat for 5 minutes, or until lightly cooked. Stir in the shallots, carrots, garlic, bouquet garni and sugar with generous 2 cups (500 ml/18 fl oz) hot water.

Season with salt and pepper and bring to a boil, then lower the heat and simmer for 15 minutes, or until the beans are tender. If the liquid evaporates, add more hot water. Take care to ensure the beans are tender but not overcooked. Serve hot.

FRIED FAVA (BROAD) BEANS

INGREDIENTS

- 1 lb 8½ oz (700 g) fresh fava (broad) beans, shelled
- 1½ tablespoons olive oil
- 4 oz (120 g) bacon, very finely chopped
- ½ red bell pepper, seeded and finely chopped
- 1 scallion (spring onion), finely chopped
- 1 clove garlic, chopped
- 1 choricero pepper, roasted, skinned and ground to a paste or pureed (see Note)
- 1 tablespoon all-purpose (plain) flour
- salt

Serves 4

Pop the fava beans out of the skins by squeezing them between your thumb and index finger. Bring a large pan of salted water to a boil. Add the beans and cook, uncovered, for about 5–10 minutes, until tender. Drain well and set aside.

Heat the oil in a skillet or frying pan. Add the bacon, bell pepper, scallion and garlic and cook over low heat, stirring occasionally, for about 6 minutes, until softened. Stir in the flour and cook, stirring constantly, for 5 minutes, or until the flour begins to brown. Add a tablespoon of the pureed choricero pepper. Stir in the fava beans and cook, stirring occasionally, for another 5 minutes, until hot. Season with salt and serve.

Note: Choricero pepper is a variety of red bell pepper widely used in Spain, particularly in the Basque region. Used both fresh and dried, it has a sweet, smoky flavor. If necessary, any kind of Spanish bell pepper or chile can be substituted.

FAVA (BROAD) BEANS WITH MORCILLA

INGREDIENTS

- 1 lb 10 oz (750 g) fava (broad) beans, shelled
- 1 tablespoon olive oil
- 1 small onion, chopped
- 11 oz (300 g) morcilla or blood sausage (black pudding), skinned and cut into small pieces
- salt

Serves 6

If using frozen fava beans, cook them according to the directions on the package. If using fresh fava beans, pop them out of their skins by squeezing them between your thumb and index finger. Bring a large pan of salted water to a boil. Add the beans and cook, uncovered, for about 5–10 minutes, or until tender.

Meanwhile, heat the oil in a skillet or frying pan. Add the onion and cook over low heat, stirring occasionally, for about 7 minutes, but do not brown. Drain the beans, add to the onion and cook over very low heat for 6 minutes. Meanwhile, heat another skillet. Add the morcilla or blood sausage and cook, stirring occasionally, for 5–8 minutes. Add it to the beans and cook, stirring occasionally, for another 10 minutes. Serve immediately.

PHOTOGRAPH PAGE 129

SPINACH FLAN

INGREDIENTS

- 3¼ lb (1.5 kg) spinach, coarse stems removed
- 2 tablespoons (25 g/1 oz) butter, plus extra for greasing
- 1 heaping (heaped) tablespoon all-purpose (plain) flour
- 1 cup (250 ml/8 fl oz) milk
- 2 tablespoons heavy (double) cream
- 4 eggs, lightly beaten
- 1 scant teaspoon nutmeg (optional)
- salt

FOR THE TOMATO BÉCHAMEL SAUCE:

- 2 tablespoons (25 g/1 oz) butter
- 1 tablespoon all-purpose (plain) flour
- 1 cup (250 ml/8 fl oz) milk
  2 tablespoons tomato paste (puree)
- salt

Serves 4–5

Preheat the oven to 350°F (180°C/GAS MARK 4). Generously grease a high-sided ring-shaped ovenproof mold. Wash the spinach in several changes of water. Drain it, then put into a pan with just the water clinging to its leaves. Add a pinch of salt and cook over medium-high heat, stirring occasionally, for 8–10 minutes. Drain well, pressing out as much liquid as possible with the back of a spoon, and chop finely to make a puree.

Melt the butter in a pan and stir in the flour. Gradually stir in the milk, a little at a time, and bring to a boil, stirring constantly. Season with salt and simmer over medium heat, stirring constantly, for 8–10 minutes, until thickened. Leave to cook for 5 minutes, then add the spinach. The resulting sauce should be very smooth. Stir in the cream, then remove the pan from the heat and add the beaten eggs, little by little. Season with salt and add the nutmeg, if desired.

Pour the mixture into the prepared mold. Put the mold into a roasting pan and pour in boiling water to come about halfway up the sides. Bake for 50–60 minutes, or until set.

Meanwhile, make the tomato béchamel sauce: melt the butter in a pan and stir in the flour. Gradually stir in the milk, a little at a time, and bring to a boil, stirring constantly. Season with salt, add the tomato paste and simmer over medium heat, stirring constantly, for 8–10 minutes, until thickened. Remove the mold from the pan and leave it to stand for 10 minutes before running a round-bladed knife around the edge. Turn out the flan onto a warm serving dish. Pour the hot sauce over it and serve immediately.

Note: The flan can also be baked in individual tart pans, in which case reduce the cooking time to about 30 minutes.

RICE WITH BEANS AND TURNIPS

INGREDIENTS

- ¾ cup (150 g/5 oz) dried navy (haricot) beans, soaked overnight in cold water and drained
- 14 oz (400 g) pig's ear, halved foot (trotter) and tail, singed to remove any hairs
- 6–8 small turnips, peeled and leaves (tops) removed
- 4 tablespoons sunflower oil
- 5 oz (150 g) bacon, chopped
- 1 onion, chopped
- 1 cup (200 g/7 oz) long-grain rice
- 1 pinch saffron
- 2 morcillas or blood sausages (black puddings), skinned and thickly sliced
- salt and pepper
  Serves 4

Put the beans in a large pan with water to cover. Bring to a boil and cook for 10 minutes, then remove the pan from the heat and drain. Return the beans to the pan, pour in 4¼ pints (2.5 litres) water. Add the ear, foot and tail, bring to a simmer and cook over medium heat about 30 minutes. Add 1 cup (250 ml/8 fl oz) water and bring back to a simmer. After 30 minutes, add another cup (250 ml/8 fl oz) water and simmer for another 30 minutes. Add the turnips and simmer for a final 30 minutes. Use a slotted spoon to remove the meat and turnips, remove the meat from the bones, cut it into pieces and set aside. Do not discard the cooking liquid.

Heat the oil in a heavy-based pan. Add the bacon and the onion and cook over low heat, stirring occasionally, for 8 minutes, or until the onion is beginning to brown. Stir in the rice, then stir in the pieces of ear, foot and tail and the turnips. Pour in 4 cups (1 litre/1¾ pints) of the reserved cooking liquid. Crush the saffron threads in a mortar with a little of the cooking liquid, then add it to the pan. Add salt and pepper to taste and mix. Bring to a boil, then lower the heat and cook, uncovered, for 20–25 minutes, until the rice is tender and the liquid has been absorbed. It should not be dry.

Meanwhile, heat a large skillet or frying pan. Add the morcilla or blood sausage slices and cook over medium heat, turning once, for about 10 minutes, until cooked through. When the rice is cooked, take it off the heat and let it stand for 5 minutes. Arrange the slices of morcilla or blood sausage on top and serve immediately.

NAVY (HARICOT) BEANS WITH PAPRIKA

INGREDIENTS

- 3 ½ cups (700 g/1 lb 8½ oz) dried navy (haricot) beans, soaked for 3 hours (if very fresh) or overnight in cold water, and drained
- ½ garlic bulb, roasted (see Note)
- 1 bay leaf
- 2 small onions
- 1 small cooking chorizo, morcilla or blood sausage (black pudding)
- 4 tablespoons olive oil
- 1 tablespoon all-purpose (plain) flour
- 1 teaspoon paprika
- salt

Serves 6

Put the beans into a pan and pour in water to cover them. Do not add salt. Cover the pan and bring to a boil, then remove the pan from the heat and drain. Return the beans to the pan, pour in fresh cold water to cover, add the roasted garlic, bay leaf, one of the whole onions and the chorizo, morcilla or blood sausage and cook for 30 minutes over medium heat. Add 1 cup (250 ml/8 fl oz) water, bring back to a boil and simmer for another 30 minutes. Repeat this step after another 30 minutes, and after 1 hour.

Meanwhile, chop the remaining onion. Heat the oil in a skillet or frying pan. Add the chopped onion and cook over medium heat, stirring occasionally, for about 10 minutes, until lightly browned. Stir in the flour and cook, stirring constantly, for about 10 minutes, until lightly browned. Stir in the paprika and 3–4 tablespoons of the cooking liquid from the beans. Remove the pan from the heat and allow to cool slightly, then transfer the mixture to a food processor and process to a puree. Stir the puree into the pan with the beans and season to taste with salt. Remove the chorizo, morcilla or blood sausage, cut into slices and return to the pan. Remove and discard the bay leaf. Ladle the solid ingredients and a little of the liquid into a soup terrine and serve immediately.

Note: To roast the garlic bulb, drizzle it with olive oil, wrap it in aluminum foil, and cook under a preheated broiler (grill), turning frequently, until softened.

POTATOES WITH BELL PEPPERS

INGREDIENTS

- 1 large red bell pepper
- 6 large potatoes, about 7 oz (200 g) each, unpeeled
- 2 cups (450 ml/¾ pint) sunflower oil
- 4 large green bell peppers, seeded and cut into large squares
- 2 hard-boiled eggs, coarsely chopped
- salt

Serves 6

Preheat the oven to 350°F (180°C/GAS MARK 4). Put the red bell pepper on a baking sheet and roast, turning occasionally, for 10–20 minutes, until the skin is blistered and charred. Remove from the oven, place in a bowl and cover with a dish towel or paper towels.

When the pepper is cool enough to handle, peel off the skin, remove the stem and seeds and cut the flesh into strips. Season with salt and set aside. Put the potatoes into a large pan of cold water and add 1 teaspoon salt. Make sure the water covers them completely. Bring to a boil, then lower the heat and cook for 20–30 minutes, until tender but not falling apart. Drain well.

Meanwhile, heat the oil in a deep skillet or frying pan. Add the green bell pepper and some salt, cover and cook over medium heat for 15–20 minutes, until tender. Remove with a slotted spoon and drain.

Preheat the oven to 400°F (200°C/GAS MARK 6). Transfer 3 tablespoons of the oil from the skillet to an ovenproof dish. Peel the potatoes, scoop a hole out of the top and a slice off the base of each one so they will stand up. Put them in a single layer in the dish. Season lightly with salt and spoon a little of the oil from the skillet on to each potato. Place a little chopped hard-boiled egg and a few strips of red bell pepper in the hollow on top of each potato. Put the green bell peppers around the edge of the dish and spoon a little more of the oil from the skillet over the potatoes. Bake for 10 minutes, or until heated through, then serve.

PATATITAS NUEVAS RELLENAS CON CABRALES

CABRALES-STUFFED NEW POTATOES

INGREDIENTS

- 8 round new potatoes
- 5 tablespoons (80 g/3 oz) butter, plus extra for dotting
- salt

FOR THE CABRALES FILLING:

- 2 oz (50 g) Cabrales or Roquefort cheese, crumbled
- 2 tablespoons (25 g/1 oz) butter
- 1 egg, beaten
- 1 pinch nutmeg
- warmed milk, to loosen
- salt
  Serves 4

Preheat the oven to 350°F (180°C/GAS MARK 4). Wash and dry the potatoes. Bake them for 30 minutes, until soft. Remove the potatoes from the oven and carefully slice off the tops. Do not switch off the oven. Using a teaspoon, carefully scoop the potato flesh into a bowl, without piercing the skins. Lightly season each skin with salt and put a piece of butter the size of a hazelnut inside each one.

Mash the potato flesh and lightly season with salt. Stir in the cheese, remaining butter, egg, nutmeg and salt to taste. Gradually add the milk until the potato mixture is firm, not runny. Fill the skins with the mixture and place in a single, fairly tight-fitting layer in a ovenproof dish. Dot a little extra butter over them and bake for another 10 minutes. Serve immediately.

Note: Many alternative fillings can be used. To stuff them with ham, bake and hollow out the new potatoes as above. Mash the potato flesh and add generous 1 cup (200 g/7 oz) diced Serrano ham. Alternatively, replace the ham with generous 1 cup (200 g/7 oz) grated cheese, or generous 200 g/7 oz chopped smoked salmon or salmon roe (keta).

POTATO FRITTERS WITH GRATED CHEESE OR NUTMEG

INGREDIENTS

- 3¼ lb (1.5 kg) potatoes, unpeeled
- 1½ tablespoons (20 g/¾ oz) butter
- 4 tablespoons milk, warmed
- 3½ oz (100 g) Gruyère cheese, grated, or a generous pinch freshly grated nutmeg
- 4 eggs
- 1 egg white
- 1⅓–2 cups (80–120 g/3–4 oz) bread crumbs
- sunflower oil, for deep-frying
- salt
- 1 quantity Tomato Sauce (see page 181)

Serves 6

Put the potatoes in a pan of cold water to cover and add 1 teaspoon salt. Bring to a boil, lower the heat and cook for about 20 minutes if they are new potatoes, or 30 minutes if larger. Drain, peel and mash while still hot. Stir in the butter, milk and Gruyère or nutmeg. Separate 3 of the eggs, reserving the whites, and beat the yolks with the remaining egg. Add to the potatoes, mix well with a wooden spoon and season to taste. Whisk the egg whites to stiff peaks and fold into the mashed potatoes.

Shape the mixture into 2-inch (5-cm) square fritters. Spread out the bread crumbs in a shallow dish and gently roll the fritters in them. Heat the oil in a deep-fryer or deep pan to 350–375°F (180–190°C) or until a cube of bread browns in 30 seconds. Add the fritters, in batches, and cook until golden brown. Drain well and keep warm until all the batches are cooked. Serve immediately, offering the tomato sauce separately.

PHOTOGRAPH PAGE 131

PATATAS BRAVAS

INGREDIENTS

- 12 small potatoes, unpeeled
- 2 tablespoons olive oil
- 1 tablespoon white-wine vinegar
- 1 pinch hot paprika
- 1 clove garlic, finely chopped
- 1 teaspoon chili powder or Worcestershire sauce
- salt

Serves 4

Bring a large pan of salted water to a boil. Add the potatoes and cook for 20–25 minutes, until tender but not falling apart. Drain and let cool, then peel and slice or dice. Transfer to a plate or tray. Mix together the oil, vinegar, paprika, garlic and the chili powder or Worcestershire sauce in a bowl. Pour the mixture over the potatoes and serve hot.

PHOTOGRAPH PAGE 128

PADRÓN PEPPER EMPANADA

INGREDIENTS

- ¼ oz (10 g) dried yeast
- 3½ cups (400 g/14 oz) all-purpose (plain) flour, plus extra for kneading and rolling
- 3 eggs, beaten
- 1 tablespoon (15 g/½ oz) butter or margarine, at room temperature
- salt

FOR THE FILLING:

- olive oil, for frying and greasing
- 3½ oz (100 g) Padrón peppers
- 3 large onions, roughly chopped
- 1 clove garlic, chopped
- 1 sprig parsley, chopped
- 7 oz (200 g) pork tenderloin (fillet), cut into thin strips
- 2 oz (50 g) chorizo, casing removed and sliced
- salt

Serves 4–5

Put the yeast and a pinch of salt into a cup of hot, but not boiling, water and stir to dissolve the yeast. Set aside until the surface is covered with small bubbles. Make the dough as described on page 367, using the flour, 2 of the eggs, yeast, butter and salt quantities given here. Roll the dough into a ball, put it into a lightly greased bowl, cover with a thick cloth and leave it to rise in a warm place for 1 or 2 hours, until it has doubled in size.

Meanwhile, preheat the oven to 350°F (180°C/GAS MARK 4). Grease a 12-inch (30-cm) mold with oil. To make the filling, heat 2 inches (5 cm) oil in a large skillet or frying pan. Add the peppers in batches and cook over medium heat for 2 minutes, stirring occasionally, until they are cooked but not too browned. Remove, drain on paper towels, sprinkle with sea salt and set aside. Pour off all but 2 tablespoons of the oil from the skillet and reserve. Add the onion to the skillet and fry over medium heat, stirring occasionally, for 6 minutes, until softened. Add the garlic and parsley and cook for another 5 minutes. Add the chorizo and cook for another 2 minutes, then remove from the heat and set aside.

Wipe out the skillet. Return 1 tablespoon of the reserved oil to the skillet and heat. Add the pork strips and cook over medium-high heat, stirring, until browned on both sides. Divide the dough into 2 slightly unequal portions. Roll out the larger one on a lightly floured surface to about ¼ inch (5 mm) thick and line the bottom and sides of the mold. Add half the chorizo mixture and level the surface. Place the pork strips on top, along with the peppers, then add the rest of the chorizo mixture. Roll out the smaller piece of dough and place over the pie to make a lid, pressing the edges together to ensure the top and bottom are securely joined.

Glaze the top of the pie with the remaining egg. Cut a small hole in the top to let steam escape. Put the pie on a baking sheet, and bake for 45 minutes, increasing the temperature slightly every 15 minutes, until the top is golden brown. Remove the pie from the oven and leave to stand for 10–15 minutes. Carefully remove from the mold or leave in the mold. Serve hot or warm, cut into wedges.

GREEN BELL PEPPERS STUFFED WITH MEAT

INGREDIENTS

- 12 green bell peppers
- generous 2 cups (500 ml/18 fl oz) sunflower oil

FOR THE FILLING:

- 2½ cups (300 g/11 oz) ground (minced) meat, half pork and half beef
- 3½ oz (100 g) Serrano ham, finely chopped
- 1 slice bread, crusts removed and soaked in hot milk
- 1 clove garlic, finely chopped
- 1 teaspoon chopped parsley
- 1 egg, lightly beaten
- 1 tablespoon white wine
- salt

FOR THE SAUCE:

- 1 large onion, chopped
- 1 large ripe tomato, seeded and quartered
- 2 carrots, sliced
- 1 tablespoon all-purpose (plain) flour
- ¾ cup (175 ml/6 fl oz) white wine
- salt

Serves 6

Cut out the stems and remove the seeds from the bell peppers. Next, make the filling: if you are mincing the meat yourself, mince the ham at the same time. Otherwise, thoroughly mix the meat and ham together in a bowl. Gently squeeze the milk out of the bread, add it to the bowl with the meat and add the garlic, parsley, egg and wine. Season with salt and mix well. Fill the bell peppers with the meat mixture, using a teaspoon, and secure with wooden toothpicks (cocktail sticks).

Heat the oil with 2 tablespoons water in a deep skillet or frying pan. Add the bell peppers, three at a time, and cook over low heat for 10 minutes. Using a slotted spoon, transfer the cooked bell peppers to a clean shallow pan, arranging them in a single layer.

Drain all but about 5 tablespoons of the oil from the skillet and reheat. Add the onion and cook over low heat, stirring occasionally, for about 10 minutes, until browned. Add the tomato and carrot and cook, stirring occasionally, for another 5 minutes. Stir in the flour and cook, stirring constantly, for 2 minutes, then stir in the wine and 4 cups (1 litre/1¾ pints) water. Simmer for 15 minutes.

Allow to cool a little, then transfer to a food processor, process until smooth and pour into the pan with the bell peppers. Season with salt and cook over low heat, stirring occasionally, for 15 minutes. If the sauce is too thick, add a little hot water. Serve in warmed, deep dishes.

Note: This dish can be made in advance and is quite delicious when it is reheated.

PHOTOGRAPH PAGE 130

PIQUILLO PEPPERS STUFFED WITH IDIAZÁBAL CHEESE

INGREDIENTS

- 8 fresh or canned red piquillo peppers
- 2 tablespoons olive oil
- 3 egg whites
- salt

FOR THE CHEESE FILLING:

- 2 tablespoons (25 g/1 oz) butter
- 2 tablespoons olive oil
- 3 tablespoons all-purpose (plain) flour
- 1 cup (250 ml/8 fl oz) milk
- 1¾ cups (200 g/7 oz) grated Idiazábal cheese, plus extra for serving
- ¾ cup (175 ml/6 fl oz) heavy (double) cream
- salt

Serves 4

If using fresh peppers, cut out the stems and remove the seeds from the peppers. Salt the peppers slightly inside. Cover the bottom of a skillet or frying pan with the oil and 2 tablespoons of water. Put the peppers in the pan, then place over low heat. Cover the pan and cook the peppers for 25 minutes, carefully turning them halfway through. If using canned peppers, drain them well and skip this step.

Meanwhile, make the filling. Melt the oil and butter in a pan, add the flour and cook for a few minutes. Gradually add the milk, stirring constantly, to form a smooth sauce. Add the cheese, stirring constantly until it melts into the sauce. Add the cream and season with salt if necessary.

Whisk the egg whites with a pinch of salt in a clean, dry bowl until stiff peaks form, then gently fold into the cheese sauce. If using fresh peppers, carefully peel off the skins without tearing the flesh. Use the cheese mixture to fill the peppers generously, allowing some of the filling to overflow. Place the peppers in an ovenproof serving dish. Preheat the oven to 400°F (200°C/GAS MARK 6) for 5 minutes before placing the dish inside for just a few minutes until the peppers are thoroughly hot. Serve immediately from the same dish with a little extra cheese grated over the top.

Note: Idiazábal is a Spanish hard cheese made from sheeps' milk. It has a slightly smoky flavor. Manchego or another full-flavored hard cheese can be substituted.

FLAN DE PIMIENTOS CON
SALSA DE ANCHOAS

BELL PEPPER MOUSSE WITH ANCHOVY SAUCE

INGREDIENTS

- 2 cups (500 ml/18 fl oz) liquid gelatin (prepared with powdered or leaf gelatin)
- 9 oz (250 g) bottled or canned roasted red bell peppers, drained and seeded
- 2 tablespoons single (light) cream
- salt and pepper

FOR THE SAUCE:

- generous ⅓ cup (100 ml/ 3½ fl oz) light (single) cream
- 5 canned anchovy fillets in oil, drained and roughly chopped
- green tops of 2 scallions (spring onions), chopped
- 2 tablespoons chopped parsley

Serves 4

Make the gelatin according to the directions on the package. If using ready-made gelatin, melt it in a heatproof bowl set over a pan of barely simmering water. Let the gelatin cool slightly, but do not allow it to set. Puree the bell peppers in a blender, then mix them with the gelatin and cream. Season lightly with salt and pepper. Pour the mixture into individual molds and place them in the refrigerator for at least 5 hours to set.

Meanwhile, prepare the sauce by beating the cream with the anchovies, scallion tops and parsley. To serve, run a knife around the inside edge of the molds, then turn out the mousses onto individual plates. Spoon the sauce around or pass it separately.

Note: Canned roasted bell peppers are very convenient for preparing mousses and flans, but if you wish to prepare red bell peppers yourself, follow the directions for Bell Pepper, Egg and Anchovy Salad (see page 61). When the bell peppers are cold, remove the skins, cut them in half lengthwise and remove the seeds, then cut the flesh into strips and puree as described above.

PHOTOGRAPH PAGE 133

PISTO

INGREDIENTS

- 5 tablespoons olive oil
- 1 lb 2 oz (500 g) red or green bell peppers, seeded and finely chopped
- 3 zucchini (courgettes), finely chopped
- 2¼ lb (1 kg) tomatoes, peeled, seeded and chopped
- 1 pinch sugar
- salt
Serves 4

Heat the oil in a large skillet or frying pan. Add the bell peppers, cover and cook over low heat, shaking the pan from time to time, for 10 minutes. Add the zucchini, tomatoes and sugar and continue cooking for another 10 minutes. Uncover the pan and simmer until all the liquid from the tomatoes has evaporated. Season with salt.

Note: This dish can be prepared in advance and reheated. It is particularly delicious served with triangles of bread fried in butter.

LEEK FLAN

INGREDIENTS

- 4 leeks, trimmed and cut into ¾-inch (2-cm) slices
- butter, for greasing
- 3 eggs
- generous 2 cups (500 ml/ 18 fl oz) milk
- 2 teaspoons cornstarch (cornflour)
- 5 oz (150 g) cooked ham
- 5 oz (150 g) Gruyère cheese, grated
- salt and pepper
Serves 6

Bring a pan of salted water to a boil. Add the leeks and cook over medium-high heat for 15 minutes, or until very tender. Meanwhile, preheat the oven to 400°F (200°C/GAS MARK 6) and generously grease an ovenproof serving dish.

Drain the leeks well. Beat the eggs and mix with the milk. Add a small amount of this mixture to the cornstarch to make a paste, then pour the cornstarch mixture into the milk mixture and season with salt and pepper. Chop the ham into small pieces. Stir in the ham, cheese and leeks, then pour the mixture into the prepared dish. Bake for 20 minutes or until set, cut into slices and serve hot or cold.

PHOTOGRAPH PAGE 132

LEEK AND RICE TART

INGREDIENTS

- 3 tablespoons olive oil, plus extra for brushing
- 4 leeks, trimmed, sliced and rinsed well
- 2 large onions, finely chopped
- 1 bay leaf
- 2 pinches dried thyme
- ¾ cup (175 ml/6 fl oz) dry white wine
- 3 eggs
- 1½ cups (350 ml/12 fl oz) milk
- ½ cup (50 g/2 oz) grated Gruyère cheese
- 1½ cups (220 g/7½ oz) cooked long-grain white rice
- salt

FOR THE SAUCE:

- 1 large red bell pepper, roasted and peeled
- ¾ cup (175 ml/6 fl oz) chicken stock
- 4 tablespoons light (single) cream
- salt and pepper

Serves 6

Preheat the oven to 350°F (180°C/GAS MARK 4) and preheat the broiler (grill). Brush an ovenproof dish with oil. Heat the oil in a pan. Add the leeks, onions, bay leaf and thyme and pan-fry over low heat, stirring occasionally, until softened and translucent. Pour in the wine, cover and simmer for 12 minutes.

Beat the eggs in a bowl, then stir in the milk and Gruyère cheese. Mix the leeks and onions with the cooked rice in another bowl and add the egg mixture, then season with salt. Spoon into the prepared dish and bake for 30 minutes.

Meanwhile, make the sauce. Remove and discard the seeds from the pepper and coarsely chop the flesh. Put the pepper and stock into a food processor and process to a puree, then pour into a pan and bring to a boil. Simmer for 2 minutes. Stir in the cream and heat gently but do not let boil. Season with salt and pepper. Turn the leek tart out onto a warm serving plate and serve immediately, cut into slices, serving the sauce separately.

FRICASSE DE SETAS
CON ANCHOAS

WILD MUSHROOM AND ANCHOVY FRICASSEE

INGREDIENTS

- 4 tablespoons olive oil
- 2¼ lb (1 kg) porcini (ceps) or other wild mushrooms, cleaned and cut into large pieces
- 12 canned anchovy fillets, drained
- 2 cloves garlic
- 1 cup (250 ml/8 fl oz) stock (homemade or ready-made)
- 1 tablespoon chopped parsley
- pepper

Serves 4

Heat the oil in a flameproof earthenware casserole or a large skillet or frying pan, add the mushrooms and pan-fry over low heat, stirring occasionally, for 10 minutes. Meanwhile, put the anchovies and garlic in a large mortar and crush them to a paste.

Stir the stock and the contents of the mortar into the mushrooms and season with pepper. Cover the pan and let simmer over low heat for 25 minutes. Sprinkle the parsley into the pan, re-cover and simmer for another 5 minutes. Serve hot, either in a serving dish or on small plates.

PHOTOGRAPH PAGE 133

ENSALADA TEMPLADA
DE SETAS Y CHAMPIÑONES

WARM PORCINI AND MUSHROOM SALAD

INGREDIENTS

- 3 tablespoons olive oil
- 1 lb 10 oz (750 g) porcini (ceps) or other wild mushrooms, cleaned and cut into thick slices
- 1 lb 2 oz (500 g) cultivated mushrooms, cleaned, peeled and cut into thick slices
- 1 clove garlic, finely chopped
- 1 tablespoon chopped parsley
- 1 tablespoon sherry vinegar
- salt and pepper

Serves 6

Heat the oil in a large skillet or frying pan or flameproof casserole over low heat. Add the porcini and cultivated mushrooms and pan-fry, stirring occasionally, for about 6 minutes. Do not allow them to brown. Add the garlic and parsley and take the pan off the heat. Sprinkle the sherry over the contents of the pan and serve warm, either in a serving dish or straight onto small plates.

RICE WITH VEGETABLES

INGREDIENTS

- 3 artichokes
- 1 lemon, halved
- ¾ cup (175 ml/6 fl oz) sunflower oil
- 2 tomatoes, peeled, seeded and chopped
- 1 onion, finely chopped
- 2 red bell peppers, halved, seeded and chopped
- 1 clove garlic
- 1 sprig parsley
- 8 almonds
- 3½ oz (100 g) green beans, trimmed, strings removed and chopped
- 3½ oz (100 g) fava (broad) beans, trimmed, strings removed and chopped
- 2 carrots, peeled and sliced
- 2 cups (400 g/14 oz) long-grain rice
- 4 cups (1 litre/1¾ pints) vegetable stock or water
- 1 pinch saffron strands
- salt
- chopped parsley, to garnish (optional)
- 2 hard-boiled eggs, shelled and sliced, to garnish (optional)

Serves 6

Squeeze the juice from one lemon half and add the juice to a large bowl of water. Break off the artichoke stems and remove the coarse outer leaves. Cut off the tips of the remaining leaves. Cut the artichokes in half lengthwise and remove and discard the chokes. Rub the artichokes with the remaining lemon half and place in the acidulated water. Bring a large pan of salted water to a boil. Add the artichokes and bring back to a boil, then lower the heat, cover and simmer for about 25 minutes, until tender. (Test by gently pulling a leaf; it should come away easily.) Drain well. Heat a little of the oil in a frying pan or skillet and pan-fry the artichokes until golden. Set aside.

Heat the remaining oil in a flameproof casserole over medium-high heat. Add the tomatoes, onion and bell peppers and pan-fry, stirring occasionally, until browned. Meanwhile, crush the garlic, parsley and almonds in a large mortar.

When the vegetables have browned, stir in the garlic mixture, along with the green beans, fava beans, carrots, rice, stock and saffron and season with salt. Bring to a boil, cover, reduce the heat to low and let cook for 15 minutes, or until the rice is tender and the stock is absorbed.

Arrange the fried artichoke pieces on top, re-cover the casserole and let rest for 5 minutes. Garnish with chopped parsley and slices of hard-boiled egg, if desired, then serve.

PHOTOGRAPH PAGE 134

RICE WITH GREEN SAUCE

INGREDIENTS

- 2 cups (400 g/14 oz) long-grain rice
- 4 tablespoons olive oil
- 1 onion, chopped
- 1 clove garlic
- several parsley sprigs, plus 1 tablespoon very finely chopped parsley
- 1 tablespoon all-purpose (plain) flour
- 5 oz (150 g) canned asparagus, drained and rinsed, or cooked fresh asparagus
- salt and pepper

Serves 6

Bring 4 cups (1 litre/1¾ pints) unsalted water to a boil. Add the rice, stir with a wooden spoon to prevent the grains sticking together and cook over high heat for 12–15 minutes, until tender. Drain the rice in a large colander and rinse well under cold running water, stirring to ensure it is well washed. Leave the rice standing in the colander until required.

Heat the oil in a skillet or frying pan over low heat. Add the onion and pan-fry, stirring occasionally, for 6 minutes, or until softened but not colored. Meanwhile, crush the garlic in a large mortar with the parsley sprigs and a little salt, and set aside.

Add the flour to the pan with the onions and stir with a wooden spoon, then slowly stir in 1 cup (250 ml/8 fl oz) cold water until a smooth sauce forms. Simmer for 2 or 3 minutes before adding a couple of tablespoons to the garlic mixture in the mortar. Stir well, then pour the contents of the mortar into the skillet and stir it in.

Strain the sauce through a strainer with large holes into a flameproof earthenware casserole over medium heat. Add the rice and stir well until it is heated through. Meanwhile, reheat the asparagus by blanching it briefly in a pan of salted boiling water. Season the rice with pepper and sprinkle the chopped parsley over it. Garnish with the asparagus, then serve immediately.

VEGETABLE EMPANADA

INGREDIENTS

- 5 tablespoons olive or sunflower oil, plus extra for greasing
- 2 scallions (spring onions), finely chopped
- 2 zucchini (courgettes), peeled and chopped
- 1 eggplant (aubergine), peeled and chopped
- 3 tomatoes, peeled, seeded and chopped
- 1 clove garlic
- 1 lb 5 oz (600 g) puff pastry, thawed if frozen
- all-purpose (plain) flour, for rolling out the pastry
- 1 egg, lightly beaten
- salt and pepper

Serves 6

Heat the oil in a large skillet or frying pan over low heat. Add the scallions and pan-fry for 5 minutes, stirring occasionally. Add the zucchini and pan-fry for another 5 minutes, then stir in the eggplant and let cook for another 15 minutes, stirring occasionally.

Meanwhile, preheat the oven to 400°F (200°C/GAS MARK 6). Add the tomatoes and garlic to the pan and season with salt and pepper. Give everything a good stir and let cook for 6 minutes, or until the liquid has evaporated. Adjust the seasoning, if necessary.

Roll out the pastry on a lightly floured surface with a floured rolling pin. Lightly grease a 12-inch (30-cm) baking sheet with oil, then line it with half the pastry, leaving half hanging over one edge. Pour in the vegetable mixture and then fold the other half of the pastry over it to form a lid.

Seal the edges of the pastry carefully, pressing them together and rolling them slightly, creating a ¾-inch (2-cm) border all the way round. Cut 2 small holes in the center to allow steam to escape during baking. Use a fork to score a pattern of squares on the top, but take care not to pierce the pastry. Use a pastry brush to glaze the top with the beaten egg. Bake the pie for 30–40 minutes, or until golden brown. Remove from the pan and serve sliced.

PHOTOGRAPH PAGE 135

VEGETABLES WITH EGGS

INGREDIENTS

- 2 red bell peppers, seeded and cut into thin strips
- 2 tomatoes, peeled, seeded and chopped
- 2 onions, chopped
- 1 bouquet garni
- lemon juice or vinegar, to taste
- 4 eggs
- salt and pepper
  Serves 4

Put the peppers, tomatoes, onions, bouquet garni and 1 cup (250 ml/8 fl oz) water in a heavy-based pan. Season with salt and pepper and cook over medium-low heat, stirring occasionally, until tender. Transfer the vegetables to a serving dish and keep warm.

Two-thirds fill a pan or deep skillet or frying pan with water. Add 1 tablespoon of the lemon juice, or a dash of vinegar, for each 4 cups (1 litre/1¾ pints) water, and bring to a boil. Carefully crack an egg into a small cup and tip it carefully into the water from just above the water level, to prevent the yolk from breaking and the white from spreading. Immediately repeat with another egg.

When the water comes back to a boil, turn the heat down to low and cook the eggs for 3 minutes in very hot but not boiling water. Remove them with a slotted spoon and keep warm while poaching the remaining eggs. Serve the eggs on top of the vegetables.

Note: The most important thing for this recipe is to use very fresh eggs, which are easier to poach, and also to ensure that the yolks remain intact when cracking the eggs. To remove excess water when transferring the eggs from the pan, hold the slotted spoon over a clean dish towel for a few seconds before placing the eggs in the vegetable dish.

OLIVE
CAVIAR
PAGE 44

MUSHROOM AND OLIVE SALAD
PAGE 51

ARTICHOKE SALAD WITH ANCHOVY DRESSING
PAGE 46

CARDOON IN
VINAIGRETTE
PAGE 50

CAULIFLOWER AND
SHRIMP (PRAWN) SALAD
PAGE 53

PRUNES WITH
ROQUEFORT,
RAISINS AND
PINE NUTS
PAGE 52

LETTUCE
HEART SALAD
PAGE 54

ROASTED MIXED
VEGETABLES
PAGE 55

ASPARAGUS, HAM AND
MAYONNAISE TAPA
PAGE 56

NAVY (HARICOT)
BEAN SALAD WITH
SAGE AND THYME
PAGE 58

ORANGE, FENNEL
AND ONION SALAD
PAGE 59

RADISH SALAD
PAGE 63

RED BELL PEPPER, EGG
AND ANCHOVY SALAD
PAGE 61

RUSSIAN
SALAD
PAGE 62

BREAD WITH
TOMATO
PAGE 63

CARROT SALAD
WITH ORANGE
PAGE 66

GREEN
SAUCE
PAGE 65

**TOMATOES FILLED
WITH SARDINES**

PAGE 64

FRIED
ARTICHOKES
PAGE 70

RICE WITH SWISS
CHARD AND NAVY
(HARICOT) BEANS
PAGE 69

RICE WITH
MUSHROOMS
AND SHERRY
SAUCE
PAGE 74

FRIED
PUMPKIN
PAGE 73

CAULIFLOWER
FRITTERS
PAGE 77

STUFFED
MUSHROOMS
PAGE 76

FRIED GREEN ASPARAGUS
WITH GARLIC, VINEGAR
AND PAPRIKA

PAGE 79

GARBANZO BEAN
(CHICKPEA) SALAD
PAGE 81

PATATAS BRAVAS
PAGE 92

FAVA (BROAD) BEANS
WITH MORCILLA
PAGE 86

GREEN BELL PEPPERS
STUFFED WITH MEAT
PAGE 94

POTATO FRITTERS
WITH GRATED CHEESE
OR NUTMEG
PAGE 92

LEEK FLAN
PAGE 97

BELL PEPPER MOUSSE
WITH ANCHOVY SAUCE
PAGE 96

WILD MUSHROOM
AND ANCHOVY
FRICASSEE
PAGE 99

RICE WITH
VEGETABLES
PAGE 100

VEGETABLE
EMPANADA
PAGE 102

EGG AND CHEESE TAPAS

COLD

HARD-BOILED EGGS WITH BLACK OLIVES

INGREDIENTS

- 4 eggs
- 8 black olives, pitted (stoned) and finely chopped
- 1 bottled or canned roasted red bell pepper, drained and finely chopped
- 1 tablespoon capers, drained, rinsed and finely chopped
- extra-virgin olive oil
- chopped parsley, to garnish
- salt
  Makes 8

To hard boil the eggs, pour enough water to cover them into a large pan, add 1 tablespoon salt and bring to a boil. Add the eggs carefully and stir gently with a wooden spoon so that when they set the yolks will be in the center. Cook medium-size eggs for 12 minutes. (Add 1 minute for bigger eggs and subtract 1 minute for smaller eggs.) Drain off the hot water, fill the pan with cold water and leave the eggs until required.

When the eggs are cool enough to handle, shell and halve them lengthwise, then scoop out the yolks with a teaspoon, without piercing the whites. Cut a thin slice off the base of each egg white half so it stays upright.

Put the yolks into a bowl and crush with a fork. Add the olives, bell pepper and capers and mix them together, then beat in enough oil to create a smooth mixture. Season with salt, but remember the capers may be salty. Using a teaspoon, fill the egg whites with the olive mixture. Leave in the refrigerator until ready to serve. Garnish with parsley just before serving.

PHOTOGRAPH PAGE 185

CURD CHEESE
AND OLIVE TAPA

INGREDIENTS

- scant 2½ cups (500 g/1 lb 2 oz)
  curd cheese
- 1¼ cups (150 g/5 oz)
  black olives, pitted (stoned)
  and chopped, plus extra
  for garnishing
- 2 shallots, finely chopped
- 1 bunch chives, finely chopped
- 3 tablespoons olive oil
- 12 x ½-inch (1-cm) slices
  French baguette
- 12 onion rings, to garnish
- pepper
  Makes 12

Put the cheese, olives, shallots and chives in a bowl and beat together until blended. Beat in the oil until smooth, then season with pepper. Cover and chill until required.

When ready to serve, spread the bread slices with the cheese and olive mixture. Garnish with an onion ring and a black olive in the center. Serve immediately or the bread will become soggy.

PHOTOGRAPH PAGE 186

CABRALES
CHEESE DIP

INGREDIENTS

- 1 generous cup (150 g/5 oz)
  crumbled Cabrales cheese
  (see Note)
- ½ cup (125 g/4 oz) plain yogurt
  Serves 6

Mash the Cabrales cheese in a bowl, then gradually stir in the yogurt. This dip can be served with thin savory crackers (biscuits) or potato chips (crisps).

Note: Cabrales is a blue cheese from the northern Spanish principality of Asturias. It is most often made with cow's milk, but may also be made with sheep's or goat's milk. Roquefort cheese is a good substitute.

HARD-BOILED EGGS WITH ANCHOVIES AND MAYONNAISE

INGREDIENTS

- 9 eggs
- 1 oz (25 g) canned anchovy fillets in oil, drained and chopped
- 1 quantity Thick Mayonnaise (see page 211)
- parsley sprigs or watercress, to garnish
- salt and pepper

Makes 18

To hard boil the eggs, pour enough water to cover them into a large pan, add 1 tablespoon salt and bring to a boil. Add the eggs carefully and stir gently with a wooden spoon so that when they set the yolks will be in the center. Cook medium-size eggs for 12 minutes. (Add 1 minute for bigger eggs and subtract 1 minute for smaller eggs.) Drain off the hot water, fill the pan with cold water and leave the eggs until required.

When the eggs are cool enough to handle, shell and halve them lengthwise, then scoop out the yolks with a teaspoon, without piercing the whites. Cut a thin slice off the base of each egg white half so it stays upright.

Mix the mayonnaise with 10 halved hard-boiled yolks and the anchovies. Season with salt and pepper, but remember the anchovies will be salty. Using a teaspoon, fill the egg white halves with the anchovy mixture and place in a serving dish. Push the remaining egg yolks through a fine strainer and sprinkle them over the top. Garnish the serving dish with sprigs of parsley or watercress and chill in the refrigerator for up to 2 hours – any longer and the mayonnaise will become dry.

HARD-BOILED EGGS WITH PEAS AND RED BELL PEPPERS

INGREDIENTS

- 12 eggs
- 2 cloves garlic
- 2 sprigs parsley
- 1 pinch saffron, dissolved in a little water
- ¼ cup (50 ml/2 fl oz) sunflower oil
- 1 large onion, chopped
- 2 tablespoons all-purpose (plain) flour
- generous 2 cups (500 ml/ 18 fl oz) tomato sauce, bottled or homemade (see page 181)
- 1 teaspoon paprika
- 14 oz (400 g) fresh or canned peas, rinsed and drained
- 2 bottled or canned roasted red bell peppers, drained and diced the same size as the peas
- salt and pepper
  Makes 24

To hard boil the eggs, pour enough water to cover them into a large pan, add 1 tablespoon salt and bring to a boil. Add the eggs carefully and stir gently with a wooden spoon so that when they set the yolks will be in the center. Cook medium-size eggs for 12 minutes. (Add 1 minute for bigger eggs and subtract 1 minute for smaller eggs.)

Drain off the hot water, fill the pan with cold water and leave the eggs until required. Meanwhile, put the garlic, parsley and saffron in a large mortar and crush. Set aside.

Heat the oil in a deep pan, add the onion and pan-fry over low heat, stirring occasionally, for 7 minutes, or until lightly browned. Stir in the flour and cook for 2 minutes, then stir in the tomato sauce. Remove the pan from the heat and stir in the paprika and 1 cup (250 ml/8 fl oz) water. Return the pan to the heat and let the sauce simmer for 15 minutes.

After the sauce has simmered for 15 minutes, add the mixture from the mortar, the peas and the bell peppers. Season with salt and pepper and let cook for another 10 minutes.

Shell and halve the eggs lengthwise. Cut a thin slice off the base of each egg white half so it does not slip in the serving dish, then arrange in the dish. Pour the sauce over the eggs and serve at room temperature.

PHOTOGRAPH PAGE 187

QUAILS' EGG SALAD

INGREDIENTS

- 7 oz (200 g) green beans, trimmed with strings removed
- 1 head of lettuce, separated into leaves, or mixed salad leaves, such as Batavia, watercress and lettuce, rinsed and patted dry
- 12 quails' eggs
- 5 oz (150 g) bottled or freshly cooked green asparagus tips, rinsed
- 4 tablespoons oil
- 4 slices bread
- 4 slices (rashers) bacon
- 2 tablespoons vinegar
- 4 teaspoons runny honey
- salt and pepper

  Serves 4

Bring a pan of salted water to a boil. Add the green beans and cook for 10 minutes, or until they are just tender. Drain them and then run under cold running water to stop them cooking. Drain again and set aside.

Meanwhile, cook the quails' eggs in another pan of boiling salted water for 3 minutes, then run them under cold running water. When they are cool enough to handle, shell them and cut them in half lengthwise. Put them in a salad bowl with the green beans and asparagus tips, then set aside.

Pan-fry the bread in the oil in a large skillet or frying pan over medium heat until golden on both sides. Remove from the skillet, cut into pieces and set aside.

Add the bacon to the skillet and pan-fry until it is crispy, then cut it into pieces. Pour the warm oil from the skillet into a small bowl and mix with the vinegar and honey. Add a pinch of salt and pepper, the fried bread and the bacon to the salad. Pour the dressing over the salad and serve.

PHOTOGRAPH PAGE 188

HUEVOS DE
CODORNIZ RELLENOS

STUFFED QUAILS' EGGS

INGREDIENTS
- 12 quails' eggs
- 3 tablespoons thick mayonnaise
- 1 teaspoon Dijon mustard
- 1 scallion (spring onion), finely chopped
- salt
Makes 12

To hard boil the eggs, pour enough water to cover them into a large pan, add 1 tablespoon salt and bring to a boil. Add the eggs carefully and stir gently with a wooden spoon so that when they set the yolks will be in the center. Cook the eggs for 3 minutes. Drain off the hot water, and fill the pan with cold running water to stop the cooking. When the eggs are cold, remove the shells and cut a little off the base of each egg so they sit in the dish.

At the fattest end of the egg, remove enough of the egg white to enable the yolk to be carefully removed. Crush all of the yolks and stir in the mayonnaise and a little mustard, then add a very little scallion. Season with salt. Using a teaspoon, generously fill the egg whites with this mixture, allowing some to overflow. Store in the refrigerator until serving.

Note: This tapa can also be made with hens' eggs. Serve on a lightly dressed bed of lettuce cut into julienne strips.

TAPA DE JAMÓN Y
HUEVOS DE CODORNIZ

HAM AND QUAILS' EGG TAPA

INGREDIENTS

- 12 quails' eggs
- 12 large slices bread
- 12 thin slices Serrano ham
- ⅓ cup (75 g/2½ oz) butter or margarine, softened, for spreading, plus extra for garnishing (optional)
- chopped parsley, to garnish
- salt

Makes 24

Put the quails' eggs into a large pan of salted water, bring to a boil and boil for 3 minutes. Drain off the hot water and fill the pan with cold running water to stop the cooking. When the eggs are cool enough to handle, shell them. Leave in a bowl of cold water if not using at once.

Using a 2-inch (5-cm) round cookie cutter, cut out 24 circles from the bread. Using the same cutter, cut out 24 circles of ham. Butter one side of each slice of bread, taking care not to tear the bread. Sprinkle the parsley over the buttered side of each circle, then top each with a circle of ham.

Drain the eggs if they are in water and pat dry, then cut each in half lengthwise. Put half an egg on top of each tapa, cut side down, then sprinkle with parsley. The tapas can be served like this, or you can garnish them with soft piped butter all around, if you like. They are best served immediately but if prepared in advance, store in the refrigerator until ready to serve.

PHOTOGRAPH PAGE 189

HARD-BOILED EGGS WITH SEAFOOD AND MAYONNAISE

INGREDIENTS

- 9 eggs
- 1⅓ cups (300 g/11 oz)
  mayonnaise, homemade
  (see page 62) or ready-made
- 9 oz (250 g) cooked mixed
  seafood, such as shrimp
  (prawns), mussels, crayfish
  and lobster, shelled and
  chopped as necessary
- salt and pepper
  Makes 18

Hard boil the eggs as described below. Shell them, but keep them whole.

Carefully remove the yolks from the eggs with a teaspoon, without piercing the whites. Finely chop the yolks. Put them in a large bowl and mix together with the mayonnaise and seafood. Season with salt and pepper. Cut a thin slice off the bottom of each egg white half so it stands up straight. Using a teaspoon, fill the egg whites with the seafood mixture. Put the filled halves on a serving dish and chill in the refrigerator before serving.

EGGS WITH MAYONNAISE AND GHERKINS

INGREDIENTS

- 4 eggs
- generous 1 cup (250 g/9 oz)
  mayonnaise, homemade
  (see page 62) or ready-made
- 1 tablespoon mustard
- 1 tablespoon white-wine vinegar
- 4 teaspoons capers, rinsed
  and drained
- 3 gherkins, sliced
- 1 roasted red bell pepper, seeded
  and chopped
- 1 tablespoon chopped scallion
  (spring onion) or parsley
- salt and pepper
  Makes 8

To hard boil the eggs, pour enough water to cover them into a large pan, add 1 tablespoon salt and bring to a boil. Add the eggs carefully and stir gently with a wooden spoon so that when they set the yolks will be in the center. Cook medium-size eggs for 12 minutes. (Add 1 minute for bigger eggs and subtract 1 minute for smaller eggs.) Drain off the hot water, fill the pan with cold water and leave the eggs until required. Shell them, but keep them whole.

Mix the mayonnaise, mustard and vinegar together, stir in the capers, gherkins, bell pepper and scallion or parsley, then season with salt and pepper. Cover the eggs with the sauce and serve, or keep in the refrigerator until required.

CHEESE AND RADISH SALAD

INGREDIENTS

- 14 oz (400 g) young Spanish cheese, such as fresh Manchego
- 7 oz (200 g) ham
- 5 radishes, sliced
- 12 walnuts, halved
- 1 tablespoon chopped parsley
- 5 oz (150 g) lettuce leaves, such as arugula (rocket), rinsed and shredded
- 2 tablespoons white-wine vinegar
- 6 tablespoons olive oil
- salt and pepper

Serves 8

Cut the cheese and ham into ¾-inch (2-cm) strips. Put the cheese, ham, radishes, walnut, parsley and lettuce leaves into a salad bowl and mix together. In a bowl, beat the vinegar with a pinch of salt with a fork, then beat in the oil and add pepper to taste. Pour the dressing over the salad and serve.

Note: If not serving the salad immediately, cover and chill the ingredients. Pour the dressing over it just before serving.

PHOTOGRAPH PAGE 190

SOFT CHEESE SANDWICHES

INGREDIENTS

- scant ½ cup (100 g/3½ oz) ricotta cheese
- scant ½ cup (100 g/3½ oz) mascarpone cheese
- 2 tablespoons heavy (double) cream
- 1 teaspoon chives, shallot or scallion (spring onion), finely chopped
- 10 slices white bread
- 10 slices rye bread

Makes 20

Beat together the cheeses until combined, then beat in the heavy cream. Stir in the chives, shallot or scallion. Remove the crusts from the bread. Spread the mixture onto the slices of white bread and place a slice of rye bread on top of each slice. Cut each sandwich diagonally in half to form 2 triangles. The sandwiches may be kept in the refrigerator for a short time before serving.

PHOTOGRAPH PAGE 191

IDIAZÁBAL CHEESE AND FRIED ONION TAPA

INGREDIENTS

- 7 oz (200 g) Idiazábal cheese, rind removed and sliced
- 1 cup (250 ml/8 fl oz) milk
- 2 teaspoons black peppercorns, lightly crushed
- 1 cup (250 ml/8 fl oz) olive oil
- 1 onion, sliced
- 6 slices of French baguette
- 1 teaspoon honey
  Serves 6

Place the cheese in a bowl, add the milk and peppercorns and let soak for 30 minutes. Drain the cheese and pat dry with paper towels. Heat the oil in a skillet or frying pan. Add the onions and cook over high heat, stirring frequently, for about 15 minutes, until they are crunchy and crispy, like French fries (chips), and all the liquid has evaporated. Remove with a slotted spoon and drain well on paper towels. Place each slice of cheese on a slice of bread and top with fried onions. Drizzle a little honey over each one and serve.

Note: Idiazábal is a hard cheese made from sheep's milk. It has a slightly smoky flavor. Manchego or other full-flavored hard cheese can be substituted.

BAKED CHEESE STICKS

INGREDIENTS

- scant ½ cup (100 g/3½ oz) butter
- ¾ cup (85 g/3 oz) all-purpose (plain) flour
- 3½ oz (100 g) Parmesan cheese, grated
- ⅔ cup (50 g/1¾ oz) bread crumbs (made from day-old bread)
- salt (optional)
  Makes about 20

Preheat the oven to 400°F (200°C/GAS MARK 6). Put the butter in a pan and melt it over low heat but do not allow it to brown, then remove the pan from the heat. Stir in the flour, then stir in the Parmesan. Season with salt, if necessary. Spread out the bread crumbs in a shallow dish. Shape scoops of the cheese mixture into long, fat sticks, about the size of your little finger. Roll the cheese sticks in the bread crumbs and place on a baking sheet. Bake for 8–10 minutes, until golden brown. Carefully transfer the cheese sticks to a wire rack (they will break easily) and let cool completely before serving.

PHOTOGRAPH PAGE 192

HARD-BOILED EGGS WITH SMOKED SALMON

INGREDIENTS

- 4 eggs
- ½ cup (120 g/4 oz) mayonnaise, homemade (see page 62) or ready-made
- 1 generous slice smoked salmon
- salt (optional)
- 3½ tablespoons (50 g/1¾ oz) bottled salmon roe (keta), drained, to garnish

Makes 8

To hard boil the eggs, pour enough water to cover them into a large pan, add 1 tablespoon salt and bring to a boil. Add the eggs carefully and stir gently with a wooden spoon so that when they set the yolks will be in the center. Cook medium-size eggs for 12 minutes. (Add 1 minute for bigger eggs and subtract 1 minute for smaller eggs.) Drain off the hot water, fill the pan with cold water and leave the eggs until required. When the eggs are cool enough to handle, shell and halve the eggs lengthwise. Cut a thin slice off the base of each egg white half so it stays upright.

Put the mayonnaise and smoked salmon in a blender and blend until well mixed. Season with salt, if necessary, as the salmon might be already salted. To improve the presentation of the eggs, use a pastry (piping) bag to pipe the salmon and mayonnaise mixture onto the halved eggs. Garnish with the salmon roe and serve. If not serving immediately, store in the refrigerator until required.

HARD-BOILED EGGS WITH RUSSIAN SALAD

INGREDIENTS
- 9 eggs
- 1 bunch watercress, to garnish

FOR THE SALAD:
- 1lb 2oz (500g) shelled peas
- 9oz (250g) carrots, diced
- 2 potatoes, unpeeled

FOR THE MAYONNAISE:
- 2 egg yolks, at room temperature
- 1½ tablespoons white-wine vinegar or lemon juice
- 1½ cups (350ml/12floz) sunflower oil
- salt
  Makes 18

First cook the vegetables. Bring a pan of salted water to a boil. Add the peas and cook for 5–10 minutes, until tender. Put the carrots in another pan, pour in water to cover and add a pinch of salt. Bring to a boil and cook for 20–30 minutes, until tender. Put the potatoes in a third pan, pour in water to cover and add a pinch of salt. Bring to a boil and cook for 20–30 minutes, until tender but not falling apart. Drain all the vegetables well and let cool. Peel and dice the potatoes.

Meanwhile, make the mayonnaise. Put the egg yolks in a bowl with 1½ teaspoons of the vinegar or lemon juice and a small pinch of salt. Stir lightly with a whisk or fork and then gradually whisk in the oil, 1–2 teaspoons at a time, until about a quarter has been added. Whisk in the remaining oil in a slow, steady stream. Add the remaining vinegar or lemon juice, then taste and adjust the seasoning by adding salt. Cover and chill until required.

While the vegetables are cooking, hard boil the eggs. Pour enough water to cover the eggs into a large pan, add 1 tablespoon salt and bring to a boil. Add the eggs carefully and stir gently with a wooden spoon so that when they set the yolks will be in the center. Cook medium-size eggs for 12 minutes. (Add 1 minute for bigger eggs and subtract 1 minute for smaller eggs.) Drain off the hot water, fill the pan with cold water and leave the eggs until required. When the eggs are cool enough to handle, shell and halve the eggs lengthwise, then scoop out the yolks with a teaspoon, without piercing the whites. Cut a thin slice off the base of each egg white half so it stays upright. Set the egg yolks aside.

Mix the mayonnaise with the vegetables. Using a teaspoon, fill the egg whites with this mixture. Push the egg yolks through a fine strainer and sprinkle them over the top. Chill in the refrigerator for 1 hour before serving. Serve garnished with watercress leaves.

PHOTOGRAPH PAGE 193

STUFFED HARD-BOILED EGGS

INGREDIENTS

- 8 eggs
- 7 oz (200 g) canned tuna, drained and flaked
- 1 onion, finely chopped
- 4 bottled or canned red bell peppers, drained and finely chopped
- 8 olives, pitted (stoned) and fincly chopped
- 4 tablespoons thick mayonnaise, plus extra to garnish
- salt
Makes 8

To hard boil the eggs, pour enough water to cover them into a large pan, add 1 tablespoon salt and bring to a boil. Add the eggs carefully and stir gently with a wooden spoon so that when they set the yolks will be in the center. Cook medium-size eggs for 12 minutes. (Add 1 minute for bigger eggs and subtract 1 minute for smaller eggs.) Drain off the hot water, fill the pan with cold water and leave the eggs until required.

Mix the tuna and onion together, then stir in the bell peppers, olives and enough mayonnaise to bind together. Season with salt and stir again.

Shell and halve the eggs lengthwise, then scoop out the yolks with a teaspoon, without piercing the whites. Cut a thin slice off the base of each egg white half so it stays upright. Finely chop the yolks and set aside.

Using a teaspoon, fill the egg whites with the tuna mixture, and garnish around the eggs with extra mayonnaise. Sprinkle the egg yolks over the eggs and chill in the refrigerator until ready to serve.

HOT

ARTICHOKE HEARTS WITH SCRAMBLED EGGS

INGREDIENTS

- 1 lemon, cut in half
- 4–6 large artichokes
- 8 eggs
- 4–5 tablespoons milk
  or heavy (double) cream
- 3 tablespoons (40 g/1½ oz)
  butter
- 1 good-size truffle
- salt
  Serves 4–6

Fill a bowl with water and squeeze the juice from half the lemon into the bowl. Cut the stems off the artichokes, trim off the tips of the leaves and remove the hard external leaves. Force the top leaves open and use a long spoon to scoop out the hairy choke. Cut the bases flat to stop them falling over when filled, rubbing each cut side with half the lemon and dropping it into the bowl of water as it is prepared.

Meanwhile, bring a large pan of salted water to a boil. Add the artichokes and when the water returns to a boil, reduce the heat to low, cover the pan and let simmer for 35 minutes, or until tender. Test by pulling off one leaf, which should come off without resistance. Drain them well, then place upside down on folded paper towels to drain. Cover with a dish towel to keep warm and set aside.

Lightly beat the eggs and place in a heatproof bowl set over a pan of barely simmering water. Add the milk and 2 tablespoons butter and cook gently, stirring constantly, until starting to set. When the eggs are creamy and almost cooked, add the remaining butter.

Place the artichokes in a dish in which they will all fit upright. Fill them generously with the scrambled eggs and place a slice of truffle on the top of each one. Serve immediately.

Note: If you only have small artichokes, allow 2 per person.

PHOTOGRAPH PAGE 194

TORTILLA DE ATÚN

TUNA TORTILLA

INGREDIENTS

- 4 tablespoons olive oil
- 1 small onion, finely chopped
- 2½ oz (65 g) canned tuna, drained and flaked
- 1 tablespoon light (single) cream
- 4 eggs
- salt and pepper
- tomato sauce, bottled or homemade (see page 181), to serve (optional)

Serves 2

Heat 2 tablespoons of the oil in a pan over medium heat. Add the onion and pan-fry for about 6 minutes until it is soft but not colored. Stir in the tuna and take the pan off the heat. Stir in the cream and season with pepper.

Heat the remaining 2 tablespoons of oil in a 9½-inch (24-cm) skillet or frying pan over high heat and swirl it around. Beat the eggs vigorously with a pinch of salt. Tip the egg mixture into the skillet and pull it from the edge of the skillet to the center with a fork or rubber spatula. Cook until the underside is set and lightly browned.

Spoon half the tuna mixture along the center of the tortilla. Fold the tortilla using a rubber spatula, then slide it onto a plate and serve immediately.

Note: You can drizzle several tablespoons of hot tomato sauce over the tortilla once it is on the plate, if desired.

TORTILLA FINA CON
ATÚN Y PIMIENTOS

THIN TORTILLAS WITH TUNA AND BELL PEPPER

INGREDIENTS

- 5 oz (150 g) green bell peppers, halved
- 5 oz (150 g) red bell peppers, halved
- 3 tablespoons olive oil
- 2 onions, finely chopped
- 1 lb 8½ oz (700 g) tomatoes, peeled, seeded and chopped
- 2 cloves garlic, crushed
- 8 eggs
- 7 oz (200 g) canned tuna, drained and flaked
- salt and pepper
- mint leaves, to garnish
  Serves 8

Preheat the broiler (grill), and broil (grill) the peppers until they are soft and the skin has blackened. Let cool between 2 plates. Peel the peppers, remove the seeds and stalks and cut the flesh into strips.

Heat 2 tablespoons of the oil in a pan over low heat. Add the onion, cover the pan, and cook for 6 minutes, or until softened but not browned, stirring from time to time with a wooden spoon. Keep the pan covered, removing the lid only to stir the onions. Add the bell peppers, tomatoes and garlic and continue pan-frying gently, uncovered, for 8 minutes, stirring occasionally. Add salt and pepper to taste.

Vigorously beat 2 eggs in a dish with a pinch of salt. Heat a little of the remaining oil in a small skillet or frying pan over high heat and when it is hot, pour in the egg. Pull it from the edge of the skillet to the center to make a thin tortilla. Place one-quarter of the vegetable mixture on top, along with one-quarter of the flaked tuna. Remove from the pan and keep warm. Prepare the remaining 3 tortillas in the same way. Serve garnished with mint.

CHEESE FRITTERS WITH TOMATO SAUCE

INGREDIENTS

- 2 tablespoons (25 g/1 oz) butter
- 1 cup (120 g/4 oz) all-purpose (plain) flour
- 4 eggs
- 5 oz (150 g) Gruyère cheese, grated
- vegetable oil, for deep-frying
- salt

FOR THE TOMATO SAUCE:

- 3 tablespoons olive oil
- 1 onion, chopped (optional)
- 2¼ lb (1 kg) ripe tomatoes, seeded and chopped
- 1 teaspoon sugar
- salt

Serves 6–12

Pour generous 1½ cups (375 ml/13 fl oz) water into a pan, add the butter and a pinch of salt and heat gently until the butter has melted. Bring to a boil, tip in the flour and stir vigorously with a wooden spoon until the mixture comes together and leaves the sides of the pan. Remove the pan from the heat and stir for about 5 minutes, until the mixture is cool. Stir in the eggs (unbeaten), one at a time, making sure each one is fully incorporated before adding the next. Stir in the Gruyère and let the mixture stand for 2 hours.

Meanwhile, make the tomato sauce. Heat the oil in a skillet or frying pan. Add the onion, if using, and cook over low heat, stirring occasionally, for about 5 minutes, until softened but not browned. (If you're not using the onion, add the tomato immediately.) Add the tomato and cook over low heat, breaking the flesh up with the edge of a skimmer or slotted spoon, for about 15 minutes. Allow the mixture to cool slightly, then transfer to a food processor and process. Add the sugar, season to taste with salt and process briefly again. Set aside.

To make the fritters, heat the vegetable oil in a large, deep pan or deep-fryer to 350–375°F (180–190°C) or until a cube of bread browns in 30 seconds. Scoop up a little of the cheese mixture on a teaspoon and use another teaspoon to carefully push it off the spoon into the hot oil. It should sink to the bottom of the pan. Repeat the process, but do not add too many fritters to the pan at the same time, as they expand considerably during cooking and it is better to fry them with plenty of space. When they are golden brown, remove them from the oil with a slotted spoon and place them in a large heatproof colander set over a baking pan in a warm oven until all the fritters are cooked. Serve the fritters in a cloth-lined dish and offer the warmed tomato sauce separately.

PHOTOGRAPH PAGE 195

TORTILLA DE COLIFLOR

CAULIFLOWER TORTILLA

INGREDIENTS
- 4 cauliflower florets
- lemon juice, for soaking
- 1 tablespoon butter
- 2 tablespoons olive oil
- 6 eggs
- salt
Serves 2

Soak the cauliflower florets in a bowl of water with the lemon juice for 20 minutes. Bring a large pan of salted water to a boil. Add the florets and boil, uncovered, for 4–5 minutes, or until tender but not too soft. Test by inserting a sharp knife into the base of a floret. Drain well and pat dry.

Melt the butter with the olive oil in a 10¼-inch (26-cm) nonstick skillet or frying pan over medium-high heat. Add the florets and stir until lightly browned. Beat the eggs vigorously with a pinch of salt. Tip into the skillet and cook, gently shaking the skillet occasionally, until the underside is set and lightly browned. Invert the tortilla onto a plate, then slide it back into the skillet, cooked side up. Cook, gently shaking the skillet occasionally, until the underside is set and golden brown. Serve immediately, in wedges.

TORTILLITAS DE CALABACÍN

ZUCCHINI (COURGETTE) TORTILLITAS

INGREDIENTS
- 1 large zucchini (courgette), peeled and quartered lengthwise
- 8 eggs
- 2 tablespoons olive oil
- 3 tablespoons grated cheese, such as Manchego or Gruyère
- 1½ tablespoons (20 g/¾ oz) butter
- salt
Makes 4

Bring a pan of salted water to a boil. Add the zucchini and boil for 10 minutes, then drain well and pat dry. Set aside. Meanwhile, preheat the oven to 400°F (200°C/GAS MARK 6). Vigorously beat 2 eggs in a dish with a pinch of salt. Heat a little oil in a small skillet or frying pan over high heat and when it is hot, pour in the egg. When it begins to set, put a strip of zucchini in the middle, cook the tortilla until set and lightly browned underneath. Sprinkle a little grated cheese over the tortilla, then fold it and place it in an ovenproof dish. Continue to make 3 more tortillas the same way. Add the butter in little pieces and put into the oven until they are golden brown. Remove from the oven and serve.

PHOTOGRAPH PAGE 196

CODDLED EGGS ON TOAST WITH SPINACH

INGREDIENTS

- 4 thick slices bread
- 1 lb 2 oz (500 g) fresh spinach
- 2 tablespoons (25 g/1 oz) butter
- generous ⅓ cup (100 ml/ 3½ fl oz) light (single) cream
- 4 eggs
- 3½ oz (100 g) cooked ham, chopped
- 2 tablespoons Gruyère cheese, grated
- salt and pepper

Serves 4

Preheat the broiler (grill) to high. Toast the bread for 2 minutes on each side, until it is golden but still soft. Do not turn off the broiler. Blanch the spinach in a large pan of salted boiling water for 1 minute, then drain it well, using a wooden spoon to press out all the liquid. Melt the butter in a pan, add the spinach and lightly pan-fry over low heat for a few minutes. Remove the pan from the heat and stir in the cream. Keep the spinach and toast warm.

Bring a pan of water with 2 tablespoons salt to a boil. Put the eggs into a wire basket and plunge them into the boiling water. When the water comes back to a boil, cook the eggs for exactly 5 minutes, then remove the pan from the heat. Run cold water in the pan until it is completely cold to prevent any further cooking.

Shell the eggs very carefully. Spread half the spinach mixture over the slices of toast and sprinkle each with the ham. Carefully place an egg on top of each, then top with the remaining spinach mixture and sprinkle with cheese. Put the slices of toast under the broiler until the cheese melts but do not let it brown. Serve immediately.

Note: The bread can also be fried in olive oil (see page 160), instead of toasting it.

PHOTOGRAPH PAGE 197

SCRAMBLED EGGS WITH ASPARAGUS AND POTATOES

INGREDIENTS

- 4½ lb (2 kg) asparagus, trimmed
- sunflower oil, for deep-frying
- 2¼ lb (1 kg) potatoes, diced
- 6 eggs, lightly beaten
- salt
  Serves 8

Cut the asparagus into 1-inch (2.5-cm) lengths. Bring a large pan of salted water to a boil, add the asparagus, cover and cook for 10–20 minutes, until tender but not falling apart. Drain well. Heat the oil in a deep skillet or frying pan to 350–375°F (180–190°C) or until a cube of bread browns in 30 seconds. Add the potato and cook for 5–8 minutes, until evenly browned. Remove with a slotted spoon, drain well, lightly season with salt and set aside.

Drain off almost all the oil from the skillet, leaving just a thin layer on the bottom, and reheat. Add the asparagus. Season the eggs with salt and then pour into the skillet. Cook, stirring frequently with a fork, for a few minutes, until the eggs are creamy. Remove the skillet from the heat and let the eggs set a little more, then add the potato. Stir well, turn the mixture out onto a warm serving dish and serve immediately.

SERRANO HAM TORTILLA

INGREDIENTS

- 1½ tablespoons olive oil
- 3½ oz (100 g) Serrano ham in one piece, diced
- 1 small onion, finely chopped
- ½ clove garlic, finely chopped
- 4 eggs
- salt
  Serves 2

Heat 1 tablespoon of the oil in a 9½-inch (24-cm) skillet or frying pan over low heat. Add the ham, onion and garlic and pan-fry for about 6 minutes, stirring occasionally, until the onion is softened but not colored.

Beat the eggs vigorously with a pinch of salt. Increase the heat to high, add the remaining oil and swirl it around until hot. Tip the egg mixture into the skillet and pull it from the edge of the skillet to the center with a fork or rubber spatula. Cook until the underside is set and lightly browned. Fold the tortilla using a rubber spatula, then slide it onto a plate and serve immediately.

**REVUELTO DE ESPINACAS,
GAMBAS Y HUEVOS**

SCRAMBLED EGGS WITH SPINACH AND SHRIMP (PRAWNS)

INGREDIENTS
- 2¼ lb (1 kg) spinach
- 1 pinch baking soda
  (bicarbonate of soda)
- 3½ tablespoons (50 g/1¾ oz)
  butter or 5 tablespoons olive oil
- 11 oz (300 g) raw shrimp
  (prawns), peeled
- 8 eggs, lightly beaten
- salt

FOR THE FRIED BREAD (OPTIONAL):
- 1 cup (250 ml/12 fl oz) olive oil
- 5 oz (150 g) day-old bread,
  thinly sliced
  Serves 6

Remove and discard the coarse stems and wash the spinach in several changes of water. Drain slightly, then put into a pan with just the water clinging to its leaves. Add a pinch of salt and cook over medium heat, stirring occasionally, for 8–10 minutes. Drain well, pressing out as much liquid as possible with the back of a spoon. Chop it finely.

Heat the butter or oil in a skillet or frying pan. Add the shrimp and cook over medium heat, stirring occasionally, for 2 minutes. Stir in the spinach and cook, stirring constantly, for 3 minutes.

Meanwhile, make the fried bread, if using. Heat the oil in a skillet over medium heat. Add the bread slices, in batches, and fry for 2 minutes until golden brown on both sides. Remove with a spatula (fish slice) and drain on paper towels.

Season the beaten eggs with salt, pour into the skillet with the shrimp and spinach and cook, stirring frequently, for a few minutes, until the eggs begin to set. Turn the mixture out onto a warm serving dish and serve immediately, garnished with triangles of fried bread, if desired.

PHOTOGRAPH PAGE 198

HARD-BOILED EGG CROQUETTES

INGREDIENTS

- olive oil, for brushing
- 6 hard-boiled eggs, shelled and halved lengthwise
- 2 eggs
- 1½–2 cups (80–120 g/ 3–4 oz) fine bread crumbs
- sunflower oil, for deep-frying
- salt

FOR THE BÉCHAMEL SAUCE:

- 2 tablespoons (25 g/1 oz) butter
- 2 tablespoons olive oil
- 4 tablespoons all-purpose (plain) flour
- 3 cups (750 ml/1¼ pints) milk
- salt

Serves 6

Brush a baking sheet with olive oil. To make the béchamel sauce, melt the butter with the oil in a pan and stir in the flour and cook, stirring constantly, for 2–3 minutes, then remove the pan from the heat. Gradually stir in the milk, a little at a time. Return the pan to the heat and bring to a boil. Add salt to taste and simmer over medium heat, stirring, for 8–10 minutes. Remove the pan from the heat. Using 2 spoons, add the pieces of egg, one at a time, and coat in béchamel sauce, then place on the prepared baking sheet. Let cool for 1 hour.

Beat the eggs in a shallow dish and spread out the bread crumbs in another shallow dish. Dip the egg pieces first in the beaten egg and then in the bread crumbs to coat. Heat the sunflower oil in a deep-fryer or saucepan to 350–375°F (180–190°C), or until a cube of bread browns in 30 seconds. Add the egg pieces, in batches, if necessary, and cook until golden brown. Remove and drain on paper towels. Sprinkle with salt and serve hot or at room temperature.

HAM AND CHEESE SOUFFLÉD TORTILLA

INGREDIENTS

- 3 tablespoons olive oil
- 4 eggs, separated
- 1 oz (25 g) Parmesan or Gruyère cheese, grated
- 2 tablespoons light (single) cream
- 5 oz (150 g) Serrano or cooked ham in one piece, finely chopped, to garnish
- butter, for greasing (optional)
- salt and pepper

Serves 2

Put the egg yolks, cheese and cream into a bowl, season with salt and pepper and stir well to form a smooth mixture. Whisk the egg whites to stiff peaks with a pinch of salt, then gently fold them into the egg yolk mixture with a rubber spatula. Add the ham, reserving a little to use later as garnish.

Heat the oil in a 9½-inch (24-cm) skillet or frying pan over high heat and swirl it around. Tip the egg mixture into the skillet and pull it from the edge of the pan to the center with a fork or rubber spatula. Cook until the underside is set and lightly browned. Fold the tortilla using a rubber spatula, then slide it onto a plate and serve immediately.

Alternatively, put the egg mixture into a baking pan greased with butter, and place it in an oven preheated to 350°F (180°C/ GAS MARK 4) for 10–15 minutes. Remove the tortilla from the pan, sprinkle the remaining ham on top and serve immediately.

TORTILLA AL HORNO

BROILED (GRILLED) TORTILLA

INGREDIENTS
- 2 bacon slices (rashers)
- 2 tablespoons olive oil
- 1 small onion, finely chopped
- 1 clove garlic, finely chopped
- 8 eggs
- 2 ripe, juicy tomatoes, thinly sliced
- 4 oz (120 g) cheese, such as Manchego, grated
- salt
- black or green olives, pitted (stoned) and halved, to garnish

Serves 4

Preheat the broiler (grill) to high. Broil (grill) the bacon slices for 5 minutes, turning once, until crisp. Remove them from the broiler pan, let drain on paper towels and finely chop, then set aside. Do not turn off the broiler.

Heat the oil in an 11-inch (28-cm) skillet or frying pan with a flameproof handle over low heat. Add the onion and garlic and pan-fry for about 5 minutes, stirring occasionally, until the onion is softened but not browned.

Beat the eggs vigorously with a pinch of salt. Increase the heat under the skillet to medium high. Tip in the eggs and cook, gently shaking the skillet occasionally, until the underside is set and lightly browned.

Arrange the tomato slices over the top, then sprinkle with the bacon and cheese and broil for 1 minute, or until the cheese is bubbling and the tortilla is set. Garnish with olives and serve immediately or at room temperature, cut into wedges.

Note: If you like, use anchovy fillets instead of bacon.

TORTILLA DE GAMBAS

SHRIMP (PRAWN) TORTILLA

INGREDIENTS

- 1½ tablespoons (20 g/¾ oz) butter
- 2 shallots, or ½ onion, very finely chopped
- 1¼ cups (150 g/5 oz) peeled shrimp (prawns)
- 1 tablespoon brandy
- 1⅓ cups (300 ml/½ pint) light (single) cream
- 1 tablespoon tomato paste (puree)
- 4 tablespoons olive oil
- 8 eggs
- salt and pepper
  Serves 4

Melt the butter in a pan with a long handle over low heat. Add the shallots or onions and pan-fry for 6 minutes, stirring occasionally, until softened but not colored. Add the shrimp and stir just until they turn opaque. Remove the pan from the heat, pour in the brandy and carefully ignite it, standing well back. When the flames die down, return the pan to the heat, stir in the cream and the tomato paste, and season with salt and pepper. Keep warm but do not boil. Set aside.

Heat 2 tablespoons of oil in a 9½-inch (24-cm) skillet or frying pan over high heat and swirl around. Beat 4 eggs vigorously with a pinch of salt. Tip the egg mixture into the skillet and pull it from the edge of the skillet to the center with a fork or rubber spatula. Cook until the underside is set and lightly browned.

Spoon half the shrimp mixture along the center of the tortilla. Fold the tortilla using a rubber spatula, then slide it onto a plate and serve immediately. Repeat with the remaining ingredients to make a second tortilla.

TORTILLA DE MARISCOS

SEAFOOD TORTILLA

INGREDIENTS

- 3 tablespoons olive oil
- 2 tablespoons finely chopped onion
- 1 tablespoon brandy
- 9 oz (250 g) shrimp (prawns), peeled, deveined and chopped
- 9 oz (250 g) jumbo shrimp (king prawns), peeled, deveined and chopped, with 4 left whole to garnish
- 8 eggs
- salt
- sprigs parsley, to garnish

Serves 6

Heat 2 tablespoons oil in an 11-inch (28-cm) skillet or frying pan over low heat. Add the onion and pan-fry for 6 minutes, stirring occasionally, until softened but not colored. Add the chopped shrimp, brandy and a little salt and quickly pan-fry for 1 minute to allow the alcohol to evaporate, but do not allow the shrimp to cook through.

Meanwhile, heat 1 tablespoon of the oil in a another pan over high heat. Add the whole jumbo shrimp, a pinch of salt and cook for a few minutes until they turn opaque. Set aside and keep warm.

Beat the eggs vigorously with a pinch of salt. Increase the heat under the skillet with the chopped shrimp. Tip in the eggs and cook, gently shaking the skillet occasionally, until the underside is set and lightly browned. Invert the tortilla onto the lid of a pan to a plate, then gently slide it back into the same skillet, cooked side up. Cook, gently, shaking the skillet occasionally, until the underside is set and golden brown. Top with the whole shrimp and garnish with parsley. Serve immediately or at room temperature, cut into wedges.

Note: Alternatively, make 2 folded tortillas, following the instructions for the Shrimp (Prawn) Tortilla (see opposite).

MUSSEL TORTILLA

INGREDIENTS

- 1 lb 2 oz (500 g) mussels, cleaned (see page 275)
- 2 tablespoons dry white wine
- 1 clove garlic, finely chopped
- 1 tablespoon finely chopped parsley, plus extra to garnish
- 1 tablespoon (15 g/½ oz) butter
- 4 tablespoons olive oil
- 8 eggs
- salt

Serves 4

Discard any cracked or open mussels that do not snap shut when tapped. Put them in a large bowl of salted water, moving them around with your hands, then drain them. Place them in a large pan over high heat with the wine, garlic, parsley, 4 tablespoons water and a pinch of salt. Cover and steam for 5 minutes, shaking the pan occasionally, or until all the mussels are open. Drain the mussels in a large colander set in the sink and leave until cool enough to handle. Discard any mussels that do not open, then remove the remainder from their shells and set aside. If any are large, cut them in half. Discard the shells.

Melt the butter in a pan over medium heat. Add the mussels and quickly stir until they are coated with the mixture and warm. Take care not to overcook them. Set aside.

Heat 2 tablespoons of oil in a 9½-inch (24-cm) skillet or frying pan over high heat and swirl around. Beat 4 eggs vigorously with a pinch of salt. Tip the egg mixture into the pan and pull it from the edge of the pan to the center with a fork or rubber spatula. Cook until the underside is set and lightly browned. Spoon half the mussel mixture along the center of the tortilla, being careful not to add the excess butter. Fold the tortilla using a rubber spatula. Sprinkle with parsley to garnish then slide it onto a plate and serve immediately. Repeat with the remaining ingredients to make a second tortilla. Serve immediately or at room temperature, cut into wedges.

POTATO AND CHEESE TORTILLA

INGREDIENTS

- 2 potatoes, scrubbed but not peeled
- 1 tablespoon (15 g/½ oz) butter
- 4 tablespoons olive oil
- 6 eggs
- 1½ oz (40 g) Gruyère cheese, grated
- salt

Serves 2

Put the potatoes in a large pan of salted water and bring to a boil, then boil for 20 minutes, or until tender. Drain the potatoes and when cold enough to handle, peel and thinly slice them.

Melt the butter with 2 tablespoons of the oil in a 10¼-inch (26-cm) skillet or frying pan over medium-high heat. Add the potatoes and sauté them, shaking the pan often, until they are golden brown. Drain the potatoes and set aside. Wipe out the skillet with paper towels if there are any bits of potato stuck to it.

In a large bowl, beat the eggs vigorously with a pinch of salt. Stir in the potatoes and cheese. Heat the remaining oil in the skillet and swirl around. Tip in the eggs and potatoes and cook, gently shaking the pan occasionally, until the underside is set and lightly browned. Invert the tortilla onto the pan lid or a plate, then gently slide it back into the same skillet, cooked side up. Cook, gently, shaking the pan occasionally, until the underside is set and golden brown. Serve immediately or at room temperature, cut into wedges.

TORTILLA DE PATATAS
A LA ESPAÑOLA

SPANISH TORTILLA

INGREDIENTS

- generous 2 cups (500 ml/ 18 fl oz) olive oil
- 2¼ lb (1 kg) potatoes, halved lengthwise and thinly sliced
- 8 eggs
- 2 tablespoons olive oil
- salt
- 1 quantity Mayonnaise (see page 62), to serve (optional)

Serves 6

Heat the olive oil in an 11-inch (28-cm) skillet or frying pan over medium heat. Add the potato slices and cook, stirring occasionally, until softened and lightly browned. Season with salt, remove from the skillet and drain well. Beat the eggs vigorously with a pinch of salt in a large bowl for 1 minute. Add the potato slices and stir with a fork. Heat 2 tablespoons olive oil in the skillet over high heat. Tip in the egg mixture and cook, gently shaking the skillet occasionally, until the underside is set and lightly browned. Invert the tortilla onto the lid of a pan or a plate, then gently slide it back into the skillet, cooked side up. Cook, shaking the skillet occasionally, until the underside is set and golden brown. Serve immediately, with mayonnaise poured over it or offered separately.

PHOTOGRAPH PAGE 199

REVUELTO CON PIMIENTOS
DE PADRÓN

SCRAMBLED EGGS WITH PADRÓN PEPPERS

INGREDIENTS

- generous ⅓ cup (100 ml/3½ fl oz) olive oil
- 3½ oz (100 g) Padrón peppers
- 3¼ lb (1.5 kg) potatoes, peeled and cut into ¾-inch (1-cm) cubes
- 6 eggs
- salt

Serves 4–6

Heat 2 inches (5 cm) oil in a large skillet or frying pan. Add the peppers, in batches, and cook over medium heat for a couple minutes, stirring occasionally, until they are cooked and lightly browned. Remove them with a slotted spoon and drain on paper towels. Season the potatoes lightly with salt. Heat the remaining oil in a skillet. Add the potatoes, in batches, and cook over medium-high heat, stirring constantly, for 15–20 minutes, or until tender and golden brown. Strain the oil into a bowl, then return just enough oil to the skillet to cover the bottom. Return the potatoes and peppers to the still-warm pan. Beat the eggs lightly with a pinch of salt. Pour them over the potatoes and peppers and cook, stirring, over high heat, until the eggs are lightly set. Pour into a serving dish and serve immediately.

LITTLE TORTILLAS WITH PISTO

INGREDIENTS

- 8 eggs
- 1 lb 10 oz (750 g) potatoes, halved lengthwise and thinly sliced
- 1¼ cups (500 ml/18 fl oz) sunflower oil
- 2 tablespoons olive oil
- salt

FOR THE PISTO:

- ⅔ cup (150 ml/¼ pint) olive oil
- 2 large onions, chopped
- 1 lb 10 oz (750 g) eggplants (aubergines), peeled and cut into ¾-inch (2-cm) cubes
- 2 green bell peppers, seeded and chopped
- 1 lb 10 oz (750 g) zucchini (courgettes), cut into ¾-inch (2-cm) dice
- 5 very ripe tomatoes, peeled, seeded and chopped
- 2 cloves garlic
- salt

Serves 6

First, make the pisto. Heat the oil in a skillet or frying pan. Add the onions and cook over low heat, stirring occasionally, for 10 minutes. Add the eggplant and cook, stirring occasionally, for another 10 minutes. Add the bell pepper and cook, stirring occasionally, for another 10 minutes. Stir in the zucchini and tomatoes, add the garlic and season with salt. Cover and simmer over low heat for 1 hour. If the pisto is very runny, remove the lid for the last 10 minutes to let some of the liquid evaporate. Remove and discard the garlic. Set the pisto aside.

Heat the sunflower oil in a skillet. Add the potato slices and cook, stirring occasionally, until softened and lightly browned. Season with salt, then drain well.

Beat the eggs vigorously with a pinch of salt in a large bowl for 1 minute. Add the potato slices and stir with a fork. Heat the olive oil in an 11-inch (28-cm) skillet over high heat. Tip in the egg mixture and cook, gently shaking the pan occasionally, until the underside is set and lightly browned. Invert the tortilla onto the lid of a pan or a plate, then gently side it back into the pan, cooked side up. Cook, gently shaking the pan occasionally, until the underside is set and golden brown. When it has cooled a little, use a round pastry cutter to cut out 2-inch (5-cm) circles. Place the little tortillas in a warm serving dish. Reheat the pisto, if necessary, and spoon it around the tortillas.

Note: The pisto can be prepared in advance and reheated.

CHICKEN LIVER TORTILLA

INGREDIENTS

- 1 oz (25 g) mushrooms
- lemon juice, for washing
- 2 tablespoons (25 g/1 oz) butter
- 3 oz (80 g) chicken livers, thawed if frozen, trimmed and coarsely chopped
- 2 tablespoons chopped parsley
- 1 tablespoon vermouth
- 2 tablespoons olive oil
- 4 eggs
- salt and pepper
  Serves 2

Wash the mushrooms with the lemon juice and water, then remove and discard the stems and thinly slice the caps. Melt the butter in a skillet or frying pan over medium-high heat. Add the livers and mushrooms and pan-fry, stirring occasionally, until the water from the mushrooms has evaporated. Stir in the parsley and stir for another minute before adding the vermouth. Season with salt and pepper, stir well and keep warm.

Heat 2 tablespoons of oil in a 9½-inch (24-cm) skillet over high heat and swirl around. Beat the eggs vigorously with a pinch of salt. Tip the eggs into the skillet and pull them from the edge of the skillet to the center with a fork or rubber spatula. Cook until the underside is set and lightly browned. Spoon the chicken liver mixture along the center of the tortilla. Fold the tortilla using a rubber spatula, then slide it onto a plate and serve immediately.

LEFTOVER CHICKEN TORTILLA

INGREDIENTS

- 4 tablespoons olive oil
- 1¾ oz (50 g) skinless leftover roast chicken, chopped
- 2 tablespoons tomato sauce, bottled or homemade (see page 181)
- 4 eggs
- salt and pepper
  Serves 2

Heat 2 tablespoons oil in a 9½-inch (24-cm) skillet or frying pan, add the chicken and tomato sauce and stir over low heat until warmed through. Beat the eggs vigorously with a pinch of salt and pepper in a large bowl, then stir in the chicken mixture. Add the remaining oil to the skillet and heat over high heat. Tip in the egg mixture and cook, gently shaking the pan occasionally, until the underside is set and lightly browned. Invert the tortilla onto the lid of a pan or a plate, then gently slide it back into the skillet, cooked side up. Cook, gently shaking the skillet occasionally, until the underside is set and golden brown. Serve immediately.

PASTEL DE TORTILLAS
CON QUESO Y JUDÍAS

TORTILLA 'CAKE' WITH CHEESE AND BEANS

INGREDIENTS

- olive oil, for frying
- 1 lb 2 oz (500 g) red bell peppers, halved, seeded and chopped
- 9 oz (250 g) green beans, trimmed
- 9 eggs
- scant 2¼ cups (500 g/1 lb 2 oz) ricotta cheese
- 2 tablespoons basil, chopped
- salt and pepper

Serves 4

Heat 2 tablespoons oil in a skillet or frying pan about 7 inches (18 cm) in diameter across the bottom. Add the bell peppers, season with salt, cover and cook, stirring occasionally, over low heat for 20 minutes, or until tender but still retaining a little bite. Remove the bell peppers from the skillet and set aside.

Meanwhile, preheat the oven to 375°F (190°C/GAS MARK 5). Grease the base of a loose-bottom pan the same size as the skillet with a little oil. Bring a large pan of salted water to a boil. Add the beans, bring back to a boil, and cook, uncovered, for 10 minutes, or until just tender, then refresh in cold water. Drain immediately, pat dry and chop.

Beat 3 eggs vigorously with a pinch of salt and pepper in a bowl. If necessary, add more oil to the skillet the bell peppers were cooked in and reheat. Tip the egg mixture into the skillet and pull it from the edge of the pan to the center with a fork or rubber spatula. Cook, shaking the pan occasionally, until the underside is set and lightly browned. Slide the tortilla onto a plate and keep warm. Make 2 more 3-egg tortillas the same way.

Set aside a few of the bell peppers and green beans to use as a garnish. Mix the rest with the cheese and basil and season with salt and pepper. Place the first tortilla in the loose-bottom pan, then cover with half the cheese mixture. Put the second tortilla on top and add the remaining cheese mixture, then put the final tortilla on top. Cover the pan with aluminum foil and bake for 25 minutes.

Remove the tortilla 'cake' from the pan, garnish with the reserved bell pepper and green beans and serve, hot or cold.

PHOTOGRAPH PAGE 201

CHEESE AND EGG CROQUETTES

INGREDIENTS

- 3 tablespoons
  (40 g/1½ oz) butter
- 2 tablespoons olive oil
- 4 tablespoons all-purpose
  (plain) flour
- 3 cups (750 ml/1¼ pints) milk
- 4 eggs
- 7 oz (200 g) Gruyère
  cheese, grated
- 3 cups (175 g/6 oz)
  bread crumbs
- vegetable oil, for deep-frying
- salt
- fresh or deep-fried sprigs
  parsley (optional)
  Serves 6–12

First, make a thick béchamel sauce. Melt the butter with the oil in a pan and stir in the flour. Gradually stir in the milk, a little at a time, and bring to a boil, stirring constantly. Add salt to taste and simmer over medium heat, stirring constantly, for 8–10 minutes, until thickened. Remove the pan from the heat and let cool slightly. Stir in 2 eggs, one at a time, making sure each one is fully incorporated before adding the next. Stir in the Gruyère cheese. Spread the mixture out on a large dish to cool for at least 2 hours.

Using 2 tablespoons, shape scoops of the mixture into croquettes. Finish forming the croquettes with your hands. Beat the remaining eggs in a shallow dish. Spread out the bread crumbs into another shallow dish. Roll each croquette lightly in the bread crumbs, then in the beaten egg and finally in the bread crumbs again, making sure that each one is evenly covered. If the croquettes are being prepared in advance, cover them with a damp dish towel to prevent them drying out.

Heat the vegetable oil in a deep-fryer or deep pan to 350–375°F (180–190°C) or until a cube of bread browns in 30 seconds. Add the croquettes, in batches of about 6 at a time, and cook until crisp and golden brown. Using a slotted spoon, transfer them to a large heatproof colander set over a baking pan and place in a warm oven until all the croquettes have been cooked. Serve immediately on a dish garnished with sprigs of fresh or deep-fried parsley, if using.

PHOTOGRAPH PAGE 200

CURD CHEESE AND GOAT CHEESE PASTRIES

INGREDIENTS

– 7 oz (200 g) puff pastry, thawed if frozen
– all-purpose (plain) flour, for rolling out the pastry
– 5 oz (150 g) goat cheese, grated or crumbled
– generous 1 cup (250 g/9 oz) curd cheese or similar
– 3 eggs
– salt and pepper
Makes 12

Preheat the oven to 400°F (200°C/GAS MARK 6). Roll out the pastry on a lightly floured surface to a thickness of ¾ inch (1.5 cm) with a lightly floured rolling pin. Put the goat cheese into a bowl, then mix in the curd cheese and the egg and season with salt and pepper. Cut the pastry into 12 x 2-inch (5-cm) squares, or use a round 2-inch (5-cm) cookie cutter to cut out 12 circles from the pastry, then turn up the edges of each piece to make a little tart shape, or use them to line small tartlet pans.

Put the pastries on a baking sheet and prick the bottom of each. Bake for 10 minutes, then remove and fill each one with the cheese mixture. Return them to the oven and continue baking for 20 minutes, or until well risen and golden brown. Serve hot.

PHOTOGRAPH PAGE 202

TORTILLA WITH LEFTOVERS

INGREDIENTS

– 1 tablespoon (15 g/½ oz) butter
– 4 tablespoons olive oil
– about 3½ oz (100 g) leftover cooked vegetables, finely chopped, or leftover cooked boneless meat or chicken, skins removed, and finely chopped
– 4 eggs
– salt
Serves 2

Melt the butter with 2 tablespoons oil in a 9½-inch (24-cm) skillet or frying pan over medium-high heat. Add the vegetables, meat or chicken and stir until warmed through. Set aside and keep warm.

Heat the remaining oil in the skillet over high heat and swirl it around. Beat the eggs vigorously with a pinch of salt. Tip the egg mixture into the pan and pull it from the edge of the pan to the center with a fork or rubber spatula. Cook until the underside is set and lightly browned. Spoon the leftovers mixture along the center of the tortilla. Fold the tortilla using a rubber spatula, then slide it onto a plate and serve immediately.

FLANECITOS DE QUESO

LITTLE CHEESE FLANS

INGREDIENTS

- butter, to grease the pans
- 4 eggs
- ¾ cup plus 2 tablespoons (200 ml/7 fl oz) light (single) cream
- 1 cup (100 g/3½ oz) Parmesan cheese, grated
- 2 slices cured ham, such as Serrano, chopped
- 1¼ cups (500 ml/18 fl oz) milk
- salt and pepper
- tomato sauce, bottled or homemade (see page 181), to serve (optional)

Serves 4

Preheat the oven to 400°F (200°C/GAS MARK 6). Line the bases of 4 individual 2¾-inch (7-cm) flan pans with aluminum foil, then grease them with the butter. Beat the eggs in a bowl, add the cream, cheese and ham and season with salt and pepper. Mix well, then gradually stir in the milk, a little at a time. Pour the mixture into the prepared individual pans. Put them in a roasting pan and pour in boiling water to come about halfway up the sides. Bake for 30 minutes, until set.

Just before serving, heat the tomato sauce, if using. Remove the roasting pan from the oven. Run a round-bladed knife around the edges of each flan and turn out onto warm serving dishes. Pour the hot tomato sauce over each, if you like, and serve immediately.

FRITOS DE QUESO
GRUYÈRE Y BACON

FRIED GRUYÈRE CHEESE WITH BACON

INGREDIENTS

- 7 oz (200 g) Gruyère cheese
- 10 thin bacon slices (rashers), rinds removed
- 2–3 tablespoons olive oil

Makes about 15

Cut the Gruyère into strips about ½-inch (1-cm) thick and a little longer than the width of the slices of bacon. Cut the slices in half. Place a piece of cheese on each half, roll up the bacon and run a toothpick (cocktail stick) through, to secure the roll.

Heat the oil in a skillet or frying pan over medium heat. Add the bacon rolls and cook, turning frequently, for 10–15 minutes, until the bacon is browned and cooked through. Drain well and serve immediately, leaving the toothpicks in place.

PHOTOGRAPH PAGE 204

GRATED CHEESE GALLETTES

INGREDIENTS

- sunflower oil, for greasing
- 1 egg
- 2¼ cups (250 g/9 oz) all purpose (plain) flour, plus extra for dusting
- generous ¾ cup (200 g/7 oz) butter, at room temperature
- 2⅓ cups (200 g/7 oz) potatoes, cooked and mashed
- 1¾ cups (200 g/7 oz) Gruyère cheese, grated
- salt, optional

Makes about 30

Preheat the oven to 325°F (160°C/GAS MARK 3). Grease 2 baking sheets with the oil. Beat the egg in a large bowl. Add all the remaining ingredients, reserving ½ cup (50 g/2 oz) of the grated cheese, and mix. Turn the mixture out onto a lightly floured surface. Gently roll it out with a lightly floured rolling pin until it is ¼ inch (5 mm) thick. Use a cookie cutter or floured wine glass to cut out circles, re-rolling the trimmings as necessary. Sprinkle a little grated cheese on top of each one.

Place them on the baking sheet and bake for about 15 minutes, until golden brown around the edges. Remove the baking sheet from the oven and loosen all the galettes with a metal spatula (palette knife). Serve at once or transfer to wire racks to cool slightly. The galettes keep for 2–3 days in an airtight container.

TOAST WITH CHEESE AND BEER

INGREDIENTS

- 4 slices of bread from a country-style loaf
- 7 oz (200 g) cheese, such as Gouda or Cheddar, finely chopped
- 4 tablespoons beer
- 1 teaspoon mustard

Makes 8

Preheat the broiler (grill) to high. Toast the bread on both sides for 2 minutes, or until golden and crisp. Cut into quarters. Do not turn the broiler off.

Heat the beer in a pan over medium heat, then add the cheese and stir until a smooth paste forms. Stir in the mustard. Spread the mixture onto the pieces of toast, then return them to the broiler and broil (grill) for about 1 minute until they are golden brown and the cheese is bubbling. Serve immediately. This is also good as a first course, accompanied by salad.

MOLDED EGGS WITH KIDNEYS IN SHERRY

INGREDIENTS

- butter, for greasing
- 1 x 11-oz (300-g) veal kidney, trimmed
- white-wine vinegar, for rinsing
- 3 tablespoons olive oil
- 1½ tablespoons all-purpose (plain) flour
- ¾ cup (175 ml/6 fl oz) dry sherry
- 4 eggs
- salt

Serves 4

Preheat the oven to 400°F (200°C/GAS MARK 6). Generously butter 4 cocottes or ramekins. Cut the kidney into large pieces and wash them, first in water with a little vinegar, then in fresh water. Dry the pieces with a cloth, then cut them into smaller pieces. Place the kidney pieces into a skillet or frying pan, cover and cook over medium heat, shaking the pan, for 2 minutes. Drain off and discard the cooking juices and set the kidney pieces aside on a plate.

Heat the oil in a pan, add the flour and cook over low heat, stirring constantly, for 8 minutes, or until it is lightly browned. Stir in the sherry and 1½ cups (350 ml/12 fl oz) water, a little at a time. Season with salt and cook, stirring constantly, for 6 minutes. Stir in the kidney pieces and cook for another 3 minutes.

Divide the kidney pieces among the prepared cocottes or ramekins, adding about 1 tablespoon of the sauce to each. Carefully break an egg into each mold, ensuring the yolk is in the center and does not break, and season with salt. Put the molds in a roasting pan and pour in boiling water to come about halfway up the side. Bake for 4–5 minutes, until the whites have set but the yolks are still runny. Serve the eggs straight from the molds or remove them carefully, making sure the yolks do not break. They can also be served cold.

TORTILLA DE SARDINAS

SARDINE TORTILLA

INGREDIENTS

- 6 fresh sardines, cleaned, rinsed and dried
- juice of 1½ lemons
- 6 tablespoons olive oil
- 1 pinch dried thyme
- 8 eggs
- 1 bunch parsley, very finely chopped
- salt and pepper

Serves 4

An hour before you plan to make the tortilla, preheat the broiler (grill) to high. Put the sardines into a baking sheet, rub them with 1 tablespoon of the oil and sprinkle 2 tablespoons lemon juice over them. Broil (grill) the sardines for about 10 minutes, turning once, until cooked through. Set aside until cool enough to handle, then remove the skins and bones. Flake the flesh into a nonmetallic bowl, then add 3 tablespoons of the oil, the remaining lemon juice and thyme and season with pepper. Gently stir together and set aside for an hour.

Drain the sardines. Beat the eggs vigorously with a pinch of salt in a large bowl. Add the flaked sardines and parsley and stir with a fork. Heat the remaining oil in an 11-inch (28-cm) skillet or frying pan and swirl around. Tip in the egg mixture and cook, gently shaking the skillet occasionally, until the underside is set and lightly browned. Invert the tortilla onto the a lid of a pan or a plate, then gently slide it back into the skillet, cooked side up. Cook, gently shaking the skillet occasionally, until the underside is set and golden brown. Serve immediately, cut into wedges.

PHOTOGRAPH PAGE 205

BREAD ROLLS WITH CHEESE SOUFFLÉ AND SALAMI

INGREDIENTS

- 12 bread rolls
- 7 tablespoons
  (100 g/3½ oz) butter
- 12 large thin slices salami
- 4 tablespoons all-purpose
  (plain) flour
- 4 teaspoons potato flour
- 1¼ cups (500 ml/18 fl oz) milk
- ¾ cup (100 g/3½ oz) Gruyère
  cheese, grated
- 5 eggs, separated
- 3 or 4 egg whites
- salt
  Makes 12

Preheat the oven to 350°F (180°C/GAS MARK 4). Remove a slice from the top of each roll and scoop out all the bread from the center. Butter the inside of each roll generously and line them with salami, cutting the slices in half if they are large. Place the rolls on a baking sheet.

Melt 5 tablespoons (80 g/3 oz) of the butter in a skillet or frying pan. Stir in the flour and potato flour and cook, stirring constantly, for 2 minutes. Gradually stir in the milk, a little at a time. Bring to a boil, stirring continuously, then lower the heat and simmer, still stirring, for another 5 minutes. Remove the pan from the heat and stir in the Gruyère cheese. Let cool slightly. Stir in the egg yolks, one at a time, then season with salt.

Whisk half the egg whites to stiff peaks in a clean, dry bowl. Gently fold into the cheese mixture. Repeat with the remaining egg whites. Spoon the soufflé mixture into the bread rolls and bake for 15 minutes. Increase the oven temperature to 425°F (220°C/GAS MARK 7) and bake for another 10 minutes, or until risen and golden brown. Transfer to serving dishes and serve immediately. A soufflé cannot wait, even a few minutes, as it will collapse.

Note: The tops of the rolls, which were cut off at the beginning, can be replaced for serving, although this will squash the soufflés a little.

CHEESE AND HAM MAGDALENAS

INGREDIENTS

- 2 eggs
- 3½ tablespoons (50 g/1¾ oz) butter
- 4 tablespoons grated cheese, such as Gruyère
- 3 heaping (heaped) tablespoons all-purpose (plain) flour
- 1 teaspoon baking powder
- 3½ oz (100 g) dry Serrano ham, not too cured, and finely chopped
Makes 12

Preheat the oven to 350°F (180°C/GAS MARK 4). Arrange 12 cupcake cases in a muffin pan or on a baking sheet. Beat the eggs in a bowl with a fork. Gently melt the butter in a pan, then add the eggs. Immediately stir in the cheese, flour, baking powder and ham. Spoon this mixture into the cupcake cases.

Bake the magdalenas for 15 minutes, then increase the heat to 400°F (200°C/GAS MARK 6) and continue baking for another 15 minutes until they begin to brown. Remove the magdalenas from the oven and immediately remove them from the cases. These are best when served recently baked and slightly warm.

PHOTOGRAPH PAGE 203

BRICK PASTRY TRIANGLES

INGREDIENTS

- 5 tablespoons ricotta cheese
- 1 oz (25 g) smoked salmon, finely chopped, plus extra to serve
- 2 teaspoons pistachio nuts, chopped, plus extra to serve
- 2 green peppercorns in brine, drained, rinsed and chopped
- 1 pinch sugar
- 7 tablespoons olive oil
- 6 x 8½-inch (22-cm) sheets brick pastry dough, or 6 large spring roll wrappers
Serves 8

Stir the cheese, smoked salmon, pistachios, peppercorns, sugar and 1 tablespoon of the oil, together in a bowl. Cut the pastry dough into strips about 1¾ inches (4 cm) wide. Put a strip of dough, shiny side down, on a work surface vertically in front of you. Put 1 teaspoon of filling in the bottom right-hand corner. Fold the pastry from the left-hand side over the filling to form a triangle. Fold the triangle upward, then to the left. Continue folding until you reach the top of the pastry. Dampen the top edge of the pastry dough with a little water and press down to seal. Continue with the remaining ingredients. Heat the remaining oil in a large skillet or frying pan. Cook the triangles over medium heat, turning once, for 5 minutes, until beginning to brown. Drain on paper towels. Serve warm or at room temperature.

MOLDED EGGS WITH TOMATOES

INGREDIENTS

- 3½ tablespoons (50 g/1¾ oz) butter, plus extra for greasing
- 2 tablespoons olive oil
- 18 oz (500 g) ripe tomatoes, peeled, seeded and chopped
- 1 bouquet garni
- 1 pinch sugar
- 8 eggs
- salt and pepper

Serves 4

Preheat the oven to 350°F (180°C/GAS MARK 4) and generously grease 4 x 3-inch (8-cm) molds with butter. Heat the oil in a skillet or frying pan, add the tomatoes, bouquet garni and sugar and season with salt and pepper, then simmer over low heat for 35 minutes, stirring occasionally and mashing the mixture with the edge of a slotted spoon. Press the sauce through a fine strainer or blend it in a blender. If it is very liquid, put it back in the skillet over high heat and allow it to boil until it thickens.

Put 5 eggs in a bowl and beat them with salt and pepper. Melt half the butter in a skillet, add half the eggs and cook over low heat, stirring with a whisk until they have the consistency of scrambled eggs. Return them to the same the bowl, then beat the remaining eggs and stir them in. Fill the molds with the egg mixture. Put the molds in a roasting pan and pour in boiling water to come about halfway up the side. Bake for about 15 minutes, until set.

Meanwhile, re-heat the sauce. Remove the molds from the pan and let cool for a few minutes, then run a round-bladed knife around the inside edge and turn out onto a warmed serving dish. Pour the hot tomato sauce over them and serve immediately.

SAVORY CUSTARDS WITH TOMATO SAUCE

INGREDIENTS

- butter, for greasing
- 7 eggs
- ½ cup (120 ml/4 fl oz) milk
- 1 pinch freshly grated nutmeg
- salt

FOR THE TOMATO SAUCE:

- 3 tablespoons olive oil
- 1 onion, chopped (optional)
- 2¼ lb (1 kg) ripe tomatoes, seeded and chopped
- 1 teaspoon sugar
- salt

Serves 4

First, make the tomato sauce. Heat the oil in a skillet or frying pan. Add the onion, if using, and cook over low heat, stirring occasionally, for about 5 minutes, until softened but not browned. (If you're not using the onion, add the tomato immediately.) Add the tomatoes and cook over low heat, breaking the flesh up with the edge of a skimmer or slotted spoon, for about 15 minutes. Allow the mixture to cool slightly, then transfer to a food processor and process. Add the sugar, season to taste with salt and process briefly again. Set aside and keep warm.

Preheat the oven to 325°F (160°C/GAS MARK 3). Grease 4 individual flan pans or ramekins with butter. Beat the eggs in a bowl, add the milk and nutmeg, season with salt and mix well. Pour the egg mixture into the prepared pans. Put them into a roasting pan, pour in boiling water to come halfway up the sides and bake for about 15 minutes, until set. Put the tomato sauce in a warm serving dish and turn the custards out on top of the sauce. Serve immediately.

PHOTOGRAPH PAGE 306

VEGETABLE TORTILLA

INGREDIENTS

- 4 tablespoons olive oil
- 1 onion, chopped
- 1 green bell pepper, halved, seeded and finely chopped
- 1 red bell pepper, halved, seeded and finely chopped
- 1 eggplant (aubergine), diced
- 1 zucchini (courgette), diced
- 2 ripe, red tomatoes, peeled, seeded and diced
- 8 eggs
- salt

Serves 4

Heat the oil in an 11-inch (28-cm) skillet or frying pan over low heat. Add the onion and pan-fry, stirring occasionally, for 4 minutes, then stir in the bell peppers, eggplant and zucchini. When everything is browned add the tomatoes, and let cook until the water has evaporated and the mixture has thickened.

Beat the eggs vigorously with a pinch of salt in a large bowl. Increase the heat under the vegetables. Tip in the egg mixture and cook, gently shaking the skillet occasionally, until the underside is set and lightly browned. Invert the tortilla onto a lid of a pan or a plate, then gently slide it back into the skillet, cooked side up. Cook, gently shaking the skillet occasionally, until the underside is set and golden brown. Serve immediately or at room temperature, cut into wedges.

Note: If you have any of this left over, it is tasty served cold with a little mayonnaise spread across the top.

PHOTOGRAPH PAGE 207

LAYERED TORTILLAS

INGREDIENTS

- 6 tablespoons olive oil
- 2 onions, finely chopped
- 6 large ripe tomatoes, peeled, seeded and chopped
- 2 cloves garlic, finely chopped
- 1 bouquet garni
- 1 green bell pepper, seeded and cut lengthwise into ¾-inch (2-cm) slices
- 2 eggplants (aubergines), halved lengthwise
- 3 shallots, finely chopped
- 2 tablespoons (25g/1oz) butter
- 1lb 2oz (500g) spinach, tough stems removed
- 15 eggs
- salt and pepper

Serves 8–10

Heat 1 tablespoon oil in a pan. Add half the onions and cook over medium heat, until softened and translucent. Add the tomatoes, the garlic, bouquet garni and salt and pepper, and cook over low heat for 30 minutes, stirring occasionally, until the liquid released by the vegetables evaporates. Remove the mixture from the pan and let cool completely, then put it in the refrigerator.

Preheat the broiler (grill) to high. Heat 1 tablespoon oil in the same pan. Add the remaining onion and cook until softened and translucent, as above. Add the pepper and cook over low heat, stirring occasionally, for 20 minutes, until tender. Remove the mixture from the pan and let cool, then put in the refrigerator. Meanwhile, use a knife to score the eggplant flesh into cubes. Drizzle with 2 tablespoons olive oil and place on a baking sheet. Broil (grill) for 15 minutes. Using a spoon, carefully remove the flesh from the skin and chop it. Heat 1 tablespoon of the oil in the same pan. Add one of the shallots and cook over medium heat, for about 5 minutes, until softened but not browned. Stir in the eggplant flesh with salt and pepper and cook over low heat, stirring occasionally, for 20 minutes. Remove the mixture from the pan and let cool, then put it in the refrigerator. Melt the butter in the pan. Add the remaining shallot and cook as above.

Wash the spinach well, drain slightly, then cook in a hot skillet or frying pan with just the water clinging to its leaves. Stir well until wilted, then remove it from the skillet, squeeze out the excess liquid, and let cool. Beat 3 of the eggs vigorously with a pinch of salt. Over medium-high heat, heat enough oil to cover the bottom of a 7-inch (18-cm) skillet. Tip the egg mixture into the pan and pull it from the edge of the pan to the center with a fork or spatula. Let the underside brown slightly. Remove from the skillet and make 4 more tortillas in the same way. Assemble by layering the tortillas and different vegetable layers, ending with a plain tortilla on top. The layered tortilla can be served as it is, or accompanied with a vinaigrette made by beating together oil, balsamic vinegar, chopped parsley, mustard and a pinch of salt.

EGG AND CHEESE

COLD

HOT

HARD-BOILED EGGS
WITH BLACK OLIVES
PAGE 139

CURD CHEESE
AND OLIVE TAPA

PAGE 140

HARD-BOILED EGGS
WITH PEAS AND
RED BELL PEPPERS
PAGE 142

QUAILS'
EGG SALAD
PAGE 143

HAM AND QUAILS'
EGG TAPA
PAGE 145

CHEESE AND
RADISH SALAD
PAGE 147

SOFT CHEESE
SANDWICHES
PAGE 147

BAKED CHEESE
STICKS
PAGE 148

HARD-BOILED EGGS
WITH RUSSIAN SALAD
PAGE 150

ARTICHOKE HEARTS
WITH SCRAMBLED EGGS
PAGE 153

CHEESE FRITTERS
WITH TOMATO SAUCE
PAGE 156

ZUCCHINI
(COURGETTE)
TORTILLITAS
PAGE 157

CODDLED EGGS ON
TOAST WITH SPINACH
PAGE 158

SCRAMBLED EGGS
WITH SPINACH AND
SHRIMP (PRAWNS)
PAGE 160

SPANISH
TORTILLA
PAGE 168

CHEESE AND
EGG CROQUETTES
PAGE 172

TORTILLA 'CAKE'
WITH CHEESE
AND BEANS
PAGE 171

CURD CHEESE
AND GOAT
CHEESE PASTRIES
PAGE 173

CHEESE AND HAM
MAGDALENAS
PAGE 179

FRIED GRUYÈRE
CHEESE WITH BACON
PAGE 174

SARDINE
TORTILLA
PAGE 177

SAVORY CUSTARDS
WITH TOMATO SAUCE
PAGE 181

VEGETABLE
TORTILLA
PAGE 182

FISH
TAPAS

COLD

AVOCADO AND (SHRIMP) PRAWN SALAD

INGREDIENTS

– 4 avocados
– juice of ½ lemon, strained
– 1 teaspoon capers, rinsed
– 4 tablespoons (50 g/2 oz) bottled salmon roe (keta), drained, to garnish
– 5 oz (150 g) cooked shrimp (prawns), peeled, to garnish

FOR THE THICK MAYONNAISE:

– 1 egg, at room temperature
– juice of ½ lemon, strained
– mustard, to taste
– 1 cup (250 ml/8 fl oz) sunflower or olive oil, or a combination
– salt
  Serves 4

Begin by making the mayonnaise. Put the egg, lemon juice, mustard, splash of oil with a pinch of salt in a blender. These ingredients should not cover the blades completely. Stir them with a spatula or the handle of a spoon, then turn on the blender for 20 seconds. Pour in all the oil, stir as before and then turn on the blender for about 35 seconds until the mayonnaise thickens. Taste and add salt or extra lemon juice, if necessary, then cover and put in the refrigerator.

Peel and halve the avocados, remove the pits (stones), then cut the flesh into cubes. Put them into a bowl and sprinkle the lemon juice over them. Stir in 3 tablespoons of mayonnaise and the capers. Transfer to a serving bowl and garnish with the cooked shrimp and salmon roe.

Note: If covered, the remaining mayonnaise will keep in the refrigerator for several days to use in other recipes.

PHOTOGRAPH PAGE 289

ANCHOVY CREAM

INGREDIENTS

- ⅔ cup (150 g/5 oz) curd cheese
- 2 oz (50 g) canned anchovy fillets in oil, drained
- a few drops Worcestershire sauce
- pepper

Makes about ¾ cup (175 g/6 oz)

Mix all the ingredients together, with pepper to taste, to form a smooth paste. This paste can be spread on bread, or served as a dip accompanied by crisps or savory crackers. Cover and chill until required.

ANCHOVY AND OLIVE TAPA

INGREDIENTS

- 1¼ cups (150 g/5 oz) black olives, pitted (stoned)
- 4 canned anchovy fillets in oil, drained
- 1 tablespoon capers, rinsed
- 2 tablespoons olive oil
- 12 slices French baguette

Makes 12

Preheat the broiler (grill) to high. Put the olives, anchovies and capers into a blender and process until a paste forms. With the motor running slowly, add the oil until blended. Cover and set aside in the refrigerator until required.

Under the broiler, toast the bread slices for 2 minutes on each side, or until golden brown. Spread the anchovy mixture on the hot toast and serve immediately or the toast will become soggy.

Note: This paste can be kept in the refrigerator for up to 3 days if stored in a sealed container.

MARINATED ANCHOVIES

INGREDIENTS

- juice of 1 lemon, strained
- 1 tablespoon sherry vinegar
- 40 canned anchovy fillets in olive oil
- 2 fresh tomatoes, peeled, seeded and chopped
- 1 tablespoon chopped herbs, such as chervil, chives, tarragon and basil
- 1 handful mixed salad greens (leaves)
- 2 bottled or canned roasted red bell peppers, seeded and cut into thin strips
- 8 tablespoons olive oil
- salt and pepper

Serves 4

Place the anchovies and their oil in a dish. Mix half the lemon juice with the vinegar and use a pastry brush to glaze the anchovies. Sprinkle one-third of the herbs over the top of the anchovies and let stand for 10–20 minutes. Mix the tomatoes with another third of the herbs, the remaining lemon juice and vinegar and salt and pepper to taste.

Put some salad greens onto serving plates, then create a fan shape on top with alternating anchovy fillets and pepper strips. Sprinkle the remaining herbs on top, pour the olive oil over the salad and decorate with the tomatoes. Serve with lightly toasted, freshly baked bread.

SALTED ANCHOVIES

INGREDIENTS

- 12 fresh anchovies
- 2¼ lb (1 kg) coarse sea salt
- 6 bay leaves
- 3 sprigs thyme
  Serves 6

Put the whole, uncleaned anchovies in a large dish and cover them with 2 handfuls of the salt, then set aside for 20 minutes.

Once salted, clean the anchovies and remove the heads, then rinse and dry them. Put the anchovies in a glass jar, layering them with the salt, bay leaves and thyme until the jar is full. The top layer should be salt. Seal the jar hermetically and let marinate for at least one month before consuming. Remove the anchovies as needed and rinse off the salt before eating them.

Note: These are good accompanied with toast, spread with butter or oil, and topped with tomato slices and a little basil.
PHOTOGRAPH PAGE 290

ANCHOVY AND TOMATO MONTADITO

INGREDIENTS

- 4 slices bread
- 4 tablespoons (50 g/2 oz) butter
- 8 canned anchovy fillets in oil, drained
- 1 generous pinch dried oregano or dried mixed herbs
- 4 very thin slices of tomato
  Serves 4

Lightly toast the bread slices and spread with the butter. Top with the anchovy fillets in a cross shape and put the slices of tomato on top. Sprinkle with the oregano or aromatic herbs.

SMOKED EEL MOUSSE

INGREDIENTS

- 1½ oz (40 g) powdered gelatin
- ⅔ cup (150 g/5 oz) curd cheese
- 7 oz (200 g) smoked eel, skin and bones removed, finely chopped
- heaping (heaped) 2½ tablespoons (40 ml/1½ fl oz) dry white wine
- 3 tablespoons black caviar or lumpfish roe
- watercress sprigs, to garnish

Serves 6–12

Prepare the gelatin according to the directions on the package, using 1¼ cups (300 ml/½ pint) water. Put a layer of gelatin about ¾ inch (2 cm) thick into the bottom of a loaf pan measuring 9½ x 4 inches (24 x 10 cm), then place it in the freezer until it sets (but do not let it freeze).

Put the cheese into a bowl and crush it well with a fork. Add the smoked eel, white wine and still-liquid gelatin and mix well. Add half the caviar and mix again. Pour this thick mixture onto the set gelatin in the pan and place in the refrigerator for at least 5 to 6 hours.

To serve, run a palette knife around the edges of the pan and turn the mousse out onto a serving dish. If it does not come out easily, soak a cloth in very hot water, wring it out and then place it over the upturned pan to heat the gelatin a little. Give the pan a shake and the mousse should fall out. Garnish the top of the mousse with the rest of the caviar, and place watercress around the edges.

Note: Extra watercress can be dressed and served as an accompaniment, as it is delicious with this mousse. If you do not have or do not like watercress, any kind of salad greens can be served and used for garnish.

ENSALADA DE
ANGULAS

ELVER SALAD

INGREDIENTS

- 1 lb 2 oz (500 g) elvers
  or gulas, rinsed
- 1 jar (100 g/3½ oz) mullet
  roe or lumpfish roe
- juice of ½ a lemon, strained
- ½ onion, finely chopped
- 2 tablespoons vodka
- dash of extra-virgin olive oil
- pepper
  Serves 4

Put the elvers or gulas and mullet roe into a bowl and pour the lemon juice over them. Add the onion and mix everything together with a fork. Pour in the vodka and oil and season with pepper. Mix again and serve.

Note: Elvers are baby eels that are three to twelve months old. Once eaten as cheap seafood, elvers are now highly prized and priced accordingly. They can also be difficult to find. Try the more economical gulas, which are imitation or 'manufactured' baby eels made from fish, and typically found in Spanish food stores.

PHOTOGRAPH PAGE 291

BARQUITAS DE ATUN
Y ANCHOAS

TUNA AND ANCHOVY TARTLETS

INGREDIENTS

- 4 quails' eggs, hard-boiled
  (see page 144)
- 5 oz (150 g) canned tuna in
  brine, drained and flaked
- 2 oz (50 g) canned anchovies
  in oil, drained
- 1¼ oz (30 g) capers, rinsed
  and drained
- 2 tablespoons mayonnaise
  homemade (see page 62)
  or ready-made
- 15 ready-made tartlet shells
  (cases), 2 inches (5 cm) across
  Makes 15 tartlets

Shell and slice the quails' eggs. Mash the tuna and anchovies in a large mortar. When the mixture is smooth, add half the capers and mash again. Transfer this mixture to a bowl. Stir in the mayonnaise and remaining capers. Spoon this mixture into the tartlet shells. Place a slice of quails' egg on top of each one.

TUNA AND POTATO SALAD

INGREDIENTS

- 2¼ lb (1 kg) new potatoes, scrubbed
- 7 oz (200 g) canned tuna in oil, drained and flaked
- 2 tomatoes, sliced
- 2 tablespoons white-wine vinegar
- 6 tablespoons extra-virgin olive oil
- salt

Serves 4–6

Place the potatoes in a pan of salted cold water and bring to a boil, then boil for 25–30 minutes until the potatoes are tender. Drain the potatoes and when they are cool enough to handle, peel and slice them. Decoratively arrange the potato slices on a plate, alternate with the tuna and tomato slices.

Beat the vinegar and a pinch of salt in a bowl until the salt dissolves, then pour the mixture over the potatoes, followed by the oil, ensuring all the ingredients are covered. Cover and chill until required.

TUNA, TOMATO AND ASPARAGUS PINCHOS

INGREDIENTS

- 1 large tomato, halved, seeded and diced
- 12 slices French baguette, about ½ inch (1 cm) thick
- 7 oz (200 g) canned tuna, drained and flaked
- 12 bottled asparagus tips, drained and patted dry

Makes 12

Put a slice of tomato on top of each slice of bread, then top with some tuna and an asparagus tip. Use a wooden toothpick (cocktail stick) to spear each together. Serve immediately or the bread will become soggy.

Note: A little mayonnaise can be placed on top of the tuna, if desired.

PHOTOGRAPH PAGE 291

SALT COD AND GARBANZO BEAN (CHICKPEA) SALAD

INGREDIENTS

- 11 oz (300 g) salt cod fillets
- 1 cup (250 ml/8 fl oz) milk
- 4 bottled artichoke hearts, drained and rinsed
- generous 2¼ cups (400 g/14 oz) canned garbanzo beans (chickpeas), drained and rinsed
- generous ¾ cup (100 g/3½ oz) black olives, pitted (stoned) and sliced
- 4 hard-boiled eggs, quartered, to garnish

FOR THE VINAIGRETTE:

- 5 tablespoons extra-virgin olive oil
- 2 tablespoons white-wine vinegar
- 1 tablespoon chopped parsley
- salt

Makes 4–8

Put the salt cod fillets in a large bowl with water to cover and let soak for 24 hours, changing the water 4 times. Drain the salt cod fillets and put them into a pan with the milk and 1 cup (250 ml/8 fl oz) water and bring to a boil. Reduce the heat and let simmer for 20 minutes. Drain well, rinse and pat dry, then cut the flesh into thin strips, carefully removing any skin and bones. Set aside.

To make the vinaigrette, beat the oil and vinegar together with a fork. Season with salt and add the parsley.

Arrange portions of the salt cod, artichoke hearts, garbanzo beans and olives on individual plates. Pour the dressing over the salad and garnish with egg quarters. Serve at room temperature.

Note: This is also delicious with green beans instead of artichokes. To add a sophisticated touch, replace the chickens' eggs with quails' eggs.

SALT COD, ORANGE, ONION AND OLIVE SALAD

INGREDIENTS

- 14 oz (400 g) salt cod, not too dry
- 1 cup (250 ml/8 fl oz) cold milk
- 4 large, juicy oranges, peeled and chopped
- generous ¾ cup (100 g/3½ oz) black olives, pitted (stoned) and halved
- 4 scallions (spring onions), chopped
- 4 tablespoons olive oil
- 1 tablespoon white-wine vinegar, with 1 teaspoon sweet paprika dissolved in it
- salt
- 3 hard-boiled eggs, sliced or cut into wedges, to garnish
  Serves 4

Preheat the oven to 350°F (180°C/GAS MARK 4). To reduce the saltiness of the cod, put it in a roasting pan and roast for about 20 minutes until it is golden brown. Pour the milk over the fish and set aside for at least one hour. Drain off the liquid, then flake the fish, carefully removing any skin and bones.

At least one hour before serving, put the oranges in a serving bowl, followed by the olives, scallions and flaked fish. Pour the oil, vinegar and ¾ cup (175 ml/6 fl oz) water over the top. Season with salt (but remember the fish is salty), then use your hands to gently mix everything together.

Cover the bowl and chill for at least one hour. Serve in the same bowl, garnished with either slices or wedges of hard-boiled egg.

PHOTOGRAPH PAGE 292

LOBSTER WITH ROMESCO SAUCE

INGREDIENTS

- 1 lobster, about 2¼ lb (1 kg), with the claws tied
- chopped parsley, to garnish
- 2 romesco or other hot dried peppers, soaked in water
- 2 tablespoons olive oil
- 1 slice bread, torn into pieces
- 4 cloves garlic
- 2 tomatoes, peeled and chopped
- 1 tablespoon almonds, lightly toasted
- 1 tablespoon sherry vinegar
- salt

FOR THE VEGETABLE STOCK:

- 2 stalks celery, coarsely chopped
- 2 carrots, coarsely chopped
- 1 onion, coarsely chopped
- 1 bouquet garni
- 1 tablespoon black peppercorns
- 1 teaspoon salt

Serves 4

Put the lobster in the freezer for at least 2 hours before cooking. To make the stock, pour scant 3¼ quarts (3 litres/5 pints) water into a large pan. Add the celery, carrots, onion, bouquet garni, peppercorns and salt. Bring to a boil and boil for 15 minutes. Plunge in the lobster so it is completely submerged, cover the pan, lower the heat and calculate the cooking time at 8 minutes per 2¼ lb (1 kg). Remove the lobster from the liquid and set aside. Do not discard the stock.

Take the pan off the heat and let cool for 20 minutes, with the lobster still inside. Remove the lobster from the pan, drain and untie. Remove the head from the lobster and reserve, then open the tail with large scissors, cutting the underside of the shell. Remove the meat in one piece and cut it into slices about ½ inch (1 cm) thick. Remove the meat from the claws.

To prepare the sauce, using a spoon, drain the peppers and remove and discard the seeds. Heat the oil in a large skillet or frying pan and pan-fry the bread, then put it to one side. Add the garlic cloves to the skillet and pan-fry until they are golden brown. Pound the garlic and bread in a mortar or process in a small blender. Add the peppers and tomatoes and pound or process again. Add the almonds and continue pounding or processing until a smooth paste forms. Stir in the vinegar. Season to taste with salt. Stir in a little water if the sauce is too thick.

Put the lobster head on the serving dish, then place the slices of meat and the meat from the claws behind it. Garnish with parsley and serve with the sauce on the side.

LOBSTER AND CRAYFISH SALAD

INGREDIENTS

- 2 lobsters, about 1 lb 5 oz (600 g) each, with the claws tied
- 16 crayfish
- 4 tomatoes
- 12 large mushrooms, chopped
- 1 truffle, cut into julienne strips
- a few tarragon leaves, chopped
- 1 tablespoon raspberry vinegar
- generous ⅓ cup (100 ml/3½ fl oz) heavy (double) cream
- salt and pepper

FOR THE VEGETABLE STOCK:

- 2 stalks celery, coarsely chopped
- 2 carrots, coarsely chopped
- 1 onion, coarsely chopped
- 1 bouquet garni
- 1 tablespoon black peppercorns
- 1 teaspoon salt

Serves 4–8

Prepare and cook the lobsters in the vegetable stock following the instructions opposite. If you don't have a pan large enough to hold the 2 lobsters, make the stock in 2 pans. Calculate the cooking time at 8 minutes per 2¼ lb (1 kg) of lobster. Remove the lobsters from the liquid and set aside. Do not discard the stock.

To prepare the crayfish, remove the central intestine and other inedible parts, then cook them in the same stock for 4 minutes. Turn off the heat, return the lobsters to the pan with the crayfish.

Remove the lobsters from the pan, drain and untie them. Remove the heads from the lobsters and open the tails with large scissors, cutting the underside of the shell and slice the meat. Remove the meat from the tail in one piece, then discard the black strip running down it. Crush the coral and reserve it. Remove the crayfish from the pan and drain, then remove the shells, reserving the heads. Chop the crayfish and lobster meat.

Cut a cross in the stem end of each tomato with a sharp knife. Put the tomatoes in a heatproof bowl and pour in boiling water to cover. Let stand for 1–2 mintues, then drain and peel off the skins. Cut the tomatoes in half, scoop out the seeds with a teaspoon and coarsely chop the flesh. Press the flesh through a fine strainer, then spoon the puree onto 4 plates and put them in the refrigerator.

Put the lobster and crayfish meat into a bowl with the mushrooms, half the truffle and the tarragon. Mix well, then sprinkle in a few drops of raspberry vinegar and bring the whole mixture together with the heavy cream. Season to taste. Spoon the mixture evenly into the center of 4 plates. Garnish with the lobster claws and the crayfish heads, then sprinkle with the crushed lobster coral. Arrange the remaining strips of truffle around the edges.

Note: The meat from a female lobster is best. A few cubes of foie gras can also be added to the mixture.

BONITO SALAD

INGREDIENTS

- 11 oz (300 g) mushrooms
- ½ lemon
- 1 bunch watercress, stems removed and the leaves rinsed and patted dry
- 7 oz (200 g) canned bonito, flaked
- 11 oz (300 g) canned palm hearts, drained, rinsed and thickly sliced
- 3 tablespoons extra-virgin olive oil
- 1 tablespoon white-wine vinegar
- 1 teaspoon soy sauce
- salt
  Serves 4

Wash the mushrooms in cold water with a few drops of lemon juice, but do not let soak. Drain well and slice, not too thinly. Set aside. To make the dressing, beat the oil, vinegar, soy sauce and a pinch of salt in a bowl with a fork. Add the watercress leaves, bonito, palm hearts and mushrooms and mix well to ensure the dressing is evenly distributed. Cover and chill until required. Serve well chilled.

Note: Palm hearts are the inner stem of the cabbage palm tree. They are sometimes available fresh, or canned in water from large supermarkets or gourmet food stores. Their flavor is much like an artichoke or the white part of a leek.

GUETARIAN BONITO SALAD

INGREDIENTS

- 2 red bell peppers
- 2 hard-boiled eggs, shelled and finely chopped
- 11 oz (300 g) canned or bottled bonito from Guetaria, drained and flaked
- 2 tablespoons mayonnaise
- salt
  Serves 4–6

Preheat the oven to 350°F (180°C/GAS MARK 4). Put the bell peppers into the oven and cook for about 25 minutes. When they are cooked, either put them onto a cutting (chopping) board and cover with a cloth, or wrap them in paper or put them between 2 plates, and leave until cool enough to handle. Peel the bell peppers by rubbing them gently with a cloth, then remove the cores and seeds and cut them lengthwise into slices. Reserve a few bell pepper stips for garnishing, then put the rest into a bowl. Add the bonito and eggs and mix together, then add the mayonnaise and toss again. Season to taste. When ready to serve, garnish with the reserved bell pepper strips on top.

CRAB TAPA

INGREDIENTS

- 3 eggs
- generous ¾ cup (175 g/6 oz) canned crabmeat, drained and shredded
- 6 tablespooons mayonnaise homemade (see page 62) or ready-made
- 6 romaine (Cos) lettuce leaves, fincly shredded
- 3½ tablespoons (50 g/2 oz) butter, at room temperature
- 18 slices French baguette
- salt and pepper

FOR THE GARNISHES:

- 4 tomatoes, halved, seeded and finely chopped
- 10 black olives, pitted (stoned) and sliced
- 4 pickled gherkins, drained and fincly chopped
  Makes 18

Put the eggs in a large pan of water, bring to a boil over high heat and boil for 10 minutes. Transfer the pan to the sink and fill it with cold running water to stop the cooking. When the eggs are cool enough to handle, shell them. Place in a bowl of cold water if not using immediately.

Meanwhile, put the crabmeat in a bowl and beat in the mayonnaise, then stir in the lettuce. Season with salt and pepper.

Spread a little of the butter on one side of each slice of bread, taking care not to tear it, then top with the crab mixture.

Drain the eggs if they are in water and pat dry. Slice each egg into at least 6 slices. Put an egg slice on top of each tapa, then garnish the tapa with tomatoes, black olives and gherkins. Serve immediately or the bread will become soggy.

PHOTOGRAPH PAGE 293

ANCHOVIES IN VINEGAR

INGREDIENTS

- 1 lb 2 oz (500 g) fresh anchovies, cleaned
- 2¼ cups (500 ml/18 fl oz) white-wine vinegar
- ¾ cup (175 ml/6 fl oz) olive oil
- 2 cloves garlic, finely chopped
- 1 tablespoon finely chopped flat-leaf parsley
- salt
  Serves 6

Open, or 'butterfly', the anchovies, then place them skin side up and press along the backbones with your thumb. Turn over and lift out the bones, then cut each anchovy in half lengthwise along the back to make fillets. Rinse well and pat dry. Place the anchovy fillets in a deep dish and add two thirds of the vinegar, ensuring they are completely covered. Let marinate in the refrigerator for about 5 hours, stirring from time to time.

Drain well, then add the garlic and parsley and season to taste with salt. Sprinkle with the remaining vinegar and leave for another 2 hours in the refrigerator before serving.

FIG, ANCHOVY AND CHEESE TAPA

INGREDIENTS

- 3 canned anchovy fillets, drained
- ½ clove garlic
- 3½ oz (100 g) goat cheese
- 2 slices thick country-style bread, quartered
- olive or sunflower oil
- 9 oz (250 g) figs, peeled and coarsely chopped
  Makes 8

Preheat the broiler (grill) to high. Pound the anchovies, garlic and cheese with a pestle in a large mortar, or process briefly in a blender, until well blended, then set aside.

Toast the bread slices for 2 minutes on each side, or until golden brown. Brush each with oil on one side, then spread with the anchovy mixture and top with pieces of fig. Serve immediately or the toast will become soggy.

COCTEL DE LANGOSTINOS

SHRIMP (PRAWN) COCKTAIL

INGREDIENTS

- 2 carrots, peeled and sliced
- 1 onion, coarsely chopped
- 6 black peppercorns
- 1 bay leaf
- 2¼ lb (1 kg) jumbo shrimp (king prawns)
- lettuce leaves, shredded, to serve
- 1 tablespoon chopped parsley, to garnish
- 3 lemons, halved, to serve

FOR THE COCKTAIL SAUCE:

- 4 tablespoons mayonnaise, homemade (see page 62) or ready-made
- 2 tablespoons light (single) cream
- 1 tablespoon tomato paste (puree)
- juice of ½ lemon, strained
- few drops of Worcestershire sauce
- salt and pepper

Serves 6

Put the carrots, onion, peppercorns, bay leaf and a large pinch of salt in a large pan of water and bring to a boil over high heat. Add the raw shrimp, lower the heat and cook for 1 minute. Take the pan off the heat and leave the shrimp in the water to cool for about 10 minutes, then drain in a colander.

Meanwhile, to make the sauce, mix together the mayonnaise, cream, tomato paste, the lemon juice and Worcestershire sauce. Season with salt and pepper and chill until required.

Peel the shrimp when they have cooled, and if they are too large cut them into 2 or 3 pieces.

To serve, make a bed of lettuce in the base of 6 small individual glasses, such as short water tumblers or sundae dishes, and top each with ½ tablespoon of the cocktail sauce. Divide the shrimp among the glasses or dishes and cover them with the remaining sauce. Sprinkle over the parsley to garnish. Leave in the refrigerator until required, then serve with lemon halves for squeezing over.

PHOTOGRAPH PAGE 294

MUSSEL BROCHETTES WITH SAUCE

INGREDIENTS

- 40–48 large mussels
- 3 eggs
- 6 tablespons all-purpose (plain) flour
- 1 cup (120 g/4 oz) stale bread crumbs
- 6 tablespoons sunflower oil

FOR THE SAUCE:

- 2 dried red bell peppers, seeded and coarsely chopped
- 1 slice bread, the size of a small egg, from the soft center of a loaf
- 2 cloves garlic
- small piece of fresh red chile, seeded if desired
- 2 tablespoons olive oil
- 1 tablespoon vinegar
- 1 very ripe tomato, peeled, seeded and chopped
- salt and pepper

Serves 4

Begin by soaking the dried bell peppers for the sauce in cold water to cover overnight. At least 3 hours before you plan to serve, drain the bell peppers and seed them, then coarsely chop.

To make the sauce, put the bread in a cup with a little warm water and let soak. Crush the garlic cloves with a little salt in a large mortar. Add the bell peppers and chile and pound. Squeeze the water from the bread, add it to the mortar and continue pounding until a creamy mixture forms. Slowly beat in the oil and vinegar, then transfer to a blender. Add the tomato, season with salt and pepper and blend until smooth. Cover and chill until required.

Prepare the mussels as described on page 275. Put the mussels in a skillet or frying pan with ¾ cup (175 ml/6 fl oz) water and a pinch of salt. Cover and cook over high heat, shaking the skillet occasionally, for 4–5 minutes until the shells have opened. Remove the skillet from the heat and strain the mussels, reserving the liquid. Discard any that remain closed. Remove the mussels from their shells and set aside.

Thread the mussels on 4 short skewers, putting 10–12 on each skewer. Beat the eggs in a shallow dish, spread out the flour in another shallow dish and put the bread crumbs in a third shallow dish. Heat the oil in a large skillet. Dip the brochettes in the flour, shaking off the excess, then in the eggs and then in the bread crumbs. When the oil is hot, add the brochettes and fry, over high heat, turning once, until golden brown. Serve the hot brochettes with the chilled sauce. If the sauce is very thick, strain the reserved cooking sauce through a cheesecloth (muslin) and use it to thin the sauce.

Note: If using wooden skewers, be sure to soak them in cold water for at least 30 minutes before cooking.

PHOTOGRAPH PAGE 295

MEJILLONES ENVUELTOS
EN ESPINACAS

MUSSELS WRAPPED IN SPINACH

INGREDIENTS

- 24 mussels
- 3 tablespoons dry white wine
- ½ clove garlic, chopped
- ¼ onion, sliced
- 24 large spinach leaves
- salt
- tomato flowers, to garnish (optional)

FOR THE VEGETABLE BUTTER:

- 1 oz (30 g) spinach leaves, washed
- ¼ oz (10 g) watercress leaves
- ¼ oz (10 g) parsley
- ¼ oz (10 g) fresh tarragon leaves
- 2 tablespoons olive oil
- 2 shallots, chopped
- 2 canned anchovy fillets
- 1 gherkin, chopped
- 1 large clove garlic, chopped
- 2 hard-boiled eggs, yolks only
- generous cup (225 g/8 oz) butter, softened
- salt

Makes 24

To make the vegetable butter, bring a pan of salted water to a simmer. Add the spinach leaves, parsley and tarragon and bring back to a boil. Boil for 1 minute, then drain the greens and pass them under a stream of cold water to stop the cooking process. Pat dry and set aside. Heat the oil in a frying pan over medium heat. Add the shallots and cook for about 6 minutes, until transluscent. Transfer to a mortar. Add the anchovies, capers, gherkin, and garlic and grind to a paste. Transfer the paste to a mixing bowl. Stir in the egg yolks, followed by the butter. Shape the butter into a block, then chill in the refrigerator to let the mixture harden.

Prepare the mussels as described on page 275. Put the mussels into a pan with the wine, garlic, onion, 3 tablespoons water and a pinch of salt. Cover and cook over high heat, shaking the pan occasionally, for 4–5 minutes, until the shells have opened. Remove the pan from the heat and lift out the mussels with a slotted spoon. Remove the mussels from their shells and discard their shells. Discard any mussels that remain closed.

Bring a kettle of water to a boil. Put the spinach leaves in another pan, taking care they do not break and that they are flat. Cover with boiling water, add a large pinch of salt and leave over high heat for a few seconds. Drain them carefully, then immediately plunge them into cold water to preserve their green color. Dry the leaves very carefully with paper towels.

Very gently spread the leaves with vegetable butter and put a mussel onto each one. Roll them up, folding in the edges of the spinach, and use a toothpick (cocktail stick) to secure them. As well as preventing them unrolling, this also makes them easier to eat. Place the spinach rolls in the refrigerator for at least 1 hour before serving. Serve on a dish garnished with tomato flowers in the center, if desired.

CUCUMBER AND ROE TAPA

INGREDIENTS

- 1 cucumber, thinly sliced
- 12 slices of bread
- butter, softened, for spreading
- 1 onion, thinly sliced
- 1 jar (100 g/3½ oz) canned mullet roe or lumpfish roe
- lemon juice, strained, to taste
- 2 hard-boiled eggs, shelled and very finely chopped

FOR THE VINAIGRETTE:

- 3 tablespoons olive oil
- 1 tablespoon white-wine vinegar
- 1 teaspoon salt
  Makes 24

Preheat the broiler (grill) to high. To make the dressing, beat the oil, vinegar and salt in a nonmetallic bowl with a fork until blended. Add the cucumber slices, then set aside.

Using a 2-inch (5-cm) round cookie cutter, cut out 24 circles from the bread. Toast the circles for 2 minutes on each side, or until golden brown. Spread one side of each slice with butter.

Drain the cucumbers. Top each toast circle with an onion slice, then add a cucumber slice. Place 1 teaspoon of roe on top of each and sprinkle with a little lemon juice. Sprinkle the hard-boiled egg around the roe. Serve immediately or the toast will be soggy.

PHOTOGRAPH PAGE 294

FISH AND SHRIMP (PRAWN) SALAD

INGREDIENTS
- 6 tablespoons olive oil
- 12 large shrimp (prawns), peeled
- 2 strips chile
- 5 oz (150 g) kingklip fillets (see Note)
- ⅔ cup (150 g/5 oz) cooked crabmeat
- juice of 2 lemons, strained
- 1 tablespoon chopped fresh mint
- 1 lettuce, shredded
- salt and pepper

Serves 4

Heat half the oil in a skillet or frying pan. Add the shrimp and chile and cook over medium heat, stirring occasionally, for a few minutes, until the shrimp are opaque. Remove from the skillet, drain well and set aside. Steam the kingklip fillets for 3 minutes. Cut the shrimp into pieces and flake the fish and crabmeat. Put the fish and crabmeat into a bowl with the remaining oil and the lemon juice and mint, season and let marinate in the refrigerator. To serve, make a bed of lettuce on a round dish and put the fish mixture on top. Pour the marinade over the salad and serve.

Note: Kingklip, also called congrio, is an eel-like fish with pink, orange, brown or black markings. It can be found off the coasts of South America and South Africa. If you can't find it, use another firm-fleshed, mild fish such as monkfish.

PHOTOGRAPH PAGE 296

OCTOPUS IN VINAIGRETTE

INGREDIENTS
- 2¼ lb (1 kg) octopus
- ⅔ cup (150 ml/¼ pint) olive oil
- 1½ tablespoons white-wine vinegar
- 1 onion, finely chopped
- 1 green bell pepper, halved, seeded and diced
- 1½ cups (250 g/9 oz) cooked or drained canned peas
- salt and pepper

Serves 6–8

First, prepare and cook the octopus (see page 282). Meanwhile, prepare the vinaigrette. Whisk together the oil and vinegar in a bowl and season to taste with salt and pepper. Stir in the onion and bell pepper and set aside. Drain the octopus well and rinse under cold running water. Remove and discard any remaining dark skin and cut the meat into medium-size pieces with kitchen scissors. Put the octopus pieces in a bowl, pour the vinaigrette over them and add the peas. Taste and adjust the marinade if necessary. Cover the bowl and let marinate in the refrigerator, stirring occasionally, for 2 hours before serving.

PASTEL DE SALMÓN

SALMON TERRINE

INGREDIENTS
- 1 package dried cream of asparagus soup
- ½ oz (15 g) powdered gelatin
- scant 2¼ cups (500 g/1 lb 2 oz) mayonnaise, homemade (see page 62) or ready-made
- 9 oz (250 g) cooked salmon, bones and skins removed, flaked
- generous 1 cup (250 g/9 oz) curd cheese
- 1 tablespoon (15 g/½ oz) butter, softened
- 3 gherkins, drained and diced
- 1 tomato, peeled, seeded and diced
- 1 bottled or canned roasted red bell pepper, drained and diced
- 1 tablespoon good-quality cognac
- 9 oz (250 g) smoked salmon slices
- salt
  Serves 12

Dissolve the dried soup in a pan with generous 2 cups (500 ml/18 fl oz) water and mix over low heat for 10 minutes. Dissolve the gelatin in the soup over low heat, according to the directions on the package, but do not allow it to boil. Remove the pan from the heat and let cool.

Put the mayonnaise, salmon, curd cheese, butter, gherkins, tomato, bell pepper, and cognac in a bowl. Season with salt and beat together. Add the asparagus soup mixture. Line a 9½ x 4-inch (24 x 10-cm) mold with slices of smoked salmon, leaving an overhang. Spoon in the salmon mixture and smooth the surface, then fold over the overhanging salmon. Cover and put the mold in the coldest part of the refrigerator for at least 12 hours to set. To serve, unmold and cut into slices.

Note: Using a plastic mold makes unmolding easier. To create a shinier finish, put a thin layer of the plain gelatin into the mold before lining it with the smoked salmon.

PHOTOGRAPH PAGE 297

PATÉ DE SALMÓN

SALMON PÂTÉ

INGREDIENTS

- 5 oz (150 g) soft center of a day-old loaf of bread
- generous 2 cups (500 ml/ 18 fl oz) milk, boiling
- 1 lb 10 oz (750 g) fresh salmon
- 2 tablespoons dry white wine
- ½ onion
- 1 bay leaf
- 3½ oz (100 g) smoked salmon
- 3½ tablespoons (50 g/2 oz) butter
- 2 tablespoons very thick tomato sauce, bottled or homemade (see page 181)
- 4 large eggs, separated
- 2 tablespoons white wine
- grated nutmeg, to taste
- salt
- mayonnaise, homemade (see page 62) or ready-made, or sweet mustard sauce, to serve

Serves 12

Tear the bread into large pieces, add them to the boiling milk and leave until they have absorbed all the liquid. Preheat the oven to 350°F (180°C/GAS MARK 4). Put the salmon in a pan with cold water to cover and add the white wine, onion, bay leaf and a pinch of salt. Put the pan over high heat and when it comes to a boil, take it off and let the salmon cool. When the water is just warm, take the salmon out of the water, remove the skin and flake the flesh, removing any bones.

Meanwhile, finely chop the smoked salmon in a blender or meat-grinder. Place the flaked salmon and smoked salmon in a bowl with the soaked bread, half the butter, the tomato sauce, the egg yolks, and nutmeg. Season with salt and mix everything well. Whisk the egg whites with a pinch of salt until stiff peaks form and fold them into to the fish mixture.

Line the base of a 9½ x 4-inch (24 x 10-cm) mold with aluminum foil and grease it well with the remaining butter, then pour the mixture into it. Put the mold into a roasting pan and pour in hot water to come halfway up the sides, taking care no water leaks into the mold. Place in the oven and bake for 1½ hours, or until a thin knife inserted in the center comes out clean.

Take the mold out of the water and let cool completely, then cover in foil, put something heavy on top, such as cans of food, and place in the refrigerator until ready to serve. To serve, unmold, cut into slices and serve with mayonnaise or a sweet mustard sauce.

Note: This dish is also delicious if the mold is lined with thin strips of zucchini (courgette) before the fish mixture is poured in.

LITTLE GLASSES OF SALMON WITH DILL SAUCE

INGREDIENTS

- 1 tablespoon walnut oil
- 1 tablespoon balsamic vinegar
- 3 ripe tomatoes, peeled, seeded and diced
- 1 lb 2 oz (500 g) smoked salmon in one piece
- freshly ground pink pepper
- salt
- 2 oz (50 g) salmon roe (keta), drained
- 1 sprig dill, to garnish

FOR THE DILL SAUCE:

- 1 egg yolk
- 1 tablespoon sugar
- 1 tablespoon chopped fresh dill
- 1 tablespoon sweet mustard
- ¾ cup (175 ml/6 fl oz) olive oil
- salt

Serves 6–8

First, make the dill sauce. Whisk the egg yolk in a bowl. Add the sugar, dill and mustard and continue whisking. Gradually whisk in the oil, little by little. Season to taste with salt and place in the refrigerator. Whisk the walnut oil and balsamic vinegar together in another bowl. Add the pink pepper and salt to taste and continue whisking until all the ingredients are amalgamated. Add the tomatoes and gently toss until they are well coated with the dressing. Divide the tomatoes between 6–8 glasses.

Cut the salmon into small cubes. Add a layer of salmon cubes to each glass and spoon the sauce over each. Top with a little salmon roe. Chill until required, then garnish with dill and serve.

Note: As a variation, puree the salmon in a blender. Mix it with a little light (single) cream, then make the salmon layer with this puree.

SARDINE ESCABECHE

INGREDIENTS

- 1 cup (120 g/4 oz) all-purpose (plain) flour
- 2¼ lb (1 kg) small or medium size fresh sardines, scaled, cleaned and boned
- 4 cups (1 litre/1¾ pints) olive oil
- 2 bay leaves
- 6 black peppercorns
- 2 cloves garlic
- 1 cup (250 ml/8 fl oz) white wine vinegar
- salt
  Serves 6

Spread out the flour in a shallow dish. Wash the sardines well and pat dry. Lightly season the fish inside and out, then close them again and dredge them in the flour, shaking off any excess. Heat the oil in a skillet or frying pan. Add the sardines, in batches, and cook, turning once, over medium-high heat. Transfer them to a deep, heatproof serving dish, on top of each other, if necessary, but not too squashed.

Through a metal sieve, strain 5 tablespoons of oil from the skillet in which the sardines were cooked. Add the bay leaves, peppercorns and garlic and cook, stirring, until they are golden brown. Take the skillet off the heat and add the vinegar and 1 cup (250 ml/8 fl oz) water. Return the skillet to the heat and bring to a boil, then simmer for 5 minutes. Pour this liquid over the sardines, ensuring that they are evenly covered. Shake the dish a little and let cool completely before covering and chilling. This dish will keep for up to 3 days in the refrigerator.

SMOKED TROUT OR SMOKED EEL TAPA

INGREDIENTS

- 5 slices bread
- 3½ tablespoons (50 g/2 oz) butter
- 7 oz (200 g) smoked trout or smoked eel fillet, finely chopped
- 1 lemon
  Makes 20

Preheat the broiler (grill) to high. Cut the bread into 4 x 1½-inch (4-cm) rounds with a cookie cutter and toast them lightly. Spread a little butter on the toasted bread rounds and top with the smoked trout or smoked eel fillet. Sprinkle 2 drops of lemon juice on each tapa.

SMOKED
TROUT PÂTÉ

INGREDIENTS

- 5 oz (150 g) soft center of a day-old loaf of bread
- generous 2 cups (500 ml/ 18 fl oz) milk, boiling
- 1 lb 10 oz (750 g) hake or whiting, cleaned
- ½ onion
- 1 bay leaf
- dash of dry white wine
- 3½ oz (100 g) smoked trout
- 3½ tablespoons (50 g/2 oz) butter
- 2 tablespoons tomato sauce, bottled or homemade (see page 181)
- 4 large eggs, separated
- 1 pinch grated nutmeg
- salt
- mayonnaise or cocktail sauce, to serve

Serves 4–6

Tear the bread into large pieces, add them to the boiling milk and leave them until they have absorbed all the liquid. Preheat the oven to 350°F (180°C/GAS MARK 4). Remove the backbone and wash the hake, then put it into a pan with cold water to cover with the onion, bay leaf and wine. Season with salt and put the pan over high heat. When it comes to a boil, take it off and let the fish cool. Take the fish out of the water, remove the skin and flake the flesh, removing any bones.

Meanwhile, very finely chop the trout in a blender or meat-grinder. Put the hake mixture and trout in a bowl with the soaked bread, half the butter, the tomato sauce, egg yolks and nutmeg. Season with salt and mix everything together well.

Whisk the egg whites with a pinch of salt until stiff peaks form and fold them into the fish mixture. Grease a 9½ x 4-inch (24 x 10-cm) mold with the remaining butter, then pour the mixture into it. Put the mold into a roasting pan and pour in hot water to come halfway up the sides, taking care no water leaks into the mold. Place the roasting pan in the oven and cook for 1½ hours, or until a thin knife inserted in the center comes out clean.

Take the mold out of the water and let cool completely, then cover in aluminum foil and place in the refrigerator until ready to serve. When ready to serve, unmold and serve with mayonnaise or cocktail sauce on the side.

FISH PÂTÉ

INGREDIENTS

- 5 oz (150 g) mixed cooked seafood, such as the meat from the claws and white parts of crabs and spider crabs, shrimp (prawns) and Norwegian lobsters (langoustines)
- 3½ tablespoons (50 g/2 oz) butter, softened
- 4 teaspoons lemon juice, strained
- ½ oz (15 g) powdered gelatin
- salt and pepper
- hot toast, to serve

Serves 4

Flake the mixed seafood into a bowl and beat in the butter, add the lemon juice and season with salt and pepper. Line the base of 4 individual molds with aluminum foil, then tip the mixture into the molds.

Prepare the gelatin with water according to the directions on the package, then pour the gelatin into each mold, covering the mixture with a thin layer. Cover and chill for 2 hours, or until set. Turn out onto individual plates. Serve with toast on the side.

SALPICÓN DE MARISCO

SEAFOOD SALPICON

INGREDIENTS

- 1 lobster, about 1 lb 5 oz (600 g), with claws tied
- 2 bay leaves
- 9 oz (250 g) large shrimp (prawns)
- 1 hard-boiled egg, chopped
- 2 bottled or canned roasted red bell peppers, drained and chopped
- handful green olives
- 6 tablespoons olive oil
- 2 tablespoons white-wine vinegar
- 1 onion, finely chopped
- ½ tablespoon chopped parsley
- salt and pepper

Serves 4–8

To kill the lobster, put it into the freezer for 2 hours before cooking. Pour scant 4¼ quarts (4 litres/7 pints) water into a pan with 1 of the bay leaves and 1 teaspoon salt. Bring to a boil and plunge in the lobster so it is completely submerged, cover the pan, lower the heat and calculate the cooking time at 8 minutes per 2¼ lb (1 kg). Remove the pan from the heat and let the lobster cool for 15 minutes.

Lift the lobster out of the water, untie it and let drain. Remove the meat from the tail. Cut open the tail on the underside of the shell with a large pair of scissors Remove the meat in one piece. Using the point of a knife, remove and discard the black intestinal tract that runs along its length. Break off the claws, then crack the shells and remove the meat. Thinly slice or finely chop all the meat.

To cook the shrimp, bring a large pan of salted water to a boil. Add the raw shrimp, reduce the heat and simmer for 2–4 minutes, depending on their size. Drain well and let cool. Peel the shrimp and discard the heads and tails.

Arrange the lobster meat and shrimp on small plates or in wide-brimmed glasses. Top with the hard-boiled egg, bell peppers and the olives. Whisk the oil and vinegar together and season with salt and pepper, then spoon over the salads. Sprinkle with the onion and parsley and serve.

Note: A sprig of thyme and a dash of white wine can be added to the water when cooking the lobster.

PAN DE MOLDE RELLENO

FILLED LOAF

INGREDIENTS

- 1 rectangular loaf of bread with a firm, crisp crust
- canned tuna, drained
- green and black olives, pitted (stoned) and chopped
- hard-boiled eggs, shelled and roughly chopped
- cooked shrimp (prawns), peeled
- tomatoes, peeled, seeded and diced
- roasted red bell peppers, well drained if from a jar, seeded and chopped
- mayonnaise, homemade (see page 62) or ready-made

Serves 12

Prepare and assemble this recipe 24 hours before you intend to serve it. There are no quantities given, as the amounts depend on the size of the loaf: you need enough mixture to fill your loaf. Use a long, sharp bread-knife to cut one end off the loaf, then use the knife to remove the bread inside, leaving at least ½ inch (1 cm) of crust all the way around the edges. Use a fork to reach down to the end if necessary, but take care not to perforate the crust. Do not throw away the bread you remove.

Flake the tuna in a bowl, then add the olives, the hard-boiled eggs, the shrimp, the tomatoes and the bell peppers. Add the quantities according to taste, then crumble in a good handful of the bread removed from the loaf. Add a little mayonnaise – 2 or 3 tablespoons should be enough – and mix everything together. Spoon the mixture back into the crust, pushing down hard with a tart tamper or pestle. The secret to the success of this dish is that the filling is very firmly packed.

Trim the slice taken off the end of the loaf so that it fits into the hole you have made, then stand the bread upright on a baking sheet in the refrigerator with something heavy on top of the 'lid', such as a can of beans. Leave for 24 hours. When ready to serve, cut into thick slices.

Note: The bread removed from the center of the loaf can be made into bread crumbs and frozen until required. Use them for coating Salmon Croquettes (see page 283) before pan-frying.

HOT

ENSALADA DE ALCACHOFAS,
PATATAS Y GAMBAS

ARTICHOKE, POTATO AND SHRIMP (PRAWN) SALAD

INGREDIENTS

– 1 lemon, cut in half
– 8 small artichokes
– 1 lb 8½ oz (700 g) potatoes
– 2 tablespoons olive oil
– 9 oz (250 g) jumbo shrimp
  (king prawns), peeled with
  tails left on
– 1 small lettuce, leaves separated,
  rinsed and patted dry

FOR THE DRESSING:

– 1 tablespoon tarragon vinegar
– 1 tablespoon lemon juice,
  strained
– 3 tablespoons olive oil
– 1 shallot, chopped
– 1 tablespoon chopped parsley
– salt and pepper

Serves 6

Fill a bowl with water and squeeze in the juice from one of the lemon halves. Cut the stems off the artichokes, then remove the hard external leaves and cut the bulbs in half lengthwise, rubbing each cut side with the remaining lemon half, and drop it into the bowl of water as it is prepared.

To make the dressing, beat all the ingredients together with a fork, and season with salt and pepper. Set aside.

Drain the artichokes. Steam the potatoes and the artichokes in a pressure cooker, or over a pan of boiling water, until tender. When the vegetables are cool enough to handle, thickly slice the potatoes and cut each artichoke into quarters. Meanwhile, heat the oil, add the shrimp and pan-fry, stirring, for 3–5 minutes until opaque.

Cut the lettuce leaves into wide strips and use them to line the bottom and side of a bowl. Add the potatoes, artichoke hearts and the shrimp in their own oil. Pour the dressing over the salad and toss. Serve immediately, while still warm.

PHOTOGRAPH PAGE 298

ARROZ CON ALMEJAS
AL AZAFRAN

SAFFRON RICE WITH CLAMS

INGREDIENTS

- 4 dozen small clams
- 2 tablespoons sunflower oil
- 2 onions, finely chopped
- 1 red bell pepper, halved, seeded and chopped
- 2 cloves garlic, finely chopped
- 2 tomatoes, peeled, seeded and chopped
- 1 tablespoon chopped parsley
- 2½ cups (500 g/1 lb 2 oz) long-grain rice
- 1 teaspoon paprika
- 2½ cups (600 ml/1 pint) chicken, vegetable or chicken stock, or water
- 1 pinch saffron threads
- salt
  Serves 6

Scrub the clams under cold running water and discard any with broken shells or any that do not snap shut when tapped. Put the clams and 4 tablespoons water in a large pan over high heat. Cover and steam for 5 minutes, shaking the pan occasionally, or until all the clams are open. Drain the clams in a colander set in the sink and leave until cool enough to handle. Discard any clams that do not open, then discard the open half shells. Set aside.

Heat the oil in a heavy-base flameproof pan over medium heat. Add the onions, bell pepper and garlic and pan-fry, stirring occasionally, for about 6 minutes until the onions are softened but not colored. Stir in the tomatoes and parsley and continue pan-frying and stirring.

Stir the rice into the tomato mixture, then add the paprika and season with salt. Stir everything together to make sure the rice grains are coated, then add the stock and bring to a boil. Stir, cover the pan, reduce the heat to low and let simmer for 12–15 minutes, or until the rice is tender and the liquid is absorbed.

Meanwhile, toast the saffron threads in a dry pan over medium heat, stirring, until you can smell the aroma. Tip them into mortar and pound to a powder. Stir the saffron powder and clams into the rice. Re-cover the pan and let stand a few minutes before serving.

PHOTOGRAPH PAGE 299

RICE WITH CLAMS IN PARSLEY SAUCE

INGREDIENTS

- 2¼ lb (1 kg) clams
- 4 tablespoons olive oil
- 1 onion, chopped
- 1 tablespoons all-purpose (plain) flour
- 1 clove garlic
- 2 sprigs parsley, plus 1 tablespoon very finely chopped parsley, to garnish
- 2 cups (14 oz/400 g) cooked short-grain rice
- 9 oz (250 g) canned or cooked asparagus, drained and warmed (optional)
- salt and pepper
Serves 4

Scrub the clams under cold running water and discard any with broken shells or any that do not shut immediately when sharply tapped. Pour ½ cup (120 ml/4 fl oz) water into a deep skillet or frying pan, add a pinch of salt and the clams, cover and cook over high heat, shaking the skillet occasionally, for 5–7 minutes, until they have opened. Remove them with a slotted spoon and discard the empty half shells and any clams that remained closed. Reserve and strain the cooking liquid. Put the clams on their half shells into a heatproof dish and keep warm.

Heat the oil in a large skillet or frying pan. Add the onion and cook over medium heat, stirring occasionally, for about 6 minutes, until it is softened and translucent. Stir in the flour and cook for 2 minutes. Gradually add the reserved cooking liquid and enough water to make it up to 1 cup (250 ml/8 fl oz) water, stirring constantly, and continue cooking for another 2 minutes.

Crush the garlic, parsley sprigs and a pinch of salt with a pestle and mortar. Add 4 tablespoons of the sauce and mix. Stir the garlic mixture into the sauce in the skillet. Strain the sauce through a sifter (sieve) into a heavy-base pan, using the back of a spoon to press any liquid from the sediment. Add the rice and the clams to the pan, and mix. Season with salt and pepper. Sprinkle the chopped parsley over the top and add the asparagus, if desired. Serve immediately.

Note: If desired, a few saffron threads can be added to the mixture in the mortar.

ALMEJAS A LA MARINERA

SAILORS' CLAMS

INGREDIENTS

- 6½ lb (3 kg) clams
- 4 tablespoons olive oil
- 1 onion, finely chopped
- 1 clove garlic, finely chopped
- 2 tablespoons bread crumbs
- ¾ cup (175 ml/6 fl oz) dry white wine
- juice of ½ lemon, strained
- 1 bay leaf
- 1 tablespoon chopped parsley, to garnish
- salt

Serves 6

Scrub the clams under cold running and water and discard any with broken shells or any that do not shut immediately when sharply tapped. Pour ¾ cup (175 ml/6 fl oz) water into a deep skillet or frying pan, add a pinch of salt and the clams, cover and cook over high heat, shaking the pan occasionally, for 5–7 minutes, until they have opened. Remove them with a slotted spoon and discard the empty half shells and any clams that remained closed. Put the clams on the half shell into a dish and keep warm.

Strain the cooking liquid into a bowl through a cheesecloth- (muslin-) lined sifter (sieve). Heat the oil in a flameproof heavy-base pan. Add the onion and garlic and cook over medium heat, stirring occasionally, for about 6 minutes, until softened but not browned. Add the bread crumbs and pan-fry. Add the wine, lemon juice, bay leaf and reserved cooking liquid. Season with salt, stir together and return the clams to the pan. Remove the bay leaf. Sprinkle the parsley over the top and serve straight from the pan.

FABES CON ALMEJAS

BEANS
WITH CLAMS

INGREDIENTS

- 2¾ cups (500 g/1 lb 2 oz)
  dried Asturian beans or lima
  (butter) beans, soaked overnight
  in cold water and drained
- 3 tablespoons olive oil
- 1 clove garlic
- 1 bay leaf
- 1 small onion
- 3–4 sprigs parsley, tied together
  with kitchen twine or thread
- 1 pinch saffron threads
- 3 tablespoons bread crumbs
- 14 oz (400 g) carpetshell, Venus
  or warty Venus clams
- dash of white-wine vinegar
- salt
  Serves 8

Put the beans into a pan and pour in cold water to cover. Bring to a boil over low heat. Meanwhile, put the oil, garlic, bay leaf, whole onion and parsley sprigs in another large pan and pour in a little cold water. When the beans come to a boil, remove the pan from the heat and drain. Tip the beans into the pan with the parsley and add cold water to cover generously. Cover and cook over low heat for 1½ hours, adding more cold water if necessary.

Crush the saffron in a mortar and stir in 2 tablespoons of the cooking liquid from the beans, then stir the saffron mixture into the pan. Sprinkle the bread crumbs over the mixture in the pan, cover and simmer gently over very low heat for another 30 minutes, until the beans are tender. (The total cooking time depends on the type and age of the beans and the softness of the water.)

Meanwhile, wash the clams in cold water with a little salt and the vinegar. Discard any with broken shells or any that do not shut immediately when sharply tapped. Put them into a skillet or frying pan or pan, add ¾ cup (175 ml/6 fl oz) water, cover and cook over high heat, shaking the skillet occasionally, for 3–5 minutes, until the shells have opened.

Remove the clams with a slotted spoon, reserving the cooking liquid. Discard any that remain shut. Remove the clams from their shells or, if you prefer, discard the empty half shells, and leave the clams on their half shell. Put the clams in a bowl and strain the reserved cooking liquid over them through a cheesecloth (muslin)-lined strainer. Set aside. About 15 minutes before you're ready to serve, add the clams and their cooking liquid to the beans. Serve in a warm deep dish.

FROGS' LEGS WITH ONIONS

INGREDIENTS

- 24 frogs' legs, skinned
- all-purpose (plain) flour, for coating
- 5 tablespoons olive oil
- 1 large onion, very finely chopped
- 1 tablespoon good-quality white-wine vinegar
- 1 tablespoon chopped parsley
- salt and pepper

Serves 8

Fill a bowl with cold water and set aside. Bring a pan of water to a boil. Add the frogs' legs and scald for 10 minutes, then immediately drain them and place in the bowl of cold water. Drain again and pat dry with paper towels. Spread out the flour in a shallow bowl. Coat the frogs' legs in the flour, shaking off any excess, then set aside.

Heat the oil in a large skillet or frying pan. Add the onion and pan-fry over low heat, stirring occasionally, for 5 minutes, or until softened but not colored. Add the frogs' legs and pan-fry for 5 minutes. Sprinkle in the vinegar and parsley and cook for another 10 minutes. Serve very hot.

PHOTOGRAPH PAGE 300

RICE WITH ANCHOVIES AND TUNA

INGREDIENTS

- 2 tablespoons sunflower oil
- 1 onion, finely chopped
- 1 clove garlic, finely chopped
- 5 oz (150 g) canned tuna in oil,
- 4 canned anchovy fillets, drained and chopped
- 1 roasted red bell pepper in oil, drained and sliced
- ¾ cup (175 ml/6 fl oz) dry white wine
- 2½ cups (600 ml/1 pint) stock
- 1¼ cups (250 g/9 oz) rice
- salt

Serves 6

Heat the oil in pan over low heat. Add the onion and garlic and pan-fry, stirring occasionally, for 6 minutes, or until softened but not browned. Drain and flake the tuna, then add to the pan along with the anchovy fillets, bell pepper and wine and let cook slowly for 15 minutes, stirring occasionally.

Meanwhile, bring the stock to a boil over high heat. Stir in the rice and season with salt, then cover, reduce the heat to low and cook for 20 minutes, or until the stock is absorbed. Stir the rice into the pan with the other ingredients and serve hot.

BREAD WITH ANCHOVIES AND OLIVES

INGREDIENTS

- 4 tablespoons sunflower or olive oil
- 2¼ lb (1 kg) onions, thinly sliced
- 1 sprig thyme
- 1⅔ cups (200 g/7 oz) black olives, pitted (stoned) and chopped
- 2 oz (50 g) canned anchovy fillets in olive oil, drained and chopped
- all-purpose (plain) flour, for kneading the dough
- salt and pepper

FOR THE DOUGH:

- 6½ cups (725 g/1 lb 9½ oz) whole wheat (wholemeal) flour, or a mixture of white and whole wheat (wholemeal)
- 1 teaspoon salt
- 1 tablespoon (20 g/1 oz) butter 20 g fresh yeast

Serves 8–10

To make the dough, sift the flour with the salt in a bowl. Add the butter and rub in with the tips of your fingers. In a separate bowl, mix the yeast with generous 2 cups (500 ml/18 fl oz) warm water. Make a well in the center of the flour and pour in the yeast mixture. Using a spoon at first and then your hands, combine the flour and yeast mixture. When the dough is firm, put it onto a lightly floured surface and knead until it stops sticking to your hands. Shape the dough into a ball and put into a bowl. Cover with a cloth or piece of greased baking paper and let it rest for 50 minutes to 1 hour, or until doubled in size.

Meanwhile, heat the oil in a large pan over low heat. Add the onions and thyme and pan-fry, stirring occasionally, for 6 minutes, or until softened but not colored. Add the olives and anchovies and continue pan-frying over low heat, stirring occasionally, for another 15 minutes, or until it forms a kind of compote. Season with salt and pepper.

Punch down the dough and knead it a few times on a very lightly floured surface. Spread the dough out thinly with your fingers on a lightly greased, shallow baking pan, then spoon over the onion mixture, cover with a cloth, and let rise for 30 minutes. Meanwhile, preheat the oven to 450°F (230°C/GAS MARK 8). Bake for 15 minutes until it rises and is golden brown. When the bread is cooked, a skewer inserted into the center of the bread should come out clean.

Note: If not eaten immediately, this dish can be reheated, in which case add a dash of oil when it is removed from the oven.

ARENQUES ASADOS
CON ANCHOAS

BROILED (GRILLED) HERRING WITH ANCHOVIES

INGREDIENTS

- 4 oz (120 g) canned anchovy fillets in oil
- 3½ tablespoons (50 g/2 oz) butter
- 8 sprigs parsley
- 6 herring, scaled, cleaned and boned
- 3 tablespoons olive oil
- 1 teaspoon mustard
- salt
  Serves 6

Preheat the broiler (grill) to high. Cut 6 anchovy fillets in half lengthwise and set aside. Drain the remainder and pound to a paste with the butter and two parsley sprigs in a mortar. Divide the paste among the herring cavities, close the fish and secure with wooden toothpicks (cocktail sticks). Mix together the oil and mustard and brush half of it over one side of each herring, then broil (grill) for about 10 minutes. Carefully turn the fish, brush with the remaining oil and mustard mixture and broil for another 5–10 minutes, until the flesh flakes easily. Transfer to a warm serving dish and garnish with the reserved anchovies in crosses and the remaining parsley sprigs. Serve immediately.

PHOTOGRAPH PAGE 300

VENTRESCA DE ATÚN
A LA VASCA

BASQUE-STYLE TUNA BELLY FILLETS

INGREDIENTS

- 4 tablespoons olive oil
- 11 oz (300 g) onions, sliced
- 5 oz (150 g) long, thin green bell peppers, seeded and chopped
- 2 cloves garlic, chopped
- 2 slices good Serrano ham, cut into thin strips
- 1 lb 2 oz (500 g) tuna belly fillets
- salt
- 1 fresh red chile, seeded and thinly sliced
- balsamic vinegar, to serve
- chives, finely snipped, to serve
  Serves 8

Heat 2 tablespoons oil in a pan. Add the onions and pan-fry over low heat, stirring occasionally, for 10 minutes, until beginning to brown. Add the green bell peppers and pan-fry, stirring occasionally, for 5 minutes. Add the garlic and a little salt and cook for 5 minutes. Add the ham strips at the end so they do not cook.

Heat the remaining oil in a skillet or frying pan. Season the tuna pieces lightly with salt and pepper, add to the pan and fry over high heat, turning several times, until they are pink in the center, or done to your liking. To serve, put the chile in the center of a warm serving dish, then drizzle with a little olive oil and sprinkle with the chives. Spoon the onion mixture over the top with the tuna fillets. It is important to cook the tuna at the last minute.

PHOTOGRAPH PAGE 301

TUNA
EMPANADILLAS

INGREDIENTS

- 1 tablespoon sunflower oil,
  plus extra for deep frying
- 1 onion, very finely chopped
- 1 x 7-oz (200-g) can tuna in
  brine, drained, or 7 oz (200 g)
  fresh tuna, very finely chopped
- 1 hard-boiled egg,
  finely chopped
- 3 tablespoons tomato
  paste (puree)
- salt

FOR THE PASTRY DOUGH:

- 2 tablespoons (1 oz/25 g) butter
- 3 tablespoons olive oil
- 2¾ cups (11 oz/300 g)
  all-purpose (plain) flour,
  plus extra for dusting
- 1 egg
- salt

Makes 12

First, make the pastry dough. Pour 1 cup (250 ml/8 fl oz) water into a pan, add the butter, oil and a pinch of salt and heat gently until the butter has melted. Once the mixture is warm but not boiling, remove the pan from the heat, add the flour and stir well. Stir in the egg. Turn the mixture out onto a floured surface and knead well (more flour can be added to the dough if necessary). Cover the dough with a clean dish towel and let to rest for at least 30 minutes.

Meanwhile, make the filling. Heat the oil in a pan. Add the onion and cook over medium heat, stirring occasionally, for about 6 minutes, until softened and translucent. Stir in the tuna, hard-boiled egg and tomato paste and combine thoroughly, then set aside. Roll out the dough thinly on a floured surface. Place mounds of the filling on half the dough and fold the other half over to cover the mounds. Cut the filled mounds into half-moon shapes, leaving a small margin around the filling. Press the pastry edges securely together with your fingers to prevent the filling from leaking when the empanadillas are deep-fried.

Heat the oil in a deep-fryer heavy-base pan to 350–375°F (180 –190°C), or until a cube of bread browns in 30 seconds. Carefully add the empanadillas, in batches, and deep-fry for 6–8 minutes, until they are golden brown. Drain on paper towels. Season lightly with salt and serve the empanadillas hot.

Note: To cut out the empanadillas you can use a crescent-shaped cookie cutter, a pastry wheel or a fine-edged glass. Use about 2 generous teaspoons of filling for each empanadilla.

BACALADITOS REBOZADOS
CON SALSA DE TOMATE

BREAD CRUMBED BABY COD WITH TOMATO SAUCE

INGREDIENTS

- 3¼ lb (1.5 kg) baby cod, cleaned and boned with heads removed, then washed and dried
- 2 eggs
- ⅓ cup (40 g/1½ oz) all-purpose (plain) flour
- 4 tablespoons sunflower oil
- salt
- 1 lemon, cut into wedges, to serve
- sprigs parsley, to garnish (optional)

FOR THE TOMATO SAUCE:

- 3 tablespoons sunflower oil
- 1 medium onion, very finely chopped
- 2¼ lb (1 kg) very ripe tomatoes
- 3 tablespoons dry white wine
- 1 bouquet garni
- 1 teaspoon sugar
- salt and pepper

Serves 10–12

To make the tomato sauce, heat the oil in a large skillet or frying pan. Add the onion and cook over low heat, stirring occasionally, for 7 minutes, or until lightly browned. Increase the heat to medium, add the tomatoes, wine, bouquet garni and sugar and cook, breaking up the tomato flesh with the side of a slotted spoon, for about 15 minutes. Remove and discard the bouquet garni. Season with salt and pepper.

Meanwhile, season the cod with salt and leave open. Beat the eggs in a shallow dish and spread out the flour in another. Heat the oil in a skillet and when it is hot, dip the fish first in the flour, shaking off any excess, and then in the beaten egg. Add to the hot oil, in batches, and pan-fry for about 10 minutes until golden brown and the flesh flakes easily. Remove with a spatula (fish slice), drain and keep warm while you pan-fry the remainder. Serve in a warmed serving dish with lemon wedges and garnished with sprigs of parsley, if desired. Serve the tomato sauce hot in a sauceboat.

PHOTOGRAPH PAGE 302

BACALADITOS CON CERVEZA

BABY COD IN BEER

INGREDIENTS

- 4 tablespoons sunflower or olive oil
- 1 large onion, thinly sliced
- 1 lb 2 oz (500 g) baby cod, cleaned, washed and dried
- 1 pinch dried herbes de Provence
- 1 cup (250 ml/8 fl oz) beer
- 2 tablespoons bread crumbs
- 1½ tablespoons (20 g/¾ oz) butter
- salt

Serves 6

Preheat the oven to 350°F (180°C/GAS MARK 4). Heat the oil in a large skillet or frying pan. Add the onion and pan-fry over low heat, stirring occasionally, for 6 minutes, or until softened but not colored. Transfer the onions to an ovenproof serving dish large enough to hold the cod in a single layer. Arrange the cod over the onion, sprinkle with the herbs and season with salt. Pour over the beer, sprinkle with the bread crumbs and put pieces of butter on top. Place in the oven and bake for 40 minutes, or until the flesh flakes easily when tested with a knife. Serve hot.

FRITOS DE BACALAO

SALT COD BITES

INGREDIENTS

- 2¼ lb (1 kg) potatoes, unpeeled
- 1 lb 2 oz (500 g) salt cod fillet
- 1 clove garlic, chopped
- 1 tablespoon chopped parsley
- 3 eggs, separated
- sunflower oil, for deep-frying
- salt

Serves 6

Put the potatoes and cod (not desalted) into a pan, cover with water and bring to a boil, then simmer for about 30 minutes, until the potatoes are tender. Lift the cod out of the pan and set aside to cool slightly. Drain the potatoes, peel and mash them in a bowl. Skin and debone the cod and flake the flesh, then mix into the mashed potatoes. Stir in the garlic and parsley and add the egg yolks one at a time. Whisk the egg whites with a pinch of salt in a clean, dry bowl until stiff, then fold into the mixture. Heat the oil in a deep-fryer or deep pan to 350–375°F (180–190°C) or until a cube of bread browns in 30 seconds. Use two spoons to shape the mixture into little balls, then add to the hot oil and cook, in batches, until golden brown. Remove with a slotted spoon, drain well and keep warm while you cook them all. Serve immediately.

SALT COD AND POTATO CROQUETTES

INGREDIENTS
– 3¼ lb (1.5 kg) potatoes
– 9 oz (250 g) salt cod fillet
– 1–2 tablespoons olive oil
– 1 clove garlic
– 2 eggs, separated
– all-purpose (plain) flour,
  for dusting
– vegetable oil, for deep-frying
– salt

FOR THE TOMATO SAUCE:
– 3 tablespoons sunflower oil
– 1 onion, chopped (optional)
– 2¼ lb (1 kg) ripe tomatoes,
  seeded and chopped
– 1 teaspoon sugar
– salt
Serves 6

If the salt cod is dried, place it in a bowl, add water to cover and let soak for about 2 hours without changing the water, then drain. If it is vacuum packed, this is not necessary.

To make the tomato sauce, heat the oil in a skillet or frying pan. Add the onion, if using, and cook over low heat, stirring occasionally, for about 5 minutes, until softened but not browned. (If you're not using the onion, add the tomato immediately.) Add the tomato and cook over low heat, breaking the flesh up with the edge of a spoon, for about 15 minutes. Allow to cool slightly, then transfer to a food processor and process. Add the sugar, season to taste with salt and process briefly. Set aside and keep warm.

To make the croquettes, put the potatoes (unpeeled) and cod in a pan and add enough water to cover generously. Bring to a boil, then simmer for about 30 minutes, until the potatoes are tender. Drain well, peel, place the potatoes in a bowl and mash well. Lift out the cod with a spatula (fish slice) and remove any remaining skin and bones, then finely flake the flesh and add to the potato.

Heat the olive oil in a small pan. Add the garlic and cook, stirring frequently, until lightly browned. Transfer to a mortar, add a pinch of salt and pound. Stir the garlic mixture into the mashed potato. Beat in the egg yolks, one at a time, making sure that each is fully incorporated before adding the next. Whisk the egg whites with a pinch of salt in a clean, dry bowl until soft peaks form. Fold the egg whites into the mashed potato. Shape the mixture into croquettes with your hands and lightly roll in flour.

Heat the vegetable oil in a deep-fryer or deep pan to 350–375°F (180–190°C) or until a cube of bread browns in 30 seconds. Carefully add the croquettes, in batches if necessary, and cook until crisp and golden brown. Using a slotted spoon, transfer them to a large colander set over a baking pan and place in a warm oven until all the croquettes have been cooked. Drain well and serve immediately, offering the tomato sauce separately.

PHOTOGRAPH PAGE 303

BRAISED POTATOES WITH SALT COD

INGREDIENTS
- 1 lb 10 oz (750 g) salt cod fillet
- 2 tablespoons (25 g/1 oz) butter
- 6 tablespoons olive oil
- 2 large onions, thinly sliced
- 1 lb 2 oz (500 g) fresh or canned tomatoes, peeled and chopped, if necessary
- 3¼ lb (1.5 kg) potatoes, peeled and cut into ¼-inch (5-mm) slices
- 1 sprig parsley
- salt (optional)

Serves 6

The night before you are going to cook the dish, soak the cod in a bowl of cold water overnight, changing the water once. (When you do this, remove the cod and thoroughly rinse the bowl before adding fresh water and replacing the fish, as salt tends to deposit on the bottom.)

The next day, drain the cod and pat dry. Remove the skin and flake the flesh. Melt the butter with the oil in a heavy-base pan. Add the onions and cook over low heat, stirring occasionally, for 5 minutes. Add the tomatoes and cook for another 10 minutes. Stir in the salt cod, potatoes and parsley and add just enough water to cover them. Taste and add salt, if necessary. Cover and simmer over low heat for 30 minutes, or until the potatoes are tender. The dish should have cooking juices but must not be too liquid.

ANCHOVIES WITH GARLIC AND CHILE

INGREDIENTS
- 2 tablespoons olive oil
- 6 slices garlic
- 2 chiles, seeded and sliced
- 12 fresh anchovies, cleaned and patted dry
- 1 tablespoon chopped parsley
- few drops white wine vinegar
- crusty or toasted bread, to serve

Serves 6

Preheat the oven to 400°F (200°C/GAS MARK 6). Heat the oil in a large ovenproof skillet or frying pan over medium-high heat. Add the garlic and chile and stir them around, then add the anchovies to the skillet in a single layer.

Put the anchovy mixture in the oven and bake for 5 minutes, or until cooked through and the flesh flakes easily. Sprinkle with the parsley and the vinegar. Serve straight from the pan with crusty or toasted bread.

PHOTOGRAPH PAGE 305

SALTEADO DE BOGAVANTE

LOBSTER FRICASSEE

INGREDIENTS

- 2 lobsters, preferably female, about 1 lb 5 oz (600 g) each
- scant 1 cup (200 g/7 oz) butter, softened
- generous ⅓ cup (100 ml/ 3½ fl oz) olive oil
- 3 cloves garlic, crushed
- 1 sprig thyme
- 4 sprigs tarragon, leaves only
- generous ½ cup (120 ml/4 fl oz) white wine
- generous ½ cup (120 ml/4 fl oz) heavy (double) cream
- generous ½ cup (120 ml/4 fl oz) red vermouth
- dash of lemon juice
- salt and pepper
  Serves 4

Preheat the oven to 350°F (180°C/GAS MARK 4). Cut the lobster in half lengthwise, remove the creamy parts and add to a bowl with half of the butter, then work the two ingredients together to form a lobster cream. Spread it over the lobster halves and season with salt and pepper. Bash the claws.

Heat the oil in a heavy-base flameproof pan with the garlic, thyme and tarragon leaves over low heat. Add the lobster halves, transfer to the oven and cook for 8 minutes, basting frequently. Take the lobsters out of the pan, transfer them to a warm serving dish and keep them warm.

Meanwhile, pour the white wine, and cream into the pan. Cook, stirring occasionally, over low heat for 5 minutes, or until reduced. Strain into a bowl, transfer the tarragon leaves to the bowl and mix with the lobster butter. Add the vermouth and lemon juice. Test and add salt and pepper to taste. Pour the sauce over the lobster and serve immediately.

Notes: This recipe can also be prepared with crayfish, in which case allow 1 lb 5 oz (600 g) to serve 2 people. Use a flat pastry brush or your fingers to coat the crayfish with the butter.

PHOTOGRAPH PAGE 304

EMPANADA DE HOJALDRE
CON BONITO EN ESCABECHE

TUNA PUFF-PASTRY PIE

INGREDIENTS

- 1 quantity Tomato Sauce, homemade (see page 181)
- 1 x 7-oz (200-g) can tuna in brine, drained
- 2 canned or bottled red bell peppers, cut into strips

FOR THE PUFF PASTRY:

- 1¾ cups (200 g/7 oz) all-purpose (plain) flour, plus extra for dusting
- ⅔ cup (120 g/4 oz) lard, softened
- ½ cup (120 g/4 oz) margarine, softened
- juice of 1 lemon, strained
- 1 egg, lightly beaten
- salt

  Makes 1 large pie

First, make the pastry. Try to prepare it in a cool place, particularly in the summer. Sift together the flour and a pinch of salt into a mound on a cool kitchen counter or a marble slab. Dot with the lard and margarine and mix lightly with a knife, then add the lemon juice and a little water (the amount depends on the type of flour, but never very much) and bring together with your fingers. Briefly knead the dough, then roll out into a rectangle. Fold each of the short sides of the dough into the middle. Let rest for 15 minutes.

Give the dough a quarter turn and roll out again to a rectangle. Fold each of the short sides of the dough into the middle and let rest for 15 minutes. Repeat this procedure of turning the dough a quarter turn, rolling out and folding 3 times, letting it rest for 15 minutes each time. Wrap the dough in aluminum foil and let rest in a cool place for at least 2 hours or overnight.

Preheat the oven to 350°F (180°C/GAS MARK 4). Divide the pastry into 2 equal pieces. Roll each piece into a circle 10 inches (25 cm) wide, ¼ inch (5 mm) thick. Spread the tomato sauce over the dough. Coarsely flake the tuna. Scatter it evenly over the dough and add the bell pepper strips, carefully leaving a ¾-inch (2-cm) margin around the edge so that the dough can be sealed around the filling. Gently place the second circle of dough over the top, pressing down around the edge to seal the pastry. Transfer to the oven and cook until lightly browned on top.

Note: You can vary the filling as much you like, although the classic recipe is a thick tomato sauce with strips of fresh, roasted or preserved red bell pepper.

PHOTOGRAPH PAGE 306

BOQUERONES RELLENOS

STUFFED ANCHOVIES

INGREDIENTS
- 24 large, fresh anchovies, cleaned and boned, then washed and dried
- 4 canned roasted red bell peppers, drained and sliced
- 1 cup (120 g/4 oz) all-purpose (plain) flour
- sunflower oil, for deep-frying
- salt and pepper

FOR THE SAUCE:
- 1 large red bell pepper
- ½ chicken stock cube
- 4 tablespoons light (single) cream
- salt and pepper
Serves 8

Preheat the oven to 350°F (180°C/GAS MARK 4). To roast the bell peppers for the sauce, put them in the oven and roast for about 25 minutes, turning them once. Remove the bell peppers from the oven, wrap them in a dish towel or paper towels and let cool, then peel off the skins, seed and chop. Meanwhile, crush the stock cube half in a mortar and dissolve it in ¾ cup (175 ml/6 fl oz) warm water. Pour into a blender, add the bell peppers and blend, then transfer to a small pan and set aside.

Meanwhile, put the anchovies on a work surface, skin side down, lightly season the fish, put a bell pepper strip inside each and close them up. Spread out the flour in a shallow dish. Heat the oil in a deep-fryer or pan to 350°F (180°C), or until a cube of bread browns in 30 seconds. Coat the anchovies with the flour, shaking off any excess, then add them to the oil, in batches, and fry until golden brown. Remove with a slotted spoon, drain well and transfer to a warmed serving dish to keep warm while you cook the remaining batches.

Just before serving, bring the sauce to a boil for a couple of minutes. Lower the heat, stir in the cream and heat through without boiling, then season with salt and pepper. Serve the fish and sauce separately.

Note: This dish can also be prepared with sardines.
PHOTOGRAPH PAGE 306

SQUID IN ITS INK

INGREDIENTS

- 2¼ lb (1 kg) small squid or cuttlefish
- ¾ cup (175 ml/6 fl oz) olive oil
- 2¼ lb (1 kg) onions, finely chopped
- 1 clove garlic, finely chopped
- 2 sprigs parsley
- 2 tablespoons tomato sauce, homemade (see page 181) or pureed canned tomatoes
- ½ cup (120 ml/4 fl oz) dry white wine
- 1 tablespoon bread crumbs (optional)
- salt
  Serves 6

Clean the squid, reserving the ink sacs in a bowl of water and leaving the body sacs whole. Put the oil, onions and garlic into a heavy-base pan and heat gently. Cook over very low heat, stirring occasionally, for about 10 minutes, until softened but not colored. Add the squid and cook, stirring occasionally, for 15 minutes.

Meanwhile, pound the parsley in a mortar, then add the squid ink. Pour this mixture into the pan, and add the tomato sauce and wine. Simmer gently for about 10 minutes. If the sauce seems too thin, stir in the bread crumbs to thicken. Season with salt and serve. This dish can be accompanied with white rice.

Note: If you can only find large squid, cut the body sacs into pieces before cooking.

SIMPLE FRIED SQUID

INGREDIENTS

- 2½ lb (1.2 kg) squid, cleaned and cut into ½-inch (1-cm) wide rings
- ¾ cup (80 g/3 oz) all-purpose (plain) flour
- sunflower oil, for deep-frying
- lemon wedges, for garnish
- salt
  Serves 6

Lightly season the squid rings with salt and coat them in the flour, shaking off any excess. Heat the oil in a deep-fryer or pan to 350–375°F (180–190°C), or until a cube of bread browns in 30 seconds. Add the squid rings, in batches, and cook until golden brown. Remove with a slotted spoon, drain well and keep warm while cooking the remaining batches. Serve the squid garnished with the lemon wedges.

Note: Bread crumbs can also be added to the flour.

PHOTOGRAPH PAGE 308

SQUID IN ITS INK WITH RICE

INGREDIENTS

- 2¼ lb (1 kg) small squid, cleaned with their ink sacs reserved
- ¾ cup (175 ml/6 fl oz) red wine
- 5 tablespoons olive oil
- 1 onion, chopped
- 1 tomato, peeled, seeded and chopped
- 1 tablespoon all-purpose (plain) flour
- 1 cup (250 ml/8 fl oz) sunflower oil
- 1 slice bread, crusts removed
- 1 clove garlic
- 1 sachet squid ink
- 2 cups (400 g/14 oz) long-grain rice
- 3 tablespoons (40 g/1½ oz) butter
- salt

Serves 6

Put the ink sacs into a bowl with half the red wine. Leave the squid body sacs whole if they are very small, or cut into pieces if larger. Heat the olive oil in a skillet or frying pan. Add the onion and cook over low heat, stirring occasionally for about 10 minutes, until lightly browned. Add the tomato and cook, stirring occasionally, for another 5 minutes. Stir in the flour and cook, stirring constantly, for 2 minutes. Gradually stir in generous 2 cups (500 ml/18 fl oz) water, a little at a time.

Heat the sunflower oil in another skillet. Add the bread and garlic and cook, stirring and turning the bread, for a few minutes, until golden brown. Transfer the fried bread and garlic to a mortar and pound together, then add to the onion and tomato mixture. Stir in the remaining red wine. Use the back of a spoon to mash the ink sacs into the wine, stir in the sachet of ink and pour the mixture into the skillet. Add the squid before the sauce comes to a boil and simmer over low heat for 1½–2 hours.

Cook and refresh the rice, pan-frying it in the butter afterwards. Spoon it into a ring mold and turn out onto a warm serving dish. Season the squid to taste with salt and spoon it and its sauce into the middle of the rice. Serve immediately. Alternatively, serve the rice on the side.

Note: To prepare this recipe using small squid or cuttlefish, allow 4–6 squid/cuttlefish per serving, depending on size. Clean the squid, chop the tentacles and use them to stuff the body sacs, then prepare and cook as above.

PHOTOGRAPH PAGE 307

SQUID, TOMATOES, GREEN BELL PEPPERS AND PAPRIKA

INGREDIENTS
- 2¼ lb (1 kg) squid
- ¾ cup (175 ml/6 fl oz) olive oil
- 1 large onion, chopped
- 2 large cloves garlic, chopped
- 1 lb 2 oz (500 g) fleshy green bell peppers, halved, seeded and cut into ¾-inch (2-cm) long pieces
- 9 oz (250 g) ripe tomatoes, peeled, seeded and chopped
- 1 tablespoon all-purpose (plain) flour
- 1 teaspoon paprika
- salt
- 1 tablespoon chopped parsley
- fried bread triangles, to serve
  Serves 4–6

Prepare the squid (see page 264), discarding the ink sacs and tentacles. Put the squid bodies in a pan and cover with salted water (squid are often over-salted, so care should be taken when adding salt) and bring to a boil. When the water comes to a boil take the pan off the heat, remove the squid, pat them dry and set aside, but do not throw away the water.

Heat the oil in a heavy-base flameproof pan. Add the onion and garlic cook over low heat, stirring occasionally, for 6 minutes, or until softened but not colored. Add the bell peppers and pan-fry, stirring, for about 5 minutes, then add the tomatoes and pan-fry, stirring occasionally, for another 5 minutes.

Meanwhile, use scissors to cut the squid into rings. Add them to the tomato and pepper mixture, then sprinkle in the flour and paprika and stir with a wooden spoon. Pour in 1½ cups (350 ml/12 fl oz) of the squid cooking water, lightly season with salt, cover the pan and cook over low heat for about 1¼ hours until the squid rings are tender.

If the water reduces too quickly add a little more, but once cooked this dish should not be too liquid. Serve garnished with the parsley and triangles of fried bread.

CRAYFISH TAIL BOCADITO

INGREDIENTS
- 24 crayfish
- 2 tablespoons olive oil
- 5 tablespoons (80 g/3 oz) butter
- 3 tablespoons brandy
- 7 tablespoons fruity white wine
- 2½ tablespoons tomato paste (puree)
- 1 clove garlic, finely chopped
- 2 sprigs parsley, finely chopped
- cayenne pepper, to taste
- 2 tablespoons single (light) cream
- 1 truffle, chopped
- 8 warm vol-au-vents shells 2 inches (5 cm) across, or 8 warm bread rolls, with the centers hollowed out
- ½ tablespoon snipped chives
- salt and pepper

FOR THE QUICK STOCK:
- 1 cup (250 ml/8 fl oz) dry white wine
- 2 carrots, chopped
- 1 onion, chopped
- 6 black peppercorns
- 2 bay leaves
- 1 sprig parsley
- 1 sprig thyme
- 1 tablespoon sunflower oil
- 1 pinch salt

Serves 4

Rinse the crayfish in cold water just before cooking (if this is done in advance, they lose all their juices). Remove the bitter intestines by twisting the central lamina at the end of the tail and pulling it so that the gut comes out whole. Put the quick stock ingredients into a pan, pour in 2 quarts (2 litres/3½ pints) water and add a pinch of salt. Bring to a boil over high heat and add the crayfish to the pan so that they are covered by the stock. Bring back to a boil and cook for 4–6 minutes, depending on the size of the crayfish. Strain the cooking liquid into a bowl through a fine strainer and reserve it. Allow the crayfish to cool slightly, and set 4 aside. Remove the heads from the remaining crayfish and peel the tails, reserving the shells. If the tails are very large, cut them into 2 or 3 pieces. Crush the shells in a mortar.

Put the shells and 2 tablespoons of the oil and 2 tablespoons (25 g/1 oz) of the butter in a pan over high heat and pan-fry, stirring constantly, for 3 minutes. Warm 2 tablespoons of the brandy in a small pan for a few seconds, carefully ignite it and pour it over the shells, stirring until the flames have died down. Stir in the white wine, the tomato paste and a little of the reserved stock. Add the garlic, parsley and cayenne pepper to taste. Cover and simmer for 10 minutes. Strain the sauce, pressing down hard to extract all the juice, or work it through a vegetable mill (mouli).

Melt the remaining butter in a skillet or frying pan. Add the crayfish tail meat, then add the remaining brandy. Cover and let simmer, but do not allow to boil. Pour the remaining stock into another pan. Add the cream and heat over medium heat. Strain this mixture over the crayfish tails. Add the truffle and mix well. Season with salt and pepper. Divide the crayfish mixture among the bread rolls or the vol-au-vent shells, spoon over the sauce and garnish with the chives.

Note: Alternatively, you can also make a béchamel sauce and add it to the crayfish puree instead of the cream.

CRAYFISH IN WINE AND TOMATO SAUCE

INGREDIENTS

- 3 tablespoons olive oil
- 2 large carrots, very finely chopped
- 1 small onion, very finely chopped
- 1 shallot, very finely chopped
- 36 large crayfish
- 1 cup (250 ml/8 fl oz) dry white wine
- 3 tablespoons brandy
- 2 very ripe tomatoes, seeded and chopped
- 1 pinch dried mixed herbs or 1 bouquet garni
- 1 pinch cayenne pepper
- 2 tablespoons (25 g/1 oz) butter
- 1 tablespoon chopped parsley
- salt and pepper

Serves 6

Heat the oil in a pan. Add the carrot, onion and shallot, cover and cook over low heat for 5 minutes. Add 1 cup (250 ml/8 fl oz) water, re-cover and cook for another 10 minutes.

Meanwhile, prepare the crayfish: wash them in plenty of cold water just before cooking (if this is done in advance, they lose all their juices). Remove the bitter intestines by twisting the central lamina at the end of the tail and pulling it so that the gut comes out whole. The crayfish are now ready to be cooked. Put them into a skillet or frying pan with the wine and a pinch of salt, cover and cook over high heat until they change color. Warm the brandy in a small pan for a few seconds, carefully ignite it (standing well back) and pour it over the crayfish, stirring until the flames have died down. Remove the skillet from the heat and set aside.

Add the tomatoes to the pan of vegetables and cook, stirring occasionally and breaking them up with the side of the spoon, for 5 minutes. Add the crayfish mixture and dried herbs or bouquet garni, season with pepper and cook for about 5 minutes, then remove the crayfish with a slotted spoon and keep warm. Cook the sauce for another 10 minutes, then pass it through a strainer into a clean pan, pressing down hard and adding a little hot water if necessary. Add the cayenne pepper, season to taste with salt and add the butter and crayfish. Sprinkle with the parsley and cook for a few minutes more. Serve immediately.

PHOTOGRAPH PAGE 309

SNAIL PASTRIES

INGREDIENTS
- all-purpose (plain) flour, for rolling out the pastry
- 1 lb 2 oz (500 g) puff pastry, thawed if frozen
- 12 canned or cooked snails, removed from their shells (see page 261)
- 1 egg, beaten with 2 teaspoons water
- 2 tablespoons (30 g/1 oz) butter
- 2 shallots, or small onions, finely chopped
- 1 cup (250 ml/8 fl oz) light (single) cream
- 1 tablespoon finely chopped parsley
- salt and pepper

Makes 12

Preheat the oven to 400°F (200°C/GAS MARK 6). Roll out the pastry on a lightly floured surface with a lightly floured rolling pin and cut into 12 small squares or circles. Cut out the center of half the shapes, then stack 2 shapes together, putting the ones with holes on top. Glaze the top of the pastries with the egg using a pastry brush. Use a knife to prick the bases, taking care not to go all the way through the pastry.

Put the pastries on a baking sheet and bake them for 10 minutes. In the meanwhile, melt the butter over low heat. Add the shallots or onions and pan-fry for 6 minutes, or until softened but not colored. Stir in the cream and leave until warm. Stir in the snails and parsley and season with salt and pepper. Fill each of the vol-au-vents with a snail and a little of the cream. Return the pastries to the oven for 5–10 minutes, until golden brown and the filling is hot. Serve immediately.

SNAILS

INGREDIENTS

- 1 lb 8½ oz (700 g) fresh or canned snails
- 2 tablespoons olive oil
- 1 onion, chopped
- 1 red or green bell pepper, seeded and chopped
- 3 tomatoes, finely chopped and seeded
- 2 tablespoons all-purpose (plain) flour
- 1 pinch paprika
- 1 bay leaf
- 2 oz (50 g) Serrano ham, diced 2 cloves garlic, finely chopped
- 5 sprigs parsley, chopped
- salt and pepper
- 1 hard boiled egg, chopped (optional)
  Serves 6

Live cultivated snails should be cooked on the day of purchase. If the shells are plugged, remove the blockage with the point of a knife. Put the snails into a large pan with the white-wine vinegar and a teaspoon of salt and leave for 2 hours. Rinse them again, changing the water once, to remove the slime.

If you are using fresh snails, put them in a large pan and pour in just enough lukewarm water to cover. Heat gently until the snails emerge from their shells, then increase the heat to high and cook for 30 minutes. Drain well, discard the shells and return the snails to the pan. Set aside. If you are using canned snails, drain and set aside.

Heat the oil in another pan. Add the onion and bell pepper. Cook over low heat, stirring occasionally, for about 10 minutes, until the onion begins to brown. Add the tomatoes and cook, stirring occasionally, for another 10 minutes. Sprinkle the flour over the mixture, stir in, then remove the pan from the heat and season with paprika to taste. Stir in sufficient water to make a fairly thick sauce and add a bay leaf. Season with salt and pepper to taste. (The mixture should be quite spicy.)

Stir in the Serrano ham, then add the garlic and parsley. Pour the sauce into the pan with the snails and heat through. If you are using canned snails, just add them to the sauce and heat through. If you like, you can add chopped hard-boiled egg.

PHOTOGRAPH PAGE 311

SNAILS WITH PARSLEY BUTTER

INGREDIENTS

- 36 fresh or canned snails
- 1 cup (250 ml/8 fl oz) white-wine vinegar
- sea salt
- ⅔ cup (200 ml/7 fl oz) dry white wine
- 1 carrot, chopped
- 1 shallot, sliced
- ½ onion
- 1 bouquet garni
- 4 black peppercorns, lightly crushed

FOR THE PARSLEY BUTTER:

- 3 tablespoons (40 g/1½ oz) butter, softened
- 2 shallots, very finely chopped
- 1 clove garlic, very finely chopped
- 2 tablespoons chopped parsley
- salt and pepper

Serves 6

Live cultivated snails should be cooked on the day of purchase. If the shells are plugged, remove the blockage with the point of a knife. Put the snails into a large pan with the white-wine vinegar and a teaspoon of salt and leave for 2 hours. Rinse them again, changing the water once, to remove the slime.

Once the snails are clean, put them into boiling water for about 10 minutes, then take them out and put them into a pan of cold water with the wine, 1 teaspoon sea salt, the carrots, shallot, onion, bouquet garni and peppercorns and bring to a boil. Cook over high heat for 1 hour. If using canned snails, skip these steps.

Meanwhile, preheat the oven to 350°F (180°C/GAS MARK 4). To make the butter, beat the ingredients together and season to taste with salt and pepper. Drain the snails. When they are cool enough to handle, remove them from their shells. Fill the shells with the butter mixture, then put one snail into each shell, covering the openings with a little more of the butter mixture. Put the stuffed snails in the oven for 8 minutes, until they are hot and the butter has melted, before serving.

BRICKS DE CHANGURRO

CRAB WITH BRICK PASTRY

INGREDIENTS

- 1 x 3¼-lb (1.5-kg) spider crab (mud crab)
- ¾ cup (175 ml/6 fl oz) white-wine vinegar
- scant ¼ cup (50 g/2 oz) salt
- 6 sheets brick or phyllo (filo) pastry, thawed if frozen, each about 8½ inches (22 cm), or 6 large spring roll wrappers
- 1 tablespoon butter, melted
- ¾ cup (175 ml/6 fl oz) oil
- 2 cloves garlic, 1 finely chopped and the other left whole
- 1 onion, finely chopped
- 2 tomatoes, peeled, seeded and chopped
- 1 teaspoon paprika
- 1 chile, seeded and finely chopped
- 1 teaspoon sugar
- ¼ cup (50 ml/2 fl oz) cognac or other brandy
- ¾ cup (175 ml/6 fl oz) dry sherry
- 1 heaping (heaped) tablespoon all-purpose (plain) flour
- 1 cup (250 ml/8 fl oz) fish stock, homemade or made using a stock cube
- ⅓ cup (25 g/1 oz) bread crumbs, made from day-old bread
- salt and pepper
  Serves 6

Cook the spider crab in advance, even the night before. Pour 4¼–5¼ quarts (4–5 litres/7–8¾ pints) water into a pan, add the vinegar and salt and bring to a boil over high heat. Plunge the crab in, cover, bring back to a boil and cook for 10 minutes. Take the pan off the heat and leave the crab to cool in the water.

Once the crab is cool, open it carefully without breaking the back shell. Remove and discard the gills. Collect any juice released in a large glass. Take out the white meat from the body and legs and flake it into a bowl. (Scoop the brown meat into a bowl and reserve this and any roe from a hen crab to use in other recipes.) Wash and dry the back shell and set aside.

Preheat the oven to 400°F (200°C/GAS MARK 6) and preheat the broiler (grill) to high. Line 12 x 2-inch (5-cm) tartlet pans with the pastry and brush with the melted butter, then set aside. Heat the oil in a pan. Add the whole garlic clove and brown over low heat. Remove the garlic from the pan and discard. Add the chopped garlic and onion and pan-fry, stirring occasionally, for about 6 minutes until softened but not colored. Add the tomatoes and pan-fry, then stir in the paprika, chile and sugar. Season with salt and let cook for a few minutes.

Warm the cognac or brandy in a small pan, carefully ignite it and leave until the flames have died down. Pour the cognac or brandy into the pan with the tomatoes and boil to reduce a little. Stir in the flour, a little at a time, then the fish stock and cook over low heat, stirring occasionally, for 10 minutes. Add the crab meat and add more seasoning, if necessary. Use this mixture to fill the crab shell. Sprinkle the bread crumbs over the top and broil (grill) to toast slightly.

Meanwhile, put the tartlet pans in the oven and bake until golden. Fill each tartlet shell with the broiled mixture. Serve warm.

SMALL CUTTLEFISH IN THEIR INK WITH GULAS

INGREDIENTS

- 2¼ lb (1 kg) small cuttlefish or squid, with the ink sacs
- ¾ cup (175 ml/6 fl oz) sunflower oil
- 2¼ lb (1 kg) onions, very finely chopped
- 1 clove garlic, very finely chopped
- 2 sprigs parsley
- 2 tablespoons tomato sauce, bottled or homemade (see page 181)
- ¼ cup (50 ml/2 fl oz) dry white wine
- 2 oz (50 g) gulas (see Note)
- 1 tablespoon day-old bread crumbs (optional)
- salt

Serves 8

To clean the cuttlefish or squid, pull the head away from the body – the intestines will come away at the same time. Cut away the ink sac from the intestines and put it in a bowl of water. Cut off the tentacles from the head and reserve, if using, and squeeze out the beak. Discard the head and beak. Remove and discard the transparent quill from the body sac and remove any remaining membrane. Rinse well under cold running water and peel off the skin. Repeat until they are all cleaned and the ink sacs reserved.

Heat the oil in a heavy-base flameproof pan. Add the onions and garlic and cook over very low heat, stirring occasionally, for 10 minutes, or until softened but not colored. Lower the heat, add the cuttlefish and cook, stirring occasionally, for 15 minutes.

Meanwhile, crush the ink sacs with the parsley. Pour the mixture into the pan, and add the tomato sauce and wine. Simmer for about 10 minutes. Heat the gulas according to the directions on the package and add them to the cuttlefish mixture. If the sauce seems too thin, stir in the bread crumbs to thicken. Season with salt and serve.

Note: Usually made from ling, a member of the cod family, gulas are white 'sausages' with a dark line down the back made from the squid ink. They are healthy and nutritious, with no cholesterol, low in calories and have a high protein content. You may find them in Spanish specialty food stores but they are not widely available outside of Spain. If you can't find gulas, you can try other seafood sausages, but follow the cooking time and temperature specified by your fish supplier or on the package.

PHOTOGRAPH PAGE 310

STUFFED CUTTLEFISH

INGREDIENTS

- 16 small cuttlefish or squid
- 2½ cups (300 g/11 oz) lean ground (minced) pork
- 2 hard-boiled eggs, chopped
- 1 tablespoon all-purpose (plain) flour, plus extra for dusting
- 1 cup (250 ml/8 fl oz) olive oil
- 1 onion, finely chopped
- ¼ cup (50 ml/2 fl oz) white wine
- 1 sprig parsley
- 1 pinch saffron powder
- salt

Serves 8

Prepare the cuttlefish or squid (see page 264). Wash the cuttlefish or squid thoroughly under cold running water, putting a finger into each body sac to ensure it is completely clean. Dry with a clean cloth. Finely chop the cuttlefish tentacles and leave the body sacs whole. Mix together the tentacles, pork and hard-boiled eggs in a bowl.

Divide the mixture among the body sacs, but do not overfill them or they will burst during cooking. Secure with trussing thread or wooden toothpicks (cocktail sticks). Spread the flour in a shallow bowl, for dusting.

Heat ⅔ cup (150 ml/¼ pint) of the oil in a skillet or frying pan. Dust the cuttlefish in flour, shaking off any excess, then add them to the skillet, in batches of four, and cook, turning occasionally, for a few minutes until lightly browned. Remove them from the skillet, drain well and set aside until they are all cooked.

Heat the remaining oil in another pan. Add the onion and cook over low heat, stirring occasionally, for about 8 minutes, until lightly browned. Stir in the flour and cook, stirring constantly, for 5 minutes, or until lightly colored. Gradually stir in the wine and 4 cups (1 litre/1¾ pints) water and add the parsley and saffron. Add the cuttlefish to the pan, cover and cook over low heat for 1 hour. Season with salt and stir. Remove and discard the trussing thread or toothpicks and serve the cuttlefish in a warmed dish with the sauce.

GALICIAN COCKLE EMPANADA

INGREDIENTS

- 2¼ cups (250 g/9 oz) cornstarch (cornflour)
- 2¼ cups (250 g/9 oz) all-purpose (plain) flour, plus extra for rolling out the dough
- 4½ lb (2 kg) cockles
- generous 2 cups (500 ml/18 fl oz) sunflower or olive oil
- 2¼ lb (1 kg) onions
- 2 cups (400 g/14 oz) fresh tomato sauce (see page 181)
- 5 roasted red bell peppers, halved, seeded and cut into ¾-inch (2-cm) strips
- salt and pepper

Serves 8–12

Three or four days before making this pie, bring a small pan of water to a boil. Stir in 3 heaping (heaped) tablespoons of the cornstarch, then set aside in a warm place and let ferment.

When the mixture is fermented and has small bubbles on the surface, heat 2 cups (450 ml/16 fl oz) water until just below boiling, then stir in the remaining cornstarch, the all-purpose flour and salt. Transfer this to a large bowl, add the fermenting mixture and stir together until a dough-like mixture forms. This will smell slightly acidic. Cover the bowl with a damp cloth and leave in a warm place until the dough doubles in size.

Meanwhile, soak the cockles in fresh water for 3–4 hours, then drain. Discard any with cracked or open shells that do not close when firmly tapped.

Preheat the oven to 350°F (180°C/GAS MARK 4). Heat the oil in a large skillet or frying pan over low heat and stir in the onions. Cover the skillet and let the onions soften without browning. Stir in the tomato sauce and continue cooking for 5 minutes. Add the cockles, cover, and cook for another 5 minutes, or until the cockles have opened, and then add the bell peppers. Season with salt and pepper, then remove the skillet from the heat and keep warm. Use a slotted spoon to scoop out the cockles. Remove them from their shells and then return them to the pan. Discard the shells.

Divide the dough into 2 portions, 1 one-third larger than the other. Roll out each portion on a lightly floured surface until approximately ¾ inch (2 cm) thick. Transfer one portion to a baking sheet, and brush with water around the rim. Add the filling, then top with the remaining piece of dough. Seal the dough, creating a ¾-inch (2-cm) border all the way around, and trim off the excess. Cut 2 little holes in the center to allow steam to escape during baking. Bake the pie for about 1 hour, or until the crust is golden brown.

ANDALUSIAN FRIED FISH

INGREDIENTS
- 2 squid
- 9 oz (250 g) fresh anchovies, cleaned
- 9 oz (250 g) whitebait
- 9 oz (250 g) small red mullet, scaled and cleaned
- 1 sole, about 7 oz (200 g), cleaned, filleted, skinned and cut into large pieces
- 2¼ cups (250 g/9 oz) all-purpose (plain) flour
- sunflower oil, for deep-frying
- salt
- lemon wedges, to garnish
  Serves 4

The secret to this dish is to fry the fish well in a thin-bottomed skillet or frying pan with a lot of oil, and then serve it immediately. Prepare and wash the squid (see page 264), reserving the tentacles, but discarding the heads and ink sacs. Cut the bodies into rings, then pat dry. Rinse all the remaining seafood under cold running water and pat dry.

Spread the flour out into a shallow dish. Heat the oil in a deep-fryer or deep pan to 350°F (180°C), or until a cube of bread browns in 30 seconds. When the oil is hot, season the fish and tentacles with salt, then coat in the flour, shaking off any excess. Carefully add the fish to hot oil, in batches, and cook until golden brown. Remove with a spatula (fish slice), drain well, transfer to a serving dish and either garnish with lemon wedges and serve at once while you cook the remaining batches, or keep warm until all the fish are cooked.

Note: This dish consists of varied fried fish which can be served as a tapa or as a main dish for a light lunch or supper. It is also good accompanied with garlic-flavored mayonnaise.

PHOTOGRAPH PAGE 312

GARLIC SHRIMP (PRAWNS)

INGREDIENTS

- 3¼ lb (1.5 kg) shrimp (prawns)
- ¾ cup (175 ml/6 fl oz) extra-virgin olive oil
- 1 fresh red chile, thinly sliced
- 3–4 cloves garlic, very finely chopped
- salt
  Serves 6

Do not wash the shrimp but peel them, leaving the tails whole. Place 2 tablespoons of the oil and a slice of chile into 6 small flameproof earthenware dishes. Divide the shrimp between the dishes and sprinkle each with garlic and salt. Put the dishes over high heat and cook for no more than 4–5 minutes, shaking the dishes occasionally, until the shrimp are opaque and cooked through. Serve immediately, covering each dish with a plate until it is put down on the table, to prevent the shrimp cooling or the oil splattering. Garlic shrimp are traditionally served in individual flameproof earthenware dishes, but they can also be cooked all together in one large pan and served on individual plates.

SHRIMP (PRAWNS) IN BRICK PASTRY

INGREDIENTS

- 2 tablespoons butter, plus extra melted butter to brush pastry
- 9 oz (250 g) leeks, trimmed and chopped
- 5 oz (150 g) soft, unripened cream cheese
- 8 sheets brick or phyllo (filo) pastry, thawed if frozen, each about 8½ inches (22 cm), or 8 large spring roll wrappers
- 24 large shrimp (prawns), peeled and deveined
- salt and pepper
  Makes 24

Preheat the oven to 350°F (180°C/GAS MARK 4). Melt the butter in a pan over medium-low heat, add the leeks and gently pan-fry until wilted and tender. Add the cheese and stir until a creamy consistency forms. Season with salt and pepper, then remove the pan from the heat.

Cut the pastry into 24 pieces. Put a little of the leek mixture and a shrimp onto each one, then fold the pastry to enclose the filling. Dampen the edges of the pastry with a little water and press down to seal. It is important that they are well sealed so the filling does not leak while being baked. Put the pastries on a baking sheet and brush with melted butter. Bake for 20 minutes, or until golden brown and crisp. Let cool slightly, then serve.

PHOTOGRAPH PAGE 313

CROQUETAS

SHRIMP (PRAWN) CROQUETTES

INGREDIENTS

- 2 tablespoons sunflower oil
- 3 tablespoons (40 g/1½ oz) butter
- 4 tablespoons all-purpose (plain) flour
- 3 cups (750 ml/1¼ pints) milk
- 1¼ cups (500 g/1 lb 2 oz) cooked, peeled and deveined shrimp (prawns)
- 2 eggs
- 3 cups (175 g/6 oz) bread crumbs
- vegetable oil, for deep-frying
- salt
- fresh or deep-fried parsley sprigs (see Note), optional

Serves 6–12

Make a béchamel sauce by heating the sunflower oil in a pan. Add the butter and when it has melted, stir in the flour with a wooden spoon. Gradually stir in the milk, a little at a time, and cook, stirring constantly, until the béchamel sauce thickens. Season with salt and stir in the shrimp, then spread the mixture out into a fish kettle or large dish to cool for at least 2 hours.

Using 2 tablespoons, shape the mixture into croquettes. Finish forming the croquettes with your hands. Beat the eggs in a shallow dish. Spread out the bread crumbs in another shallow dish. Roll each croquette lightly in the bread crumbs, then in the beaten egg and finally in the bread crumbs again, making sure that each one is evenly coated. If the croquettes are being prepared in advance, cover them with a damp dish towel to prevent them from drying out.

Heat the vegetable oil in a deep-fryer or deep pan to 350–375°F (180–190°C) or until a cube of day-old bread browns in 30 seconds. Carefully add the croquettes, in batches of about six at a time, and cook until crisp and golden brown. Using a slotted spoon, transfer them to a large colander set over a baking pan and place in a warm oven until all the croquettes have been cooked. Serve immediately on a dish garnished with sprigs of fresh or deep-fried parsley.

Note: If desired, tie parsley sprigs together with thread and pan-fry in moderately hot oil for an attractive garnish.

MARINATED SHRIMP (PRAWN) BROCHETTES

INGREDIENTS
- 24 long, thin strips raw zucchini (courgette)
- 24 large, fat shrimp (prawns), peeled and de-veined

FOR THE MARINADE:
- 1 red bell pepper, halved, seeded and diced
- 3 cloves garlic, chopped
- grated zest of 1 lime
- juice of 3 limes, strained
- 4 tablespoons oil
- coarse sea salt
  Serves 4

To make the marinade, crush the bell pepper pieces and garlic with a pinch of salt in a large mortar. Transfer to a nonmetallic bowl and add the lime zest and juice and oil. Add the shrimp and leave them to marinate for at least 30 minutes in the refrigerator.

Preheat the broiler (grill) to high. Wrap a zucchini strip around each shrimp, then thread 2 shrimp onto metal skewers. Brush generously with remaining marinade and broil (grill), turning once, until the shrimp are opaque and the zucchini are golden brown.

Note: As an alternative, instead of using raw zucchini, blanch the strips for 1 minute, then drain and put into cold water to stop them cooking. Pat them dry before wrapping around the shrimp. The shrimp are also delicious if a little freshly ground pink pepper is added to the marinade. Alternatively, instead of using zucchini, the marinated shrimp can be cooked whole, with the shells intact, on a griddle or in the oven. To add a touch of color, tie them with a strip of chive.

SHRIMP (PRAWN) AND BÉCHAMEL TOASTS

INGREDIENTS

- 1 lb 2 oz (500 g) raw shrimp (prawns), shelled and deveined
- 2 tablespoons (25 g/1 oz) butter
- 3 tablespoons olive oil
- 1 heaping (heaped) tablespoon all-purpose (plain) flour
- 2 cups (500 ml/18 fl oz) milk
- 1 pinch curry powder
- 12 small slices bread
- 2 oz (50 g) Gruyère cheese, grated
- salt

Serves 6

If the shrimp are quite large, cut them in half. Set aside. Preheat the oven to 350°F (180°C/GAS MARK 4). Melt the butter with the oil in a pan over low heat. Add the shrimp and cook, stirring occasionally, for 3–4 minutes, until pink and cooked through. Using a slotted spoon, transfer the shrimp to a plate. Stir the flour into the pan, then gradually add the milk, a little at a time, stirring constantly with a whisk or wooden spoon. Simmer gently for 10 minutes, then stir in the curry powder, if using, and season to taste with salt. Add the shrimp and mix well before spreading the mixture on the bread slices. Sprinkle the Gruyère on top, place on a baking sheet and bake for about 5 minutes, until golden brown. Transfer to a large dish and serve immediately.

JUMBO SHRIMP (KING PRAWNS)

INGREDIENTS

- 9 oz (250 g) jumbo shrimp (king prawns), unpeeled
- 1 bay leaf
- 1 tablespoon olive oil
- 1 clove garlic, chopped
- 1 onion, chopped
- 1 leek, sliced
- 1 sprig fresh tarragon
- 2 tablespoons fried tomato
- 2 tablespoons brandy
- boiled rice or pasta
- salt

Serves 4

Peel the shrimp and put the tails in a dish and cover with plastic wrap (clingfilm). Put the heads and shells in a pan, pour in 1 cup (250 ml/8 fl oz) water, add the bay leaf and a pinch of salt and bring to a boil. Lower the heat and simmer for 20 minutes. Heat the oil in a skillet. Add the garlic, onion and leek and cook over low heat, stirring occasionally, for 5 minutes. Add the tarragon and tomato and cook for 3 minutes, then add the jumbo shrimp and cook for 4 minutes, or until opaque. Add the brandy and carefully ignite, standing well back. Transfer the shells mixture to a food processor, discarding the bay leaf. Process to a puree and strain it over the shrimp. Heat through briefly, taste and adjust the seasoning, if necessary, and serve immediately with rice or pasta.

RICE WITH JUMBO SHRIMP (KING PRAWNS)

INGREDIENTS

- ½ chicken stock cube, dissolved in generous 2½ cups (750 ml/1¼ pints) boiling water
- 1 cup (200 g/7 oz) short-grain rice
- ¾ cup (175 ml/6 fl oz) olive oil
- 1 lb 2 oz (500 g) shelled peas
- 1 small onion, finely chopped
- 1 clove garlic, finely chopped
- 2 large, ripe tomatoes, peeled, seeded and chopped
- 1 pinch saffron
- 2 tablespoons finely chopped parsley
- 2¼ lb (1 kg) jumbo shrimp (king prawns), unpeeled but rinsed
- salt

Serves 6

Bring the stock to a boil in a pan. Add the rice, stir with a wooden spoon to prevent the grains clumping together and cook over high heat for 12–15 minutes, until tender. Drain the rice in a large colander. Leave the rice standing in the colander until required.

Heat 1 tablespoon of the oil in a heavy-base pan. Add the peas, cover and let cook until tender, then set aside and keep warm.

Meanwhile, heat the remaining oil in a paella pan or shallow heavy-base flameproof pan over low heat. Add the onion and garlic and pan-fry, stirring occasionally, for 8 minutes, or until the onions start to brown. Add the rice and stir it around for a couple minutes until all the grains are coated.

Pour in the boiling stock, tomatoes, saffron, parsley, shrimp and the peas. Stir well and season with salt. Bring to a boil, then reduce the heat to low, and let cook, uncovered and without stirring, until the rice is tender. The rice should not be dry, so add a little extra boiling water, if necessary.

PHOTOGRAPH PAGE 314

LANGOSTINOS EMPANADOS
Y FRITOS

BREADED JUMBO SHRIMP (KING PRAWNS)

INGREDIENTS
- 36 jumbo shrimp (king prawns) peeled
- 2 eggs
- ½ cup (50 g/2 oz) all-purpose (plain) flour
- 2 cups (120 g/4 oz) bread crumbs
- sunflower oil, for deep-frying
- scant 2¼ cups (500 g/1 lb 2 oz) mayonnaise, homemade (see page 62) or ready-made
- salt and pepper
Serves 6

Bend the shrimp to straighten them, season with salt and pepper and let stand for about 10 minutes. Meanwhile, beat the eggs in a shallow dish. Spread out the flour in another shallow dish and spread out the bread crumbs in a third. Heat the oil in a deep-fryer or pan to 350–375°F (180–190°C), or until a cube of bread browns in 30 seconds.

One at a time, coat the shrimp in the flour, then in the beaten egg and, finally, in the bread crumbs. Thread them onto 6 metal skewers, submerge in the hot oil and cook for 5–6 minutes, until golden brown. Remove from the oil and drain, then serve immediately, offering the mayonnaise separately.

MEJILLONES FRITOS

FRIED
MUSSELS

INGREDIENTS

- 2¼ lb (1 kg) mussels, cleaned (see page 275)
- ¾ cup (175 ml/6 fl oz) dry white wine, plus 1½ tablespoons
- 1 cup (120 g/4 oz) all-purpose (plain) flour
- generous ⅓ cup (100 ml/ 3½ fl oz) cold milk
- 1½ tablespoons olive oil
- ½ teaspoon baking powder
- sunflower oil, for deep-frying
- salt

Serves 8

Discard any cracked or open mussels that do not snap shut when tapped. Place the mussels, wine and ¾ cup (175 ml/6 fl oz) cold water in a large pan over high heat. Cover and steam for 5 minutes, shaking the pan frequently, or until the mussels are open. Drain the mussels in a large colander set in the sink and leave until cool enough to handle. Discard any mussels that are not open, then remove the remainder from their shells. Put them on a plate and cover with a damp cloth to prevent them drying out. Discard the shells.

Put the flour into a bowl and make a well in the center. Pour in the milk, the oil, the 1½ tablespoons wine and a pinch of salt. Lightly stir together until just mixed. When it is time to fry the mussels, add the baking powder and stir well.

Heat enough oil for deep-frying in a deep-fryer to 350°F (180°C), or until a cube of bread browns in 30 seconds. Stir the mussels into the batter, then use tongs to drop them in the hot oil and fry for one minute or so until they are golden brown and rise to the surface. Work in batches, if necessary. Use a slotted spoon to remove the mussels from the oil and drain on paper towels. Serve hot.

MUSSEL, BACON AND MUSHROOM PINCHOS

INGREDIENTS

- 6½ lb (3 kg) large mussels
- 9 oz (250 g) mushrooms
- juice of ½ lemon
- 9 thin slices (rashers) of bacon
- sunflower oil, for brushing
- salt

Serves 6

Holding each mussel in your hand with the wide part of the shell near your fingers and the pointed end in the palm of your hand, scrape the mussel shells with a knife and pull off the 'beards'. Wash the mussels carefully under cold running water. Strain the mussels and discard any with broken shells or any that do not shut immediately when sharply tapped.

Preheat the oven to 400°F (200°C/GAS MARK 6). Put the mussels into a pan with 1 cup (250 ml/8 fl oz) water (for 4½–6½ lb/2–3 kg mussels) and a pinch of salt. Cover and cook over high heat, shaking the pan occasionally, for 4–5 minutes, until the shells have opened. Remove the pan from the heat and lift out the mussels with a slotted spoon. Drain, discarding any mussels that remain closed. Remove them from their shells.

Separate the mushroom caps from the stems and sprinkle with the lemon juice. Cut the bacon into pieces twice the size of the mussels and fold them in half. Thread 6 skewers so that there is a mushroom cap at both ends and in the middle with pairs of mussels alternating with the folded pieces of bacon in between. Season the brochettes with salt and brush with the oil. Place the brochettes in a roasting pan or ovenproof dish so that the skewers are resting on the rim. Bake, turning the brochettes occasionally, for 8–10 minutes, until cooked through. Serve immediately.

PHOTOGRAPH PAGE 314

MUSSEL AND BACON TAPA

INGREDIENTS

- 24 mussels, cleaned
  (see page 275)
- 6 slices (rashers) bacon, each
  cut into 4 pieces
- 2 tablespoons (25 g/1 oz) butter
- 6 slices thick country-style
  bread, quartered
- chopped parsley, to garnish
  Makes 24

Discard any cracked or open mussels that do not snap shut when tapped. Place the mussels and 4 tablespoons water in a large pan over high heat. Cover and steam for 5 minutes, or until the mussels open. Drain the mussels in a large colander set in the sink and leave until cool enough to handle. Discard any mussels that are not open, then remove the remainder from their shells and set aside. Discard the shells.

Pan-fry the bacon in half the butter for 5 minutes, or until crunchy, then remove from the pan, drain on paper towels and keep warm.

Melt the remaining butter in the same pan over medium-low heat. Add the mussels and stir until they are just warmed and coated with the butter. Take care not to overcook or they will be tough.

Place a mussel on each piece of bread, then top with a piece of bacon. Garnish with a sprinkle of parsley and serve hot or warm. Serve immediately or the bread will become soggy.

RICE WITH MUSSELS AND FAVA (BROAD) BEANS

INGREDIENTS

- 2¼ lb (1 kg) mussels, cleaned (see page 275)
- 11 oz (300 g) baby clams, scrubbed
- ¾ cup (175 ml/6 fl oz) dry white wine
- 1 lb 2 oz (500 g) unshelled fava (broad) beans
- 1 cup (200 g/7 oz) rice
- ⅔ cup (150 ml/¼ pint) heavy (double) cream
- 1½ tablespoons (20 g/¾ oz) butter
- 1 onion, finely chopped
- 1 clove garlic, finely chopped
- salt
- chopped chives, to garnish (optional)
- 1 lemon, cut into wedges, to serve

Serves 4–6

Discard any open mussels or clams that do not snap shut when tapped. Wash the mussels carefully in water with a pinch of salt – do not let them soak, but move them around in the water with your fingers. Use a slotted spoon to transfer them to a skillet or frying pan, then clean the clams the same way and put them in the pan. Add the wine and the same amount of cold water, then cover and cook over high heat, shaking the pan occasionally, until they are all open. Discard any mussels and clams that are not open. Use a slotted spoon to remove the mussels and clams from the pan and set aside until cool enough to handle, then remove from the shells. Discard the shells. Strain the cooking liquid through fine cheesecloth (muslin) and set aside.

Bring a small pan of salted water to a boil and boil the beans for 10 minutes, or until tender. Drain well and keep warm.

Bring 6⅓ cups (1.5 litres/2½ pints) unsalted water to a boil in another pan. Add the rice, stir with a wooden spoon to prevent the grains clumping together and cook over high heat for 12–15 minutes, until tender. Drain the rice in a large colander and rinse well under cold running water, stirring to ensure it is well washed. Leave the rice standing in the colander until required.

Meanwhile, combine the cream and a generous ¾ cup (200 ml/7 fl oz) of the reserved cooking liquid in a small pan and simmer until reduced and the flavors are concentrated. Season with salt and keep warm.

Melt the butter in a pan over low heat. Add the onion and garlic and pan-fry for 6 minutes, stirring occasionally, until softened but not browned. Add the rice and stir until coated, then spoon it onto a serving dish or pack it into a ring-shaped mold and turn out onto a serving dish. Put the beans, mixed with the mussels and baby clams, on the top or in the center. Garnish with the chopped chives, if using, and serve with lemon wedges for squeezing over.

PHOTOGRAPH PAGE 315

MUSSELS WITH GARLIC AND PARSLEY BUTTER

INGREDIENTS
- 4½ lb (2 kg) large mussels
- ¾ cup (175 ml/6 fl oz) white wine
- 1 shallot, chopped
- 1 pinch mixed dried herbs
- salt

FOR THE GARLIC AND PARSLEY BUTTER:
- generous 1 cup (250 g/9 oz) butter, softened
- 2 cloves garlic, very finely chopped
- 3 tablespoons chopped parsley

Serves 6

Preheat the oven to 400°F (200°C/GAS MARK 6). Holding each mussel in your hand with the wide part of the shell near your fingers and the pointed end in the palm of your hand, scrape the shells with a knife and pull off the 'beards'. Scrub under cold running water and discard any mussels with broken shells or any that do not shut immediately when sharply tapped.

Put the mussels into a pan, pour in the wine and ¾ cup (175 ml/ 6 fl oz) water and add the shallot, dried herbs and a pinch of salt. Cover and cook over high heat, shaking the pan occasionally, for 4–5 minutes, until the shells have opened.

Remove the pan from the heat and lift out the mussels with a slotted spoon. Discard any that remain closed. Divide the mussels on the half shells, open side uppermost, among 6 individual ovenproof plates. Beat the butter with the garlic and parsley until thoroughly combined. Using a round-bladed knife, place a little of the flavored butter on each mussel, covering it well. Put the dishes into the oven for just 3 minutes, until the garlic and parsley butter has melted. Serve immediately.

PHOTOGRAPH PAGE 317

MERLUZA EN SALSA VERDE

HAKE IN
GREEN SAUCE

INGREDIENTS

- 1 lb 10 oz (750 g) hake, cleaned, filleted and cut into 6 pieces
- 1 cup (250 ml/8 fl oz) olive oil
- 3 cloves garlic, chopped
- 1 tablespoon chopped parsley
- 1 bay leaf
- generous ¾ cup (225 g/8 oz) peeled and diced potatoes
- salt and pepper
  Serves 6

Briefly submerge the pieces of hake in a bowl of cold water. Remove them from the bowl and place them in a pan. Add enough water to cover and place the pan over high heat. When the water is just about to start boiling, take the fish out, pat dry and remove any bones, taking care not to damage the flakes. Do not discard the cooking liquid.

Heat the oil in a flameproof heavy-base pan. Add the garlic, parsley and bay leaf. Stir, then add the potatoes, a little pepper and a little of the cooking liquid from the fish. Cover the pan and cook over medium-high heat for 5–10 minutes, until the potatoes are almost tender.

Season the hake lightly with salt and add to the pan, adding a little more cooking liquid to ensure the fish is just covered. Re-cover the pan and cook for 20 minutes, shaking the pan gently from time to time to mix everything up. Remove the bay leaf before serving.

HAKE CHEEKS PIL-PIL-STYLE WITH POTATOES

INGREDIENTS

- 12 hake cheeks, skinned and boned
- generous ⅓ cup (100 ml/3½ fl oz) virgin olive oil
- 2 potatoes, peeled and sliced
- 1 clove garlic, sliced
- fresh red chile, seeded if desired, sliced
- salt

Serves 6

Ask your fish supplier to skin and bone the hake cheeks. Heat the oil in a heavy-base flameproof pan. Add the potatoes and cook over low heat, turning them over occasionally, until they begin to soften. Use a spatula (fish slice) to remove them from the oil, drain on paper towels and set aside to keep warm.

Pan-fry the garlic and the chile in the same oil until softened but not colored–the amount of chile depends on personal taste, so there is no quantity given in the recipe. Whether you seed the chile or not is also up to you. Remove both them from the oil and set aside.

Season the hake cheeks with salt. Re-heat the oil and when it is hot, add the cheeks and move the pan in a circular motion until the sauce thickens. Put the slices of potato into the sauce, then arrange the garlic and the chile on the cheeks. Serve when the potatoes are hot.

Note: Alternative ways to serve cheeks are to coat them in flour and beaten egg before pan-frying them, or serve them in parsley sauce.

PHOTOGRAPH PAGE 313

ARROZ DE PESCADORES

FISHERMAN'S RICE

INGREDIENTS

- ¾ cup (175 ml/6 fl oz) sunflower oil
- 6 cloves garlic, 4 left whole and 2 finely chopped
- 2 dry chiles, halved lengthwise and seeded
- 1 onion, chopped
- 4 tomatoes, chopped
- 1 pinch saffron strands
- 2¼ lb (1 kg) varied fish, such as monkfish, red bream and squid, cleaned, prepared as necessary and cut into bite-size pieces
- generous 2¼ cups (500 g/1 lb 2 oz) short-grain rice
- salt
  Serves 6

Heat half the oil in a shallow heavy-base flameproof pan over medium heat. Add the 4 whole garlic cloves and the chiles and pan-fry, stirring, until they are browned. Take care with the oil, as chiles burn very easily. Use a slotted spoon to remove them from the pan and set aside.

Stir the onion into the hot oil and pan-fry. Add three-quarters of the tomatoes and leave both ingredients to pan-fry. Crush the remaining garlic in a mortar with the saffron and salt, which prevents the garlic slipping, then add a little water. Pour this into the tomato mixture.

Add the fish to the pot with 2⅔ quarts (2.5 litres/4½ pints) cold water and season with salt. Slowly bring to a boil, then reduce the heat to low and let simmer over low heat for a couple of minutes, just until all the fish is cooked through. Remove the pot from the heat and gently strain. Keep the fish warm and reserve the cooking liquid.

Heat the rest of the oil in a skillet or frying pan over medium heat. Add the remaining tomatoes and pan-fry. Add the chopped garlic and the rice and stir around, pan-frying everything together for a couple of minutes. Stir in 5 cups (1.2 litres/2 pints) of the reserved fish stock and taste to see if the dish needs seasoning, but the stock should be quite salty. Bring to a boil, then let simmer for about 25 minutes until the rice is tender and the liquid has been absorbed. Let stand for 3 or 4 minutes and serve the rice in one dish and the fish in another.

PHOTOGRAPH PAGE 316

OCTOPUS WITH PAPRIKA

INGREDIENTS
- 2¼ lb (1 kg) octopus
- ¾ cup (175 ml/6 fl oz) olive oil
- 1 pinch hot paprika
- salt (optional)

Serves 6

To tenderize the octopus it best to freeze it before cooking. To cook it, bring a large pan of salted water to a boil, add the frozen octopus and cook for about 35 minutes, or until tender. You will need to test it, as the length of time depends on the age and size of the octopus. Drain well and rinse under cold running water. Remove and discard any remaining dark skin and cut the meat into small pieces with kitchen scissors.

Place the pieces in a bowl, pour the oil over them, season with salt, if desired, and sprinkle with hot paprika to taste. Mix well to ensure the octopus is thoroughly coated and serve immediately. If this is not possible, transfer the octopus and oil to a heatproof bowl, cover with aluminum foil and keep warm in the oven until needed.

Note: As a variation, you can also heat ¾ cup (175 ml/6 fl oz) olive oil in a pan, add 1 oz (25 g) roughly chopped onion and 1 garlic clove and cook over low heat for 10 minutes. Remove the onion and garlic with a slotted spoon and discard. Remove the pan from the heat and stir in sweet paprika to taste. Add the flavored oil to the octopus pieces, mix well and serve immediately.

PHOTOGRAPH PAGE 318

CROQUETAS DE SALMÓN

SALMON CROQUETTES

INGREDIENTS

- 3 tablespoons (40 g/1½ oz) butter
- 2 tablespoons olive oil, plus enough for deep-frying
- 3 tablespoons all-purpose (plain) flour
- 2 cups (450 ml/16 fl oz) cold milk
- 12 oz (350 g) boneless, skinless cooked salmon, shredded
- about 3 cups (175 g/6 oz) fine fresh bread crumbs
- 2 eggs
- salt

Serves 6

Melt the butter with the 2 tablespoons oil in a pan. Stir in the flour and cook, stirring, for 1 minute, then slowly pour in the milk, stirring. Simmer for 10 minutes until thickened. Mix in the salmon and season with salt. The sauce should be quite thick. Spread the mixture out in a fish kettle or on a plate and let cool for at least 2 hours.

Use a wet tablespoon to scoop up a small amount of the mixture, then use your wet hands to shape it into balls or wine-cork shapes. Do not make them too large or they will be difficult to eat.

Place the bread crumbs on a plate and beat the eggs in a shallow dish. Roll a croquette in the bread crumbs so it is evenly coated, then roll it in the eggs and roll again in the bread crumbs. Set aside and repeat with the remaining ingredients.

Heat enough oil for deep-frying in a deep-fryer to 350°F (180°C), or until a cube of bread browns in 30 seconds. Carefully place the croquettes in the hot oil and fry for about 2 minutes, or until they are golden brown. Work in batches, if necessary. Use a slotted spoon to remove the croquettes from the oil and drain on paper towels. Serve hot.

SALMON AND POTATO EMPANADA

INGREDIENTS

- 2 tablespoons olive oil
- 1 onion, finely chopped
- 1 lb 5 oz (600 g) puff pastry, thawed if frozen
- all-purpose (plain) flour for rolling out the pastry
- 4 potatoes, peeled and thinly sliced
- 9 oz (250 g) smoked salmon in one piece, flaked
- generous ¾ cup (200 ml/7 fl oz) heavy (double) cream
- 1 egg, beaten
- salt and pepper
  Serves 4–8

Preheat the oven to 350°F (180°C/GAS MARK 4). Heat the oil in a skillet or frying pan over low heat. Add the onion and pan-fry, stirring occasionally, for 6 minutes, or until softened but not colored. Set aside.

Divide the dough into 2 portions, one one-third larger than the other. Roll out each on a lightly floured surface with a lightly floured rolling pin. Use the larger one to line a 10½-inch (26-cm) pie dish. Put half the potatoes in a layer in the dish, then spread the onions over the top, followed by the salmon. Arrange the remaining potatoes on top, season with salt and pepper and pour the cream over.

Brush the rim of the pastry with water, then top with the remaining pastry to cover the pie. Seal the pastry, creating a ¾-inch (2-cm) border all the way round, and trim off the excess. Cut 2 little holes in the center to allow steam to escape during baking. Use a pastry brush to glaze the top with beaten egg. Bake the pie for 45 minutes–1 hour, or until golden brown.

Note: You could also make smaller, individual empanadillas, but you will need to reduce the cooking time slightly.

PHOTOGRAPH PAGE 319

SARDINE EMPANADILLAS

INGREDIENTS

- 6 fresh sardines, scaled, cleaned, boned and filleted
- 2 tablespoons sunflower oil, plus extra for deep-frying
- 1 onion, very finely chopped
- 3 tablespoons tomato paste (puree)
- 1½ slices sandwich loaf, crusts removed, soaked in hot milk and squeezed
- 2 tablespoons chopped flat-leaf parsley
- salt and pepper

FOR THE PASTRY DOUGH:

- 2¾ cups (300 g/11 oz) all-purpose (plain) flour, plus extra for dusting
- 2 tablespoons (25 g/1 oz) butter
- 3 tablespoons sunflower oil
- 1 egg
- salt

Makes 12

First, make the pastry dough. Pour 1 cup (250 ml/8 fl oz) water into a pan, add the butter, oil and a pinch of salt and heat gently until the butter has melted. Once the mixture is warm but not boiling, remove the pan from the heat, add the flour and stir well. Stir in the egg. Turn the mixture out onto a floured surface and and knead well (more flour can be added to the dough if necessary). Cover the dough with a clean dish towel and let rest for at least 30 minutes.

Meanwhile, lightly sprinkle the sardine fillets with salt. Heat the oil in a large skillet or frying pan. Add the sardines and pan-fry for about 5 minutes on each side, until golden brown and cooked through, but not too dry. Drain on paper towels and set aside. Add the onion to the skillet and cook over medium heat, stirring occasionally, for about 6 minutes, until softened and translucent. Stir in the tomato paste, soaked bread and parsley. Season with salt and pepper and mix the ingredients together.

Roll out the dough thinly on a floured surface. Cut out 12 circles of dough, each one large enough to enclose a sardine fillet. Divide the filling among the dough circles, leaving a small margin around each one. Place a sardine fillet on one side of each circle. Fold over the dough and press the edges securely together with your fingers to prevent the filling leaking out when the empanadillas are deep-fried.

Heat the oil in a deep-fryer or heavy-base pan to 350–375°F (180–190°C), or until a cube of bread browns in 30 seconds. Carefully add the empanadillas, in batches, and deep-fry for 6–8 minutes, until golden brown. Drain on paper towels. Season lightly and serve the empanadillas hot.

BREAD WITH SARDINES

INGREDIENTS

- 4 sardines in oil, drained
- 1 heaping (heaped) tablespoon mayonnaise flavored with lemon juice
- 12 slices bread from a large, round loaf
- 1 large, ripe tomato, halved
- salt
- 1 small onion, very thinly sliced, to garnish

Serves 12

Preheat the broiler (grill) to high. Remove the skin and backbone from the sardines, then flake the flesh into a bowl and stir in the mayonnaise. Set aside.

Toast the bread on both sides for 2 minutes, or until golden and crisp. Rub the cut side of the tomato halves over the pieces of toast, pressing down, until only the skins remain. Season each piece lightly with salt, then spread with the sardine mixture. Garnish with very thin onion rings and serve while the toast is still hot.

CUTTLEFISH IN SAUCE

INGREDIENTS

- 4 cuttlefish, about 2¼ oz (65 g) each, cleaned (see page 264)
- 2 sprigs parsley, chopped
- olive oil, for brushing
- salt

FOR THE SAUCE:

- 2–3 cloves garlic
- 1 egg yolk, at room temperature
- 1 cup (250 ml/8 fl oz) olive oil
- dash of lemon juice
- salt

Serves 4

To make the sauce, crush the garlic with a little salt to a paste in a mortar. Transfer to a bowl, add the egg yolk, then gradually whisk in the oil, 1–2 teaspoons at a time, until about a quarter has been added. Whisk in the remaining oil in a slow, steady stream, stirring constantly and always in the same direction, to bring the sauce together. It should be thick. When it is ready add lemon juice and season with salt. Set aside.

Bring a large pan of water to a boil. Add the cuttlefish, submerge, and simmer for 5 minutes, then drain and dry them.

Heat a griddle over high heat. Brush the cuttlefish with oil and cook for 10 minutes, turning them occasionally. When they are tender, transfer to a warm serving platter, season with salt and sprinkle with parsley. Serve accompanied with the sauce.

SOLDADITOS DE PAVÍA

LITTLE PAVIAN SOLDIERS

INGREDIENTS

- 1 lb 2 oz (500 g) skinless salt cod fillet, cut into strips
- 2 teaspoons paprika
- juice of 1 lemon, strained
- about 2 cups (500 ml/18 fl oz) olive oil
- all-purpose (plain) flour, for dusting
- 1 egg
- 1 pinch freshly ground black pepper

Serves 4–8

Put the cod strips in a bowl and add water to cover. Let soak, changing the water once, for 24–48 hours. Drain well and pat dry thoroughly with paper towels. Mix together the paprika, pepper and lemon juice in a large bowl and stir in ¾ cup (175 ml/6 fl oz) of the oil. Add the cod strips and mix well. Cover and let marinate, stirring occasionally, for at least 2 hours. Drain the cod and pat dry with paper towels.

Heat the remaining oil in a deep-fryer or deep skillet or frying pan to 350–375°F (180–190°C), or until a cube of bread browns in 30 seconds. Spread out the flour on a shallow dish and lightly beat the egg in another shallow dish. Roll each strip of fish in the flour, shaking off any excess, then roll in the beaten egg. When the oil is hot, add the cod, in batches, and cook for 5 minutes until golden brown. Remove with a slotted spoon, drain on paper towels, then transfer to a warm oven while you cook the remaining strips. Serve immediately.

PHOTOGRAPH PAGE 319

FISH

COLD

HOT

AVOCADO AND SHRIMP
(PRAWN) SALAD
PAGE 211

SALTED
ANCHOVIES
PAGE 214

TUNA, TOMATO AND
ASPARAGUS PINCHOS
PAGE 217

ELVER SALAD
PAGE 216

SALT COD, ORANGE,
ONION AND OLIVE SALAD
PAGE 219

CRAB TAPA
PAGE 223

294

SHRIMP (PRAWN)
COCKTAIL
PAGE 225

CUCUMBER AND
ROE TAPA
PAGE 228

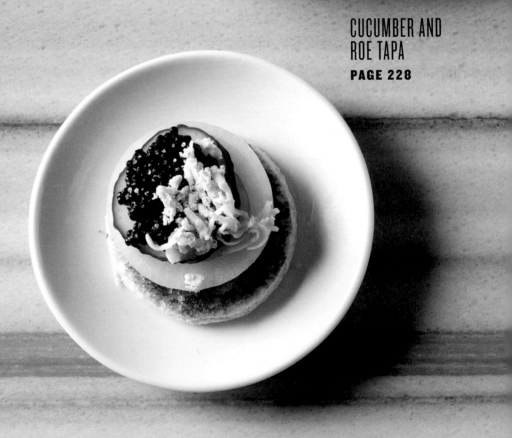

MUSSEL BROCHETTES
WITH SAUCE
PAGE 226

FISH AND SHRIMP
(PRAWN) SALAD
PAGE 229

SALMON
TERRINE
PAGE 230

ARTICHOKE, POTATO
AND SHRIMP (PRAWN)
SALAD

PAGE 239

SAFFRON RICE
WITH CLAMS
PAGE 240

BROILED (GRILLED)
HERRING WITH
ANCHOVIES
PAGE 246

FROGS' LEGS
WITH ONIONS
PAGE 244

BASQUE-STYLE
TUNA BELLY FILLETS
PAGE 246

BREAD CRUMBED
BABY COD WITH
TOMATO SAUCE
PAGE 248

SALT COD AND
POTATO CROQUETTES

PAGE 250

LOBSTER
FRICASSEE
PAGE 252

ANCHOVIES WITH
GARLIC AND CHILE
PAGE 251

TUNA PUFF-
PASTRY PIE
PAGE 253

STUFFED
ANCHOVIES
PAGE 254

SQUID IN ITS
INK WITH RICE
PAGE 256

SIMPLE
FRIED SQUID
PAGE 255

CRAYFISH IN WINE
AND TOMATO SAUCE
PAGE 259

SMALL CUTTLEFISH IN
THEIR INK WITH GULAS

PAGE 264

SNAILS
PAGE 261

ANDALUSIAN
FRIED FISH
PAGE 267

SHRIMP (PRAWNS)
IN BRICK PASTRY
PAGE 268

HAKE CHEEKS PIL-PIL-
STYLE WITH POTATOES
PAGE 280

314

MUSSEL, BACON AND
MUSHROOM PINCHOS
PAGE 275

RICE WITH
JUMBO SHRIMP
(KING PRAWNS)
PAGE 272

RICE WITH MUSSELS
AND FAVA (BROAD)
BEANS
PAGE 277

FISHERMAN'S
RICE
PAGE 281

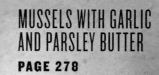

MUSSELS WITH GARLIC
AND PARSLEY BUTTER
PAGE 278

OCTOPUS WITH
PAPRIKA
PAGE 282

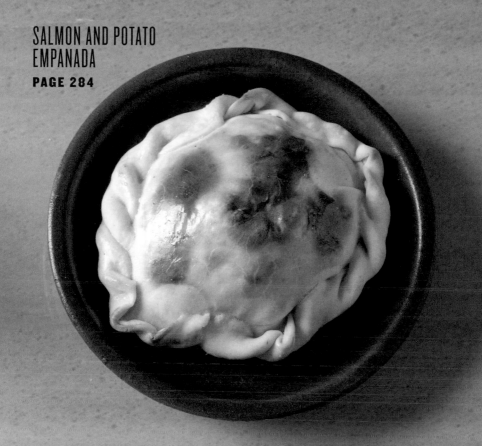

SALMON AND POTATO
EMPANADA
PAGE 284

LITTLE PAVIAN
SOLDIERS
PAGE 287

MEAT TAPAS

COLD

CHORIZO TAPA

INGREDIENTS

- 3 tablespoons (40 g/1½ oz) butter, softened, for spreading
- 12 thin slices French baguette
- 4 oz (120 g) chorizo, casings removed and sliced diagonally
- 3 or 4 tomatoes, halved, seeded and coarsely chopped
- 24 black olives, pitted (stoned) and sliced
- finely chopped parsley, to garnish

Makes 12

Spread a little butter on one side of each slice of bread, taking care not to tear it. Top with one or two slices of chorizo, then add some tomato and a few olive slices to each. Garnish with parsley. Serve immediately or the bread will become soggy.

SPICY CHORIZO AND GHERKIN PINCHOS

INGREDIENTS

- 12 canned anchovy fillets, drained
- 6 oz (175 g) spicy chorizo, casings removed and cut into 12 slices
- 2 pickled gherkins, cut into 12 slices
- 12 pickled onions, drained
- 1 fresh red chile, seeded and cut into 12 slices

Makes 12

Roll up each of the anchovy fillets. Put a slice of chorizo on a short wooden skewer or toothpick (cocktail stick), followed by a piece of gherkin, an anchovy, a pickled onion and a little chile.

PHOTOGRAPH PAGE 370

SERRANO, HAM PÂTÉ

INGREDIENTS

- a little pork fat, to grease the pan
- 2 tablespoons fine fresh bread crumbs, plus extra for the mold
- 5 oz (150 g) Serrano ham in one piece, chopped
- 1 boneless, skinless roasted chicken breast, about 12 oz (350 g), finely chopped
- 3⅓ cups (400 g/14 oz) ground (minced) beef
- 2 eggs, beaten
- ¾ cup (175 ml/6 fl oz) good-quality sherry
- salt and pepper

Serves 4–6

Preheat the oven to 350°F (180°C/GAS MARK 4). Grease a 10 x 5-inch (25 x 12-cm) mold with the pork fat and sprinkle with the bread crumbs, then tip out the excess.

Set aside. Mix the ham and chicken together, then add the minced beef, eggs, sherry and bread crumbs. Season with salt and pepper and stir until well blended. Spoon this mixture into the prepared mold, smooth the surface and then tap the mold against the work surface several times to knock out any air trapped inside.

Put the mold into a roasting pan, add enough hot water to come halfway up the sides of the mold and cover with aluminum foil. Put in the oven and cook for 2 hours. Remove the pan from the oven and let the pâté cool. When it is almost cold, place a heavy object, such as a can of beans, on top of the foil and leave for another 2 hours. Turn the pâté out of the mold, cut into thin slices and serve.

SERRANO HAM WITH MELON MOUSSE

INGREDIENTS
- 3 gelatin leaves
- 3 small melons, preferably cantaloupe, halved
- 1 cup (250 ml/8 fl oz) heavy (double) cream, whipped
- 12 thin slices Serrano ham
- salt and pepper
  Serves 6

Put the gelatin leaves in a bowl of cold water and let soak for 5 minutes. Meanwhile, remove the seeds from the melon and scoop out the flesh with a melon baller or teaspoon, taking care not to break the skins. Put the skins into the refrigerator, and put the flesh into a blender and blend. Put a small amount of the melon puree in a small pan and warm it through over low heat. Squeeze out the gelatin leaves, add to the pan and stir well to dissolve. Stir in the remaining melon puree and let cool.

Whisk the cream to stiff peaks and fold it into the melon mixture. Season with salt and pepper. Pour the mixture into the melon shells and put in the refrigerator for 4 hours. Serve each melon half on a separate plate with 2 slices of ham. Serve chilled.

PHOTOGRAPH PAGE 371

MELON BALLS WITH HAM

INGREDIENTS

- 12 thin slices Serrano ham
- 1 melon, such as cantaloupe, halved and seeded
  Makes 24–36

Depending on the width of the slices of ham, cut them into 2–3 slices lengthwise. Using a melon baller, cut 24 balls from the melon flesh. Wrap each ball in a piece of ham, and secure the ends with a toothpick (cocktail stick), which will make the melon balls easier to pick up and eat.

PHOTOGRAPH PAGE 373

PORK SALAD

INGREDIENTS

- 1 lb 9 oz (750 g) leftover roast pork, cut into bite-size pieces
- 3 gherkins, chopped
- 2 tomatoes, peeled and quartered
- 2 hard-boiled cooked eggs, shelled

FOR THE SAUCE:

- 2 tablespoons white-wine vinegar
- 1 teaspoon mustard
- 6 tablespoons oil
- 1 tablespoon chopped parsley
- 1 hard-boiled egg, chopped
  Serves 4

Combine the pork, gherkin, tomatoes and eggs in a salad bowl. Prepare the vinaigrette by mixing together all the ingredients, then pour it over the salad just before serving.

PHOTOGRAPH PAGE 369

TERRINA DE POLLO
Y JAMÓN

CHICKEN AND HAM TERRINE

INGREDIENTS

- 1 x 2½-lb (1.2-kg) chicken, giblets reserved
- 4 tablespoons olive oil
- 1 small onion, cut into 4 wedges
- 5 oz (150 g) Serrano ham, finely chopped
- 3½ oz (100 g) thinly sliced lean bacon
- 2 tablespoons brandy
- 1 bay leaf
- 1 sprig thyme
- salt and pepper

FOR THE JELLIED STOCK:

- 1 calf's foot, cut into pieces
- 2 carrots, chopped
- 1 leek, trimmed and rinsed well
- 2 stalks celery
- 1 bay leaf
- 5 tablespoons white wine
- salt

Serves 8–10

First, make the stock. Pour scant 3¼ quarts (3 litres/5¼ pints) water into a pan and add the calf's foot, carrot, leek, celery, bay leaf and the chicken giblets. Pour in the wine, season with salt and bring to a boil. Lower the heat to medium and cook for 1½ hours. Remove the pan from the heat and strain the liquid into a bowl. Discard the contents of the strainer. Let the liquid cool completely and if a layer of fat forms on top, remove it with a spoon.

Cut the chicken in half lengthwise. Heat the oil in a pan. Add the chicken and onion, season with salt and pepper and cook, turning the chicken occasionally, for 20 minutes. Remove the pan from the heat and let cool. Remove the skin from the chicken, cut the meat into very small pieces and mix it with the ham in a bowl. Preheat the oven to 350°F (180°C/GAS MARK 4). Line the base of a 9½ x 4-inch (24 x 10-cm) terrine mold with the bacon, then make a layer of the chicken and ham mixture and pour in a little of the stock. Continue making layers of chicken and ham, followed by more stock, until the mold is full. Pour in the brandy and put the bay leaf and thyme on top. Put the lid on the mold, place it in a roasting pan and pour in boiling water to come halfway up the sides. Bake for 1 hour.

Remove the mold from the roasting pan, take off the lid and let cool. If necessary, add a little more stock to cover the meat. Leave the mold in the refrigerator for at least 6 hours, until completely set. Remove and discard the bay leaf and thyme. Turn the terrine out onto a serving dish and discard the bacon. The terrine can be served with a salad.

PHOTOGRAPH PAGE 372

ENROLLADO DE POLLO

CHICKEN ROLL

INGREDIENTS

- 1 egg
- 1 lb 2 oz (500 g) boneless, skinless chicken breast, chopped
- 2 cups (120 g/4 oz) fresh bread crumbs
- 2 cloves garlic, finely chopped
- 1 sprig parsley, finely chopped
- all-purpose (plain) flour, for rolling
- 2 slices cooked ham, cut into ¼-inch (5-mm) strips
- 1 bottled or roasted red bell pepper, drained, peeled, and cut into ¼-inch (5-mm) strips
- 12 black olives, pitted (stoned) and sliced
- 5 tablespoons olive oil
- 1 onion, chopped
- ¾ cup (175 ml/6 fl oz) white wine
- 1½ cups (350 ml/12 fl oz) chicken stock

Serves 6

Beat the egg in a large bowl. Add the chicken, all but 1 tablespoon of the bread crumbs, half the garlic and the parsley. Using your hands, mix together well, then gather up and shape the mixture into one large ball. Press it out into a rectangle on a clean, lightly floured, dish towel or plastic wrap (clingfilm). Place alternate slices of ham and strips of bell pepper on top, add the olives and and then use the dish towel or plastic wrap to help roll it up. Sprinkle some flour on a plate and roll the chicken roll in it to coat evenly. Gently tap off any excess.

Heat the oil in a deep skillet or frying pan. Add the chicken roll and pan-fry, gently turning, until golden all around. Remove from the skillet and set aside. Add the onion, remaining garlic clove and reserved bread crumbs to the oil in the skillet and pan-fry, stirring occasionally, until the onion is softened but not browned. Stir in wine and chicken stock. Return the chicken roll to the pan, cover with a lid, and let cook over low heat for 40 minutes, or until tender and cooked through.

Take the chicken roll out of the skillet and let cool completely. Process all the ingredients left in the skillet in a blender, then transfer to a small pan and bring to a boil for a minute, then let cool. When ready to serve, cut the roll into slices and serve it with the sauce.

SALAMI AND CHEESE TAPA

INGREDIENTS
- butter, softened, for spreading
- 3 white or whole wheat (wholemeal) slices bread
- 12 slices salami
- 6 oz (175 g) Manchego cheese, rind removed and cut into 24 cubes

Makes 12

Spread a little butter onto one side of each slice of bread, then cut into quarters. Roll up each slice of salami like a cone. Put the rolled salami on top of the bread and fill it with little cheese cubes. Secure each cone in position with a toothpick (cocktail stick).

PHOTOGRAPH PAGE 374

VEAL TERRINE WITH SHERRY

INGREDIENTS
- ½ cup (100 g/3½ oz) lard, plus extra for greasing
- 4¼ cups (500 g/1 lb 2 oz) ground (minced) veal
- 1 large boneless, skinless chicken breast, cooked and coarsely chopped
- 1 tablespoon bread crumbs
- 2 eggs, lightly beaten
- ½ cup (120 ml/4 fl oz) dry sherry
- 5 oz (150 g) Serrano ham, in one slice, cut into thin strips
- salt and pepper
- watercress or lettuce, to garnish (optional)

Serves 4–6

Preheat the oven to 350°F (180°C/GAS MARK 4). Grease a terrine mold with the lard. Put the lard, veal, chicken, bread crumbs, eggs and sherry into a bowl. Season with salt and pepper and mix together. Make alternate layers of the meat mixture and strips of ham in the prepared mold. Cover the mold with aluminum foil, put it into a roasting pan and pour in boiling water to come halfway up the sides of the pan. Bake for 2 hours.

Remove the mold from the roasting pan and let cool slightly, then place something heavy on top, such as a can of beans, until the terrine has cooled completely. To serve, run a palette knife around the edge of the terrine and turn out onto a serving dish. Garnish with watercress or lettuce, if you like, and serve cut into slices.

PHOTOGRAPH PAGE 375

HOT

MEATBALLS

INGREDIENTS
- 4¼ cups (500 g/1 lb 2 oz) ground (minced) beef
- 1 sprig parsley, chopped
- 1 clove garlic, very finely chopped
- 1 egg, lightly beaten
- 4 tablespoons bread crumbs
- 3 tablespoons white wine
- ⅓ cup (40 g/1½ oz) all-purpose (plain) flour
- generous 2 cups (500 ml/18 fl oz) sunflower oil
- salt

FOR THE SAUCE:
- 4 tablespoons olive oil
- 3½ oz (100 g) onions, chopped
- 2 ripe tomatoes, chopped
- 1 small pinch saffron threads
- salt and pepper

Serves 10

Put the beef, parsley, garlic, egg, bread crumbs, wine and a pinch of salt into a bowl and mix well. Shape the mixture into small balls, rolling them between the palms of your hands. Lightly coat the meatballs in the flour.

Heat the oil in a skillet or frying pan. Add the meatballs, in batches, and cook over medium heat, turning frequently, until golden brown all over. Using a slotted spoon, transfer the meatballs to a pan, arranging them in a single layer.

To make the sauce, heat the oil in another skillet. Add the onion and cook over low heat, stirring occasionally, for about 5 minutes. Add the tomato and cook, stirring occasionally and breaking it up with the side of the spoon, for 6–8 minutes. Stir in generous 2 cups (500 ml/18 fl oz) water and season with salt and pepper. Bring the sauce to a boil, let cool slightly, then pass it through a food mill or process in a food processor. Pour the sauce over the meatballs. Crush the saffron threads in a mortar, then stir in generous ⅓ cup (100 ml/3½ fl oz) water and pour the mixture into the pan. Simmer the meatballs in the sauce for 15–20 minutes, then serve.

Note: You can also make the meatballs with ground veal or a mixture of ground beef and pork. Simmer veal meatballs for 10 minutes only.

PHOTOGRAPH PAGE 376

PINCHOS DE ALBONDIGAS
CON PISTO

MEATBALL PINCHOS WITH PISTO

INGREDIENTS

- 1¼ cups (500 g/1 lb 2 oz) ground (minced) beef
- 1 egg, beaten
- 4 tablespoons bread crumbs
- 2 tablespoons white wine
- 1 sprig parsley, finely chopped
- 1 teaspoon cumin
- 1 pinch curry powder
- ⅓ cup (40 g/1½ oz) all-purpose (plain) flour
- generous 2 cups (500 ml/ 18 fl oz) sunflower oil
- salt

FOR THE PISTO:

- ½ cup (120 ml/4 fl oz) olive oil
- 2 large onions, very finely chopped
- 3 eggplants (aubergines), peeled and cut into ¾-inch (2-cm) cubes
- 2 green bell peppers, halved, seeded and diced
- 4 zucchini (courgettes), peeled and cut into ¾-inch (2-cm) cubes
- 1 lb 2 oz (500 g) ripe tomatoes, peeled, seeded and chopped
- 2 cloves garlic
- salt

Serves 10

To make the pisto, heat the oil in a large, deep skillet or frying pan. Add the onion and cook over low heat, stirring occasionally, for 10 minutes. Add the eggplants and cook, stirring occasionally, for another 10 minutes. Add the bell pepper and cook for another 10 minutes. Stir in the zucchini and tomatoes, add the garlic and season with salt. Cover and simmer over low heat for 1 hour. If the pisto is very runny, remove the lid for the last 10 minutes to allow some of the liquid to evaporate. Remove and discard the garlic before serving.

Meanwhile, 15 minutes before the end of the cooking time, prepare the meatballs. Put the beef, egg, bread crumbs, wine, parsley, cumin, curry powder and a pinch of salt into a bowl and mix well. Shape the mixture into small balls, rolling them between the palms of your hands. Lightly coat the meatballs in the flour.

Heat the oil in a large skillet. Add the meatballs, in batches, and cook over medium heat, turning frequently, until golden brown all over and cooked through. Drain the meatballs carefully on paper towels, then thread them onto wooden skewers before serving on a bed of pisto.

Note: The pisto can be prepared in advance and reheated.

BROCHETAS DE POLLO
CON ESPECIAS Y MIEL

CHICKEN BROCHETTES WITH SPICES AND HONEY

INGREDIENTS
- juice of 4 lemons, strained
- 4 teaspoons curry powder
- 2 teaspoons paprika
- 2 teaspoons ground cumin
- 2 teaspoons ground ginger
- 1 star anise
- 4 boneless, skinless chicken or turkey breasts, about 5 oz (150 g) each, cut into cubes
- 1 onion, into large pieces
- 1 red bell pepper, halved, seeded and cut into cubes
- 3 tablespoons runny honey olive oil, for brushing the pan
- basmati rice, cooked, to serve
Makes 6

Put the lemon juice in a large nonmetallic bowl and stir in the curry powder, paprika, cumin, ginger and star anise. Heat the honey in a small pan, then add the spice mixture and stir together. Pour the mixture back into the bowl, add the chicken pieces and stir to mix, ensuring all the pieces are well covered. Cover and let marinate in the refrigerator for 2 hours. Remove the bowl from the refrigerator about 20 minutes before you plan to cook.

Fill 6 skewers by alternating cubes of meat with pieces of pepper and onion. Heat a ridged cast-iron pan or skillet or frying pan over very high heat until you can feel the heat rising. Brush the skillet with olive oil. Add the brochettes and cook for about 15 minutes, turning occasionally and basting with the reserved marinade, until the meat is tender and the juices are clear when you insert the tip of a sharp knife. Set the brochettes aside and keep warm. Pour the rest of the marinade into the skillet, bring to a boil and let caramelize before pouring it over the brochettes. Serve with basmati rice.

PHOTOGRAPH PAGE 377

WOODCOCK TOASTS

INGREDIENTS
- 3½ tablespoons (50 g/2 oz) butter, plus extra for pan-frying bread
- 8 thick slices bread
- 2 woodcock giblets
- 2 thick slices (rashers) bacon
- 5 chicken livers, thawed if frozen, trimmed
- 1 pinch mixed herbs
- 3 tablespoons chicken stock
- 1 tablespoon Madeira
- 3 egg yolks, lightly beaten
- grated nutmeg, for sprinkling
- salt and pepper

Makes 32

Preheat the oven to 350°F (180°C/GAS MARK 4). Melt a little of the butter in a large skillet or frying pan. Add the bread slices, in batches, and pan-fry over medium-high heat until lightly browned on both sides, then set aside. Put the giblets into a pan with the bacon, remaining butter, chicken livers and herbs. Pan-fry over medium-high heat, stirring with a wooden spoon, until the chicken livers are cooked through.

Take the pan off the heat and let the mixture cool, then chop everything finely and work it through a fine strainer with the back of a wooden spoon into a bowl. Add the stock, Madeira and egg yolks and season with salt and pepper. Spread the mixture onto the slices of fried bread, covering them generously, and cut each slice into quarters. Place on a baking sheet and put into the oven for about 10 minutes, or until hot. Sprinkle with nutmeg before serving.

Note: If you cannot find woodcock giblets, add an additional 2 chicken livers to the recipe instead.

RICE WITH BACON, SAUSAGES AND BONITO

INGREDIENTS

- 1¼ cups (250 g/8 oz) long-grain rice
- 2 tablespoons sunflower oil
- 4 frankfurters, quartered
- 2 thick slices (rashers) bacon, cut into strips
- 1 green bell pepper, halved, seeded and finely chopped
- 1 large scallion (spring onion), finely chopped
- 2 stalks celery, thinly sliced
- scant ½ cup (50 g/2 oz) black olives, pitted (stoned) and halved
- 7 oz (200 g) canned bonito or tuna, flaked
- soy sauce, to taste

Serves 8

Bring 5 cups (1.2 litres/2 pints) unsalted water to a boil. Add the rice, stir with a wooden spoon to prevent the grains sticking together and cook over high heat for 12–15 minutes, or until tender. Drain the rice in a large colander and rinse well under cold running water, stirring to ensure it is well washed. Leave the rice standing in the colander until required.

Heat the oil in a large skillet or frying pan over medium-high heat. Add the sausages and bacon and pan-fry, stirring occasionally, until cooked through. Add the bell pepper and scallion, reduce the heat to low, and cook, stirring frequently, until the onion is softened but not colored.

Stir the rice into the pan and pan-fry it for a few minutes, then add the celery, olives and the bonito. Season with soy sauce, stir well and serve hot.

PHOTOGRAPH PAGE 378

MADRID-STYLE TRIPE

INGREDIENTS
- 2 small onions
- 3¼ lb (1.5 kg) prepared tripe, cut into bite-size pieces
- 5 oz (150 g) andouille sausage
- 1 lb 2 oz (500 g) snout
- 1 calf's or ox foot, 1 lb 10 oz (750 g)
- 1 bay leaf
- ½ chile, seeded
- 10 black peppercorns
- 4 cloves
- 1 pinch freshly grated nutmeg
- 2 cloves garlic, chopped
- 2 tomatoes, peeled, seeded and chopped
- 4 tablespoons olive oil
- 1 teaspoon paprika
- 2 chorizo sausages, about 5 oz (150 g) in total
- salt

Serves 8

Cut one of the onions into 4 pieces and chop the other. Put the tripe into a pan, pour in water to cover and bring to a boil. When it reaches a full boil, drain off the water and add fresh water to cover. Add the andouille, snout, calf's or ox foot, bay leaf, chile, peppercorns, cloves, nutmeg, the pieces of onion, garlic and tomato. Cook for about 1½ hours, until the tripe is tender.

Heat the oil in a skillet or frying pan. Add the chopped onion, paprika and chorizo. Cook, stirring occasionally, for 10 minutes, then add to the tripe and cook for 1 hour more. Season with salt, remove the skillet from the heat and let cool. Cut the andouille sausage into slices and cut the meat off the calf's or ox foot and the snout, and return the meat to the pan. Reheat before serving.

Note: This dish should be prepared a day in advance and refrigerated, as it is much better when reheated. The quantity of tripe listed is the minimum that should be prepared in order for the dish to be tasty.

PINCHO DE CARNE ADOBADA

MARINATED MEAT PINCHOS

INGREDIENTS
- 1 teaspoon paprika
- 1 clove garlic, crushed
- 1 pinch oregano
- 1 lb 5 oz (600 g) tender boneless meat, such as beef or lamb fillet, cut into bite-size cubes
- olive oil
- salt

Serves 6

Mix the paprika, garlic, oregano and a little water together in a deep bowl, and beat with a fork. Add the meat and stir it around, adding extra water if necessary, until it is completely covered. Cover and marinate in the refrigerator for up to 4 hours, then drain it thoroughly and let it come to room temperature before cooking.

Thread the meat onto 6 skewers. Heat a ridged cast-iron skillet or frying pan or griddle over high heat until very hot. Brush the skillet with a little oil, then add the skewers and cook, turning occasionally, until the meat is cooked to your liking and slightly charred on the edges. Work in batches, if necessary. Remove the skewers from the pan and sprinkle with salt before serving.

PHOTOGRAPH PAGE 379

**PAN DE MOLDE
CON CARNE PICADA**

TOAST WITH GROUND (MINCED) BEEF

INGREDIENTS
- 4 tablespoons olive oil
- 1 small onion, chopped
- 1 shallot, chopped
- 2½ cups (300 g/11 oz) ground (minced) beef
- 1 heaping (heaped) tablespoon capers, drained and rinsed
- 4 large, thick slices bread
- 2¾ oz (75 g) Gruyère cheese, grated
- salt

FOR THE BÉCHAMEL SAUCE:
- 1 tablespoon (15 g/½ oz) butter or margarine
- 1 tablespoon olive oil
- 2 tablespoons all-purpose (plain) flour
- 1 cup (250 ml/8 fl oz) milk
- 1 tablespoon dry sherry
- salt

Makes 16

Heat the oil in a deep skillet or frying pan. Add the onion and shallot and cook over low heat, stirring occasionally, for 10 minutes, until they begin to brown. Stir in the ground beef and capers and mix everything together, breaking up the meat with the side of a wooden spoon. Continue cooking until browned.

Meanwhile, preheat the oven to 350°F (180°C/GAS MARK 4). Make the béchamel sauce. Melt the butter with the oil in a pan and stir in the flour. Gradually stir in the milk, a little at a time, and bring to a boil, stirring constantly. Add salt to taste and simmer over medium heat, stirring constantly, for 8–10 minutes, until thickened. Stir in the sherry. Stir this sauce into the ground beef mixture. Spread the mixture on the slices of bread, cut each slice into quarters and sprinkle with the Gruyère cheese. Place on a baking sheet and bake in the oven for about 5 minutes, until golden brown. Transfer to a serving dish and serve immediately.

PORK FILLETS IN WINE

INGREDIENTS

- 1 lb 7 oz (640 g) pork fillet, cut into 8 slices
- 1 tablespoon potato flour
- 2 tablespoons (30 g/1 oz) butter
- generous 2 cups (500 ml/ 18 fl oz) good red wine
- 2 shallots, finely chopped
- 2 tablespoons thick tomato sauce, homemade (see page 248) or bottled
- 1 teaspoon meat extract
- salt and pepper
  Serves 8

Preheat the oven to 350°F (180°C/GAS MARK 4). Season the pork slices on both sides, then coat them in the potato flour and shake off any excess.

Heat the butter in a flameproof heavy-base pan over high heat. Add the pork and cook for 2 minutes, turning to brown both sides. Add the wine, shallots, tomato sauce, meat extract and a generous ⅓ cup (100 ml/3½ fl oz) water to the dish. Season with salt and pepper. Cover the dish, transfer to the oven and cook for 15 minutes. Remove the pork fillets, cover them with aluminum foil and keep them warm. Place the pan on the stove over high heat and cook for 5 minutes, to allow the sauce to thicken. Remove from the heat, return the pork to the dish and let stand for 2 minutes before serving.

PHOTOGRAPH PAGE 381

CHORIZO COOKED IN WINE

INGREDIENTS

- 14 oz (400 g) semi-cured cooking chorizo
- 4 cups (1 litre/1¾ pints) dry red or white wine
  Serves 4

Slice the chorizo into ¾-inch (2-cm) slices. Heat a heavy-base pan and add the chorizo. Cover with the wine, bring to a boil, then lower the heat and let cook until nearly all the wine has evaporated. Serve hot, spearing each slice with a cocktail stick (toothpick).

POTATOES WITH CHORIZO

INGREDIENTS

- 2 tablespoons olive oil
- 3 cloves garlic, lightly crushed
- 2 teaspoons paprika
- 1 small onion
- 1 bay leaf
- 6 black peppercorns
- 10 pieces cooking chorizo (see Note)
- 1 lb 2 oz (500 g) potatoes
- salt

Serves 10

Heat the oil in a skillet or frying pan. Add the garlic and cook, stirring occasionally, for a few minutes, until it begins to brown. Remove the skillet from the heat and stir in the paprika, then pour the contents of the skillet into a flameproof heavy-base pan. Pour in 6⅓ cups (1.5 litres/2½ pints) water, add the onion, bay leaf, peppercorns and chorizo and bring to a boil. Lower the heat, cover and simmer for 1 hour.

Insert a knife a little way into each potato and twist slightly as you pull it out to split the potato. Add the potatoes to the casserole. If there is not enough liquid to just cover the potatoes, add a little water. Season to taste with salt, re-cover the casserole and simmer for 45 minutes. Remove the casserole from the heat and let stand for 5 minutes before serving.

Note: For this recipe it is best to use the long thin cooking chorizo; the softer type used for stews rather than the kind intended for slicing and eating raw. The pieces of chorizo (one per serving) should each be about 1½ inches (4 cm) long.

PHOTOGRAPH PAGE 380

RICE WITH TENDER RABBIT

INGREDIENTS

- 1 lemon, cut in half
- 3 artichokes
- 6 tablespoons sunflower oil
- 1 rabbit, oven-ready and cut into pieces
- 2 oz (50 g) rabbit or chicken liver, thawed if frozen and trimmed
- 3½ oz (100 g) onions, chopped
- 2 cloves garlic, chopped
- 9 oz (250 g) tomatoes, peeled and chopped
- 1¼ cups (150 g/5 oz) peeled, cooked shrimp (prawns)
- 6 cooked crayfish
- 6 cooked crabs
- 1 pinch saffron threads
- ½ cup (120 ml/4 fl oz) dry white wine
- 2½ cups (500 g/1 lb 2 oz) long-grain rice
- salt

Serves 8

Squeeze the juice of half the lemon into a bowl of water. To prepare the artichokes, cut of the stems, trim the tips of the leaves and remove the hard external leaves, then cut them in half and scrape out the central hairy chokes. Rub each cut side with the remaining lemon half and drop it in the water as it is prepared.

Heat 2 tablespoons of the oil in a paella pan or shallow ovenproof casserole over medium heat. Pat the artichokes completely dry and pan-fry until golden brown. Remove them from the pan and set aside.

Add the remaining oil to the pan, then add the rabbit and liver and pan-fry until browned on all sides. Remove them from the pan and set aside. Add the onion and one of the garlic cloves to the remaining oil in the pan and pan-fry over low heat, stirring occasionally, for about 10 minutes until golden brown. Add the tomatoes, artichokes, shrimp, crayfish and crabs, and return the rabbit to the pan.

Crush the liver in a large mortar with the remaining garlic and the saffron, then add the white wine to thin the mixture. Pour it over the other ingredients and stir everything together.

Add the rice and pan-fry gently, then add 6⅓ cups (1.5 litres/2½ pints) boiling water – using a little more than 2 parts liquid to 1 part rice – and season with salt. Bring to a boil, then reduce the heat and let cook, uncovered and without stirring, until the rice is tender. The rice should not be dry, so add a little extra boiling water if necessary.

LAMB CUTLETS WITH BÉCHAMEL SAUCE

INGREDIENTS

- 12 lamb cutlets
- sunflower oil, for pan-frying
- 2 eggs
- 1 cup (50 g/2 oz) fresh
  bread crumbs
- salt

FOR THE BÉCHAMEL SAUCE:

- 2 tablespoons (25 g/1 oz) butter
- 2 tablespoons sunflower oil
- 2 tablespoons all-purpose
  (plain) flour
- 2¼ cups (500 ml/18 fl oz) milk
- salt

Serves 4

First, make the béchamel sauce. Melt the butter with the oil in a skillet or frying pan. Stir in the flour and cook, stirring constantly, for 2 minutes. Gradually stir in the milk, a little at a time. Season with salt and cook, stirring constantly, for about 10 minutes, until thickened. Remove the pan from the heat and let cool.

Meanwhile, scrape away the meat and connective tissue from the top 2 inches (5 cm) of the chop bones. Season the meat with salt. Heat 6 tablespoons oil in a skillet or frying pan. Add the lamb chops, in batches, and cook over medium heat for about 3 minutes on each side, or until cooked to your liking. Remove them from the skillet and set aside. Reserve the oil in the skillet. Brush a work surface or cutting (chopping) board with oil. Holding the chops by the bone, dip them, one at a time, into the béchamel sauce to coat. Put them onto the oiled work surface or chopping board and let cool.

Beat the eggs in a shallow dish and spread out the bread crumbs in another shallow dish. Add enough oil for pan-frying to the reserved oil in the skillet and heat, or transfer the reserved oil and enough oil for deep-frying to a deep-fryer and heat to 350–375°F (180–190°C), or until a cube of bread browns in 30 seconds. Coat each lamb chop, first in the beaten egg and then in the bread crumbs. Add to the hot oil, in batches, and cook until golden brown all over. Remove with a spatula (fish slice), drain and keep warm while you cook the remaining batches. Serve immediately.

FRIED LAMB CHOPS

INGREDIENTS

- 24 lamb chops
- 2 cloves garlic
- 1¼ cups (500 ml/18 fl oz) sunflower oil
- salt

Serves 8

Scrape away the meat and the connective tissue from the top 2 inches (5 cm) of the chop bones. Crush the garlic in a large mortar with a pinch of salt. Rub the mixture all over the chops. Heat the oil in a large skillet or frying pan. Add the chops, in batches, and cook over medium heat for about 3 minutes on each side, or until cooked to your liking. (Take care, as the chops can cause the oil to spit.) Remove the chops from the skillet and keep warm until they are all cooked. Serve immediately. These are delicious accompanied by French fries (chips) or a salad.

FRIED DATE AND BACON PINCHOS

INGREDIENTS

- 20 dates
- 20 slices (rashers) thin rindless bacon
- 2–3 tablespoons peanut or groundnut oil

Makes 20

Slit the dates along the longest sides and carefully remove and discard the pits (stones). Wrap each date in a strip of bacon and secure with a wooden toothpick (cocktail stick). Heat the oil in a skillet or frying pan, add the bacon rolls and cook, turning occasionally, for about 10 minutes, until the bacon is cooked through and lightly browned. Drain well and serve immediately.

PHOTOGRAPH PAGE 382

FABADA

BEAN STEW

INGREDIENTS

- 2¾ cups (500 g/1 lb 2 oz) dried Asturian beans or lima (butter) beans, soaked for 3 hours or overnight in cold water and drained
- 1 large onion, cut into 4 pieces
- 2 cloves garlic
- ⅔ cup (150 ml/¼ pint) olive oil
- ½ pig's ear
- 1 pig's tail or pig's foot (trotter)
- 1 teaspoon paprika
- 1 Serrano ham hock, about 3½ oz (100 g)
- 2 chorizo sausages
- 3½ oz (100 g) fat (streaky) bacon
- 2 Asturian blood sausages (black puddings)
- 1 pinch saffron threads
- salt

Serves 8

Put the beans into a pan and pour in cold water to cover. Bring to a boil over low heat, then remove the pan from the heat and drain. Return the beans to a clean pan, pour in fresh cold water to cover and add the onion, garlic, oil, pig's ear, pig's tail or foot and the paprika. Mix well and, if necessary, add more cold water to cover the contents of the pan. Bring to a boil over low heat and cook for 30 minutes. Add the ham hock and chorizo sausages and cook for another 30 minutes. Add the bacon and cook for 30–60 minutes more, until the beans are almost tender. Add the blood sausages and cook for a final 30 minutes.

Remove the ham hock, cut it into bite-size pieces, and return the pieces to the pan. Crush the saffron in a mortar and stir in 2 tablespoons of the cooking liquid from the beans, then stir into the stew. Season to taste with salt and serve.

Notes: It is not usual to serve the tail or the ear, although some people like them and leave them in the stew. If you wish to serve the ear, cut it into fine strips first. This bean stew is much better made the previous day and reheated. To thicken the stew, remove a ladleful of beans, transfer to a blender or food processor and process to a puree, then add to the stew.

PHOTOGRAPH PAGE 383

CROQUETAS DE
JAMÓN DE YORK

HAM CROQUETTES

INGREDIENTS

- 2 tablespoons sunflower oil
- 3 tablespoons (40 g/1½ oz) butter
- 4 tablespoons all-purpose (plain) flour
- 3 cups (750 ml/1¼ pints) milk
- 2 eggs
- 3 cups (175 g/6 oz) bread crumbs
- vegetable oil, for deep-frying
- salt
- fresh or fried parsley sprigs (see Note, optional)

FOR THE FILLING:

- 7 oz (200 g) York ham, very finely chopped, or 5 oz (150 g) Serrano ham, finely chopped

Serves 8

First, make a béchamel sauce. Heat the sunflower oil in a pan. Add the butter and when it has melted, stir in the flour with a wooden spoon. Gradually stir in the milk, a little at a time, and cook, stirring constantly, until the béchamel sauce thickens. Season with salt and stir in the ham, then spread the mixture out in a large, shallow dish to cool for at least 2 hours. Using 2 tablespoons, shape scoops of the mixture into croquettes. Finish forming the croquettes with your hands.

Beat the eggs in a shallow dish. Spread out the bread crumbs in another shallow dish. Roll each croquette lightly in the bread crumbs, then in the beaten egg and finally in the bread crumbs again, making sure that each one is evenly covered. Heat the vegetable oil in a deep-fryer or deep pan to 350–375°F (180–190°C), or until a cube of bread browns in 30 seconds. Carefully add the croquettes, in batches of about 6 at a time, and cook until crisp and golden brown. Using a slotted spoon, transfer them to a large colander set over a baking pan and place in a warm oven until all the croquettes have been cooked. Serve immediately on a dish garnished with sprigs of fresh or fried parsley.

Note: To prepare fried parsley as a garnish, tie parsley sprigs together with thread and pan-fry in moderately hot oil.

PHOTOGRAPH PAGE 384

RICE WITH HAM AND CHORIZO

INGREDIENTS

- 2½ cups (500 g/1 lb 2 oz) long-grain rice
- 3 tablespoons sunflower oil
- 1 onion, finely chopped
- 3½ oz (100 g) Serrano ham in one piece, finely diced
- 3½ oz (100 g) chorizo, casing removed and finely diced
- 1⅔ cups (250 g/9 oz) canned, frozen or fresh shelled peas, rinsed and drained
- salt
- 3½ oz (100 g) Parmesan cheese, grated, to serve

Serves 6

Bring 4 cups (1 litre/1¾ pints) unsalted water to a boil. Add the rice, stir with a wooden spoon to prevent the grains sticking together and cook over high heat for 12–15 minutes, until tender. Drain the rice in a large colander and rinse well under cold running water, stirring to ensure it is well washed. Leave the rice standing in the colander until required.

Heat the oil in a large skillet or frying pan over low heat. Add the onion and pan-fry, stirring occasionally, for 8 minutes or until it starts to brown. Add the ham and chorizo and cook, stirring frequently. Add the rice, mixing it in well with a wooden spoon to ensure everything heats through evenly. Cook for about 5 minutes, then add the peas, season with salt and stir again.

Transfer the rice to a warmed serving dish and serve the grated cheese separately.

PHOTOGRAPH PAGE 385

HAM EMPANADILLAS

INGREDIENTS

- 7 oz (200 g) Serrano ham, chopped
- vegetable oil, for deep-frying

FOR THE PASTRY:

- ½ cup (120 ml/4 fl oz) dry white wine
- 2 tablespoons (25 g/1 oz) butter
- 2 tablespoons (25 g/1 oz) lard
- 2¾ cups (300 g/11 oz) all-purpose (plain) flour, plus extra for dusting
- salt

Makes 30

First, make the pastry. Pour the wine into a pan and add ½ cup (120 ml/4 fl oz) water, the butter and lard. Heat gently, stirring, until the fat has melted. Once the mixture is warm but not boiling, remove the pan from the heat, sift in the flour and a pinch of salt and stir well with a wooden spoon. Turn out the dough onto a floured surface and knead well until smooth. Form the dough into a ball, put it on a plate, cover with a clean dish towel and let rest for about 2 hours.

To make the empanadillas, roll out the dough thinly on a floured surface. Cut the dough into rounds using a cookie cutter or a fine-edged glass. Place a little of the chopped ham on one side of the round. Fold the other half over to cover them and make a half moon shape. Press the pastry edges securely together with your fingers to prevent the filling leaking out when the empanadillas are deep-fried. Heat the oil in a deep-fryer to 350–375°F (180–190°C), or until a cube of bread browns in 30 seconds. Carefully add the empanadillas, in batches, and deep-fry for 6–8 minutes, until golden brown. Drain on paper towels. Season lightly with salt and serve them hot.

MIGAS

INGREDIENTS

- 1 lb 2 oz (500 g) day-old white bread, cubed
- 1¼ cups (300 ml/½ pint) olive oil
- 7 oz (200 g) semi-salted pork side (belly), cubed
- 7 oz (200 g) chorizo, casing removed and sliced
- 3 cloves garlic, sliced
- 1 teaspoon paprika
- salt

  Serves 6

Pour 2 tablespoons water over the bread cubes, add a little salt, then stir together, cover with a cloth and let stand for 30 minutes.

Heat the oil in a flameproof heavy-base pan or a large skillet or frying pan. Add the pork and pan-fry until brown and cooked through. Remove using a slotted spoon and set aside. Pan-fry the chorizo in the same oil, then remove and set aside. Finally, pan-fry the garlic in the same oil, until golden brown. Add the bread and paprika and continue stirring for 15 minutes so that the 'crumbs' stay loose and become crisp. Serve with the chorizo and pork side. Migas is also excellent with fried eggs.

PHOTOGRAPH PAGE 387

RICE WITH HAM

INGREDIENTS

- 3 tablespoons sunflower oil
- 14 oz (400 g) boiled leg ham (gammon), diced
- 5 oz (150 g) cured ham, diced
- 3 cups (600 g/1 lb 5 oz) long-grain rice
- 6⅓ cups (1.5 litres/2½ pints) chicken stock
- ½ teaspoon meat extract
- 2 sprigs parsley
- 2 tomatoes
- salt

  Serves 6

Preheat the oven to 350°F (180°C/GAS MARK 4). Heat the oil in a large flameproof heavy-base pan. Add both types of ham and stir around until lightly fried. Stir in the rice, then add the chicken stock, meat extract, and parsley sprigs. Grate the tomatoes over the pan so you capture all the juices. Bring to a boil and stir well, then reduce the heat to low, cover and cook for 15 minutes.

Without uncovering, transfer the pan to the oven and leave for another 5 minutes. Remove the pan from the oven, season with salt and leave the rice to stand, covered, for 5 minutes, then stir with a fork. Remove the parsley sprigs, if possible, then serve, straight from the pan.

ARROZ CON HIGADITOS

RICE WITH CHICKEN LIVERS

INGREDIENTS

– generous ¼ cup (65 g/2½ oz) butter
– 1 onion, finely chopped
– ¾ cup (150 g/5 oz) long-grain rice
– 2 shallots, finely chopped
– ½ cup (120 ml/4 fl oz) port
– 1 lb 2 oz (500 g) chicken livers, thawed if frozen, trimmed, and with any green parts removed
– 1 cup (250 ml/9 fl oz) tomato sauce, bottled or homemade (see page 181)
– salt and pepper

Serves 2

Melt half the butter in a skillet or frying pan over low heat. Add the onion and pan-fry, stirring occasionally, for 6 minutes, or until softened but not colored. Stir in the rice and season with salt, then pour in 1¼ cups (300 ml/½ pint) water and bring to a boil. Reduce the heat to low, cover the skillet and simmer for the time recommended on the package until all the liquid is absorbed and the rice is tender. Remove the skillet from the heat and transfer the rice to 4 individual molds or leave in the skillet. Set aside and keep warm.

Meanwhile, melt the remaining butter in a skillet over low heat. Add the shallots and pan-fry, stirring occasionally, for 3 minutes. Add the port and simmer for 2 minutes. Add the chicken livers and cook for 6 minutes in the sauce. Season with salt and pepper. Heat the tomato sauce in another pan.

To serve, turn the rice out of the molds, or shape into small piles, onto 4 warmed dishes. Serve the chicken livers and tomato sauce on the side.

LITTLE CHICKEN LIVERS

INGREDIENTS
- 4 tablespoons olive oil
- 2 onions, chopped
- 1 lb 5 oz (600 g) small chicken livers, trimmed
- 6 fl oz (175 ml) dry white wine
- salt and pepper
- triangles of fried bread, to serve (optional)
  Serves 6

Heat the oil in a nonstick skillet or frying pan. Add the onion and cook over low heat, stirring occasionally, for 6 minutes, or until softened but not colored. Add the chicken livers, season with salt and pepper and cook, turning occasionally, for 10 minutes. Stir in the wine, cover the skillet and cook for another 15 minutes. Serve immediately, with triangles of fried bread, if desired.

CHICKEN LIVERS WITH GRAPES

INGREDIENTS
- 1 tablespoon (15 g/½ oz) butter
- 3 tablespoons sunflower oil
- 1 lb 5 oz (600 g) chicken livers, trimmed
- 2 shallots, finely chopped
- 4 tablespoons rum, brandy or Madeira
- 14 oz (400 g) seedless white grapes, peeled (if desired)
- salt and pepper
  Serves 4

Melt the butter with the oil in a skillet or frying pan, add the chicken livers and pan-fry over low heat, turning occasionally, for about 10 minutes until they are golden brown on the outside but not overcooked on the inside. Lift out with a slotted spoon, set aside and keep warm. Add the shallots to the oil remaining in the skillet and pan-fry over low heat, stirring occasionally, for 6 minutes, or until softened but not colored. Pour the rum, brandy or Madeira into the skillet and cook for 3 minutes over medium heat, stirring constantly. Add the grapes, reduce the heat a little and allow to warm through. Return the livers to the skillet just long enough to heat up and season with salt and pepper. Serve the livers in a warmed dish, surrounded by the grapes and covered with the juices from the skillet.

PHOTOGRAPH PAGE 386

EMPANADA DE HOJALDRE
CON MAGRO DE CERDO
Y MORCILLA

PORK AND MORCILLA EMPANADA

INGREDIENTS

- vegetable oil, for pan-frying
- 1 quantity tomato sauce, bottled or homemade (see page 181), to serve
- 14 oz (400 g) lean pork, cut into cubes
- 1 morcilla or blood sausage (black pudding), cut into ¾-inch (2-cm) thick slices

FOR THE PASTRY:

- 1¾ cups (200 g/7 oz) all-purpose (plain) flour, plus extra for dusting
- ⅔ cup (120 g/4 oz) lard, softened
- ½ cup (120 g/4 oz) margarine, softened
- juice of 1 lemon, strained
- 1 egg, lightly beaten
- salt
  Makes 1 empanada

First, make the pastry dough. Sift together the flour and a pinch of salt into a mound on a marble slab. Dot with the lard and margarine and mix lightly with a knife, then add the lemon juice and a little water (the amount depends on the type of flour, but never very much) and bring together with your fingers. Briefly knead the dough on a lightly floured work surface, then roll out into a rectangle. Fold each of the short sides of the dough into the middle. Let rest for 15 minutes. Turn the dough 90° and roll out into a rectangle again. Fold each of the short sides of the dough into the middle and let rest for 15 minutes. Repeat this procedure of turning the dough a quarter turn, rolling out and folding three times, leaving it to rest for 15 minutes each time. Wrap the dough in plastic wrap (clingfilm) and let rest in a cool place for at least 2 hours or overnight.

Preheat the oven to 425°F (220°C/GAS MARK 7). Heat a little oil in a skillet or frying pan and add the pork and morcilla. Cook for 5 minutes, or until cooked through and lightly browned. Roll out the dough on a lightly floured surface into a large circle. Spread the tomato sauce over the dough and scatter the pork and morcilla on top. Fold one side of the dough over the filling to meet the other side. Leave a ¾-inch (2-cm) border of pastry around the whole pie and press to seal it with a fork or your fingertips. Place on a dampened baking sheet. Prick the pie in several places with a skewer to allow steam to escape during cooking. You can also make a decorative pattern with a knife blade, if you like. Brush with the beaten egg to glaze, and bake for about 30 minutes, until puffed up and golden brown.

Note: To make a chicken empanada, try adding chopped cooked chicken breast and strips of roasted red bell pepper.

PHOTOGRAPH PAGE 388

CHICKEN AND BELL PEPPER EMPANADA

INGREDIENTS

– 1 quantity pastry (see page 351)
– 14 oz (400 g) chicken breast
– 4 bottled or canned roasted red bell peppers, chopped
– 1 quantity tomato sauce, bottled or homemade (see page 181), to serve
– 1 egg, lightly beaten
  Makes 1 empanada

First, make the pastry dough (see page 351) and let rest overnight. Preheat the oven to 425°F (220°C/GAS MARK 7). Heat a little oil in a skillet and add the chicken. Cook for 10 minutes, or until cooked through. Roll out the dough on a lightly floured surface into a large circle. Spread the tomato sauce over the dough and scatter over the chicken. Top with a layer of bell peppers. Fold one side of the dough over the filling (see page 351). Brush with the beaten egg and bake for about 30 minutes, until puffed up and golden brown.

PHOTOGRAPH PAGE 394

RICE WITH MORCILLA

INGREDIENTS

– ½ cup (75 g/3 oz) lard
– 9 oz (250 g) lean bacon in one piece, diced
– 3 morcillas or blood sausages (black puddings), casings removed and sliced
– 3 red tomatoes, peeled, seeded and chopped
– 2 cloves garlic, chopped
– 5 cups (1.2 litres/2 pints) chicken or vegetable stock
– 2½ cups (500 g/1 lb 2 oz) long-grain rice
– 1 small pinch saffron threads
– 1 large tomato, sliced
– 1 sprig parsley
– salt and pepper
  Serves 8

Preheat the oven to 350°F (180°C/GAS MARK 4). Melt the lard in an ovenproof heavy-base pan. Stir in the bacon, morcilla, tomatoes and garlic and season with salt and pepper. Stir lightly and let cook for 5 minutes, stirring occasionally.

Meanwhile, bring the stock to a boil over high heat. Stir the rice into the pan, mixing it in well, then add the saffron, tomato and parsley. Return the liquid to a boil, cover the pan and put it in the oven for about 20 minutes, or until the rice is tender and the stock is absorbed. Serve as soon as it is taken out of the oven.

PHOTOGRAPH PAGE 389

MORCILLA IN BRICK PASTRY

INGREDIENTS

- 2 morcillas or blood sausages (black puddings), casing removed and cut in half lengthwise, then each half cut into 3 pieces
- 4 sheets brick or phyllo (filo) pastry, each about 8½ inches (22 cm), or 4 large spring roll wrappers
- olive or sunflower oil, for deep-frying
- mint or basil leaves, to garnish
  Makes 12

Put one piece of blood sausage at the end of a sheet of pastry and roll it up, folding in the side edges after one complete roll to completely enclose the filling. Dampen the edge of the pastry with a little water and press down to seal. Use the remaining ingredients to make a total of 12 pastries. Heat the oil in a deep-fryer or heavy-base pan to 350–375°F (180–190°C), or until a cube of bread browns in 30 seconds. Carefully add the pastries, in batches, and deep-fry for 6–8 minutes, until they are golden brown. Drain on paper towels. Season lightly with salt and serve hot.

Note: Look for ultra-thin sheets of brick pastry in North African food stores, but if you can't find it, Chinese spring roll wrappers from supermarkets or Asian food stores will work. This versatile recipe also makes an excellent first course when the rolls are made a bit larger and is delicious served with scrambled eggs alongside.

FRIED MORCILLA PINCHOS

INGREDIENTS

- 1 tablespoon sunflower oil
- 12 thick slices morcilla or blood sausage (black pudding)
- 12 slices French baguette, toasted
  Makes 12

Preheat the broiler (grill) to high. Put the oil into a large skillet or frying pan, and add the slices of morcilla while the oil is still cold – do not put the slices on top of each other. Cover the skillet and cook over a medium-high heat until the morcilla no longer makes a crackling sound. Take the skillet off the heat, turn each of the slices over and cook them on the other side. In the meantime, lightly toast the bread.

To serve, place a piece of morcilla on each slice of toasted bread and hold it in place with a toothpick (cocktail stick). Serve hot.

PICADILLOS

INGREDIENTS

- ½ cup (120 ml/4 fl oz) olive oil
- 3¼ lb (1.5 kg) boneless stewing beef, such as chuck, cut into small pieces
- 9 oz (250 g) fat (streaky) bacon, cut into small pieces
- 1 onion, chopped
- 1 clove garlic, chopped
- 9 oz (250 g) tomatoes, peeled, seeded and chopped
- scant ½ cup (50 g/2 oz) pine nuts
- 1 pinch grated nutmeg
- 1 stick cinnamon
- ¾ cup (175 ml/6 fl oz) white wine
- 1 pinch saffron strands
- salt and pepper
- triangles of fried bread, to serve
- 2 hard-boiled eggs, shelled, to serve

Serves 6

Heat the oil in a flameproof heavy-base pan. Add the beef and bacon and cook, stirring occasionally, over low heat until golden. Remove from the pan with a slotted spoon and set aside. Add the onion and the garlic to the oil and cook for 3–4 minutes, then add the tomatoes and continue cooking for about 5 minutes, breaking down the tomatoes with the side of the spoon. Return the beef and bacon to the pan and add the pine nuts, nutmeg and cinnamon. Season with salt and pepper, then sprinkle in the wine.

Crush the saffron in a mortar and dissolve it in ¾ cup (175 ml/ 6 fl oz) water, then pour it into the pan with the meat. Continue cooking, partially covered, over low heat, stirring occasionally, for about 2 hours, until the meat is tender and most of the liquid has reduced. There should be just enough liquid left to keep the dish moist. Spoon into a warm serving dish and serve garnished with the fried bread, and the eggs cut into wedges or chopped and sprinkled over the top.

PHOTOGRAPH PAGE 391

POLLO AL AJILLO

GARLIC CHICKEN

INGREDIENTS

- 3½ lb (1.6 kg) chicken pieces
- 1 cup (250 ml/8 fl oz) olive oil
- 4 cloves garlic
- salt
  Serves 6

Season the chicken pieces with salt. Heat the oil in a large skillet or frying pan. Add the pieces of chicken, in batches, and cook over medium heat, turning frequently, for 8–10 minutes, until golden brown all over. Add the garlic cloves and let it cook for another 20 minutes, stirring occasionally with a wooden spoon. Cover the skillet and cook over low heat for 15 minutes, or until the chicken is cooked. To check this, pierce the thickest part of the meat with the point of a sharp knife; if the juices run clear and the meat is no longer pink, the chicken is cooked. Remove garlic and pour out a little of the oil so the dish is not too oily. Transfer to a warm serving dish and spoon the skillet juices over the chicken. Serve immediately.

ARROZ CON POLLO Y JUDÍAS VERDES

RICE WITH CHICKEN AND GREEN BEANS

INGREDIENTS

- ¾ cup (175 ml/6 fl oz) sunflower oil
- 1 chicken, about 4½ lb (2 kg)
- 9 oz (250 g) green beans, trimmed and chopped
- 5 oz (150 g) tomatoes, peeled, seeded and chopped
- 1 teaspoon paprika
- 2½ cups (500 g/1 lb 2 oz) long-grain rice
- 1 pinch saffron strands, in 1 tablespoon hot water
- salt
  Serves 8

Heat the oil in a flameproof heavy-base pan over medium-high heat. Cut the chicken into serving-size pieces and pan-fry until they are golden on each side. Add the beans and tomatoes and cook for 5 minutes. Sprinkle the paprika over the top and stir in the rice. Pour in 5 cups (1.2 litres/2 pints) water and add the saffron. Season with salt and bring to a boil. Reduce the heat to low, cover and cook for 20 minutes, or until the rice is tender and the stock is absorbed. Let stand for 5 minutes before serving.

PHOTOGRAPH PAGE 390

CHICKEN WINGS WITH GARLIC, PARSLEY AND LEMON JUICE

INGREDIENTS

- 12 chicken wings
- 1 cup (250 ml/8 fl oz) olive oil
- juice of 3 lemons, strained
- 4–5 cloves garlic, chopped
- several sprigs parsley, chopped
- salt

Serves 4–6

Lightly salt the chicken wings. Heat the oil in a large skillet or frying pan. Add the chicken wings, in batches, and cook over medium heat, turning frequently, for 12–15 minutes, until evenly browned and cooked through. Check that the wings are cooked by piercing one with the point of a sharp knife; if the juices run clear and the meat is no longer pink, the chicken is cooked. Drain the skillet, reserving about 2 tablespoons oil. Stir in the lemon juice. Add the garlic and parsley and cook for 5 minutes.

Serve the chicken wings immediately with the skillet juices spooned over them. These are good accompanied with French fries (chips) or a green salad.

CHICKEN AND PRUNE BROCHETTES

INGREDIENTS

- 16 prunes, pitted (stoned)
- generous ⅓ cup (100 ml/3½ fl oz) cognac or other brandy
- 1 lb 2 oz (500 g) boneless, skinless chicken breasts, cut into cubes
- 5 tablespoons sunflower oil
- few drops of lemon juice
- 3½ oz (100 g) pheasant or other game pâté
- 8 mushrooms, trimmed
- 8 slices (rashers) bacon
- salt and pepper

Serves 4

Put the prunes into a bowl and pour half the cognac over them, then let marinate for a couple of hours. At the same time, put the chicken pieces into another bowl with the oil, remaining cognac and salt and pepper to taste. Cover and and marinate in the refrigerator. Remove from the refrigerator before you plan to cook.

Meanwhile, wash the mushrooms in a bowl of water with the lemon juice. Remove from the water, pat dry and set aside. Preheat the broiler (grill) to high. Remove the prunes from the marinade, stuff each with the pâté and seal them by wrapping each one in bacon. Spear alternate pieces of chicken, prune and mushroom onto 4 long skewers. Use a pastry brush to glaze them with the oil and cognac mixture. Put the brochettes under the broiler and broil (grill) for 8–10 minutes, turning occasionally, until the meat is tender and the juices run clear when the thickest part of the meat is pierced with a knife.

PHOTOGRAPH PAGE 393

KIDNEYS IN SHERRY

INGREDIENTS

- 2 tablespoons all-purpose (plain) flour
- 4 tablespoons olive oil
- ¾ cup (175 ml/6 fl oz) dry sherry
- 2¼ lb (1 kg) veal kidneys, trimmed and cleaned
- salt

Serves 6

Put the flour into a skillet or frying pan and cook over medium heat, stirring constantly, for about 10 minutes, until it begins to brown. Stir in the oil, then add the sherry, generous 2 cups (500 ml/18 fl oz) water and a pinch of salt. Cook for 5 minutes. Add the kidneys, lower the heat and cook for about 10 minutes, stirring occasionally, until cooked to your liking. Serve immediately.

CHICKEN WITH PINE NUTS, BELL PEPPERS AND TOMATOES

INGREDIENTS

- 2 onions, chopped
- 3¼–4 lb (1.5–1.8 kg) chicken pieces
- 4 tomatoes, peeled, seeded and chopped
- 3 green bell peppers, seeded and thinly sliced into rings
- 1 tablespoon bread crumbs
- scant ½ cup (50 g/2 oz) pine nuts
- ¼ teaspoon mixed dried herbs or 1 bouquet garni
- 2 cloves garlic
- ¾ cup (175 ml/6 fl oz) olive oil
- 2 chicken stock cubes
- ¾ cup (175 ml/6 fl oz) white wine
- salt and pepper

Serves 6–8

Preheat the oven to 350°F (180°C/GAS MARK 4). Put the onion into a flameproof heavy-base pan, place the pieces of chicken on top and add the tomato and bell pepper. Sprinkle with the bread crumbs, pine nuts and dried herbs or bouquet garni, and season with salt and pepper. Put the garlic cloves among the pieces of chicken, pour the oil over the top and mix well. Put the pan in the oven and cook for 15 minutes.

Dissolve the stock cubes in 3 tablespoons hot water. Remove the casserole from the oven, stir well and add the wine and stock. Return to the oven and cook, stirring occasionally, for another 20–30 minutes. Remove and discard the bouquet garni, if used, and try to put the rings of bell pepper back on top of the chicken, then check that it is done by piercing the thickest part of the meat with the point of a sharp knife; if the juices run clear and the meat is no longer pink, the chicken is cooked. Serve immediately, straight from the pan.

PHOTOGRAPH PAGE 392

**ARROZ MELOSO
RABO DE TORO**

STICKY
OXTAIL RICE

INGREDIENTS
- 1 oxtail, about 3¼ lb (1.5 kg)
- 3½ oz (100 g) carrots,
  halved lengthwise
- 1 onion, studded with a few
  cloves
- 2 peppercorns
- ½ bay leaf
- ¾ cup (175 ml/6 fl oz)
  dry white wine
- 2 tablespoons sunflower oil
- 1 onion, finely chopped
- 1 clove garlic, finely chopped
- scant 1¼ cups (250 g/9 oz)
  short-grain rice
- salt and pepper
- 1 fresh truffle, shaved, to garnish
  (optional)
  Serves 4

Put the oxtail in a pan with 6⅓ cups (1.5 litres/2½ pints) water and bring to a boil, skimming the surface as necessary. Reduce the heat to low, add the carrots, onion, peppercorns and bay leaf and season with salt. Let simmer, partially covered, for a couple hours until the meat comes away from the bone easily. Top off with extra water, if necessary.

Remove the oxtail from the liquid when it is tender and set aside. Leave the liquid to simmer until thickened, then strain it to obtain a smooth texture. Carefully take the meat off the bone, trying to keep the pieces in their original round shape.

Heat the oil in a large skillet or frying pan over low heat. Add the onion and garlic and pan-fry, stirring occasionally, for 10 minutes, or until golden brown. Meanwhile, strain the cooking liquid and set aside. Add the rice and pan-fry for about 10 minutes. Add the cooking liquid little by little, stirring continuously until all the liquid has been absorbed. This will take about 20 minutes. The rice should be creamy but just slightly hard in the center. Season with salt and pepper and serve hot with the oxtail meat arranged over the top. Garnish with the shaved truffle, if you like.

GOLDEN RICE

INGREDIENTS

- 1 pig's foot (trotter), cut in half
- 1 pig's ear, hairs singed off
- 5 oz (150 g) unsmoked fat (streaky) bacon, in one piece
- generous 1 cup (250 g/9 oz) garbanzo beans (chickpeas), soaked overnight in water to cover and drained
- 1 onion
- 1 stalk celery
- 2 morcillas or blood sausages (black puddings), total weight about 11 oz (300 g)
- a few saffron strands, crushed in a mortar with 2 tablespoons water
- 6 tablespoons sunflower oil
- 3 or 4 cloves garlic, crushed
- 9 oz (250 g) tomatoes, peeled, seeded and chopped
- 2 parsley sprigs, finely chopped
- 2 cups (400 g/14 oz) long-grain rice
- salt
Serves 6

Put the pig's ear and foot with the bacon into a large pan. Pour in scant 2⅔ quarts (2½ litres/4⅓ pints) cold water and bring to a boil. When the water begins to boil, add the garbanzo beans, onion and celery, then reduce the heat and let simmer for 1½ hours, skimming the surface as necessary. Then add the morcilla and saffron and season with salt. Continue simmering for another 30 minutes.

Strain the ingredients, reserving the stock. Remove any skin and rinds and finely chop the pork pieces. Remove the casings from the morcilla and slice them. Set both aside. Preheat the oven to 350°F (180°C/GAS MARK 4). Heat the oil in a flameproof heavy-base pan. Add the garlic and pan-fry, stirring occasionally, until golden brown. Stir in the tomatoes and parsley, then add the meat and blood sausage slices and let simmer for a few minutes, stirring. Stir in the rice, garbanzo beans and 4 cups (1 litre/1¾ pints) of the reserved stock and season with salt.

Return the liquid to the boil and stir, then cover the pan and transfer to the oven for 20 minutes, or until the rice is tender, the stock is absorbed and the top is golden brown. Leave the rice to stand for 5 minutes, then lightly stir with a fork to separate the grains. Serve the straight from the pan.

PHOTOGRAPH PAGE 395

SOBRASADA TAPA

INGREDIENTS

- 3½ oz (100 g) sobrasada, casing removed, if necessary
- 4 tablespoons (50 g/2 oz) butter
- 12 slices French baguette
- toasted almonds, to serve
  Makes 12

Preheat the oven to 400°F (200°C/GAS MARK 6). Mix the sobrasada with a little butter. Preheat the broiler (grill) and lightly toast the slices of baguette on both sides, or toast in a toaster. Spread them with the sobrasada mixture while they are still warm. Finely chop the toasted almonds and sprinkle on top of each toast. Put the slices on a baking sheet and bake for 5–10 minutes.

Note: If you cannot obtain sobrasada (a cured pork sausage spiced with paprika, made in Mallorca) use ordinary sausage meat instead. Add sweet smoked and hot Spanish paprika to the meat, then beat in the butter, then proceed as above.

CALF'S LIVER AND BACON PINCHOS

INGREDIENTS

- 1 lb 10 oz (750 g) calf's liver, trimmed and cut into cubes
- 6 medium-thick slices (rashers) of bacon, cut into squares
- olive oil, for brushing
- 6 thin slices bread
- salt
  Serves 6

Preheat the oven to 425°F (220°C/GAS MARK 7). Season the liver with salt, then thread the cubes of liver onto skewers, alternating them with the squares of bacon. Brush the brochettes with oil. Put the slices of bread in a roasting pan and balance the ends of the skewers on the rim of the pan, so that the bread catches the cooking juices. Cook in the oven, turning occasionally, for about 20 minutes, until the liver is just firm and the bacon is brown. Transfer the bread to a serving dish and put the brochettes on top.

PHOTOGRAPH PAGE 397

VEAL AND VEGETABLE ROLLS

INGREDIENTS

– 12 thin bacon slices (rashers)
– 6 thin slices of veal flank,
  pounded
– 4 stalks celery, cut into
  thin pieces
– 2 carrots, peeled and cut
  into julienne strips
– 4 tablespoons olive oil
– 1 tablespoon all-purpose
  (plain) flour
– ¾ cup (175 ml/6 fl oz) dry
  white wine
– 1 bay leaf
– salt and pepper
  Serves 6

Cut the bacon slices to the same length as the veal fillets. Season the veal slices with salt and pepper and place 2 slices of bacon on each slice of veal and top with a stick of celery and some julienne strips of carrot. Roll up each veal slice and secure with a wooden toothpick (cocktail stick) or tie with fine kitchen string.

Heat the oil in a deep skillet or frying pan with a tight-fitting lid. Carefully add the veal rolls to the pan, in two batches if necessary, and cook over medium heat, turning frequently to ensure even browning, for 4–5 minutes until golden brown all over. Remove with a slotted spoon, drain and set aside.

Stir in the flour and cook, stirring constantly, for 2 minutes. Gradually stir in the wine, a little at a time, then stir in ¾ cup (175 ml/6 fl oz) water. Add the bay leaf and return the veal rolls to the pan and add ¾ cup (175 ml/6 fl oz) water to cover them. Season and bring to a boil. Lower the heat to medium, cover and cook for 30 minutes to 1 hour, until the veal rolls are tender. Just before serving, lift out the veal rolls and remove and discard the toothpicks or string and place on a warm serving dish. Discard the bay leaf. Season the sauce with salt and pepper, if necessary, and bring the sauce to a boil, then pour over the meat.

Note: This dish is delicious accompanied by a salad of raw celery with vinaigrette.

ARROZ BLANCO
CON TERNERA

WHITE RICE
WITH VEAL

INGREDIENTS
- 3¼–4½ lb (1.5–2 kg)
  breast of veal
- 2 carrots, thickly sliced
- 1 onion, studded with 2 cloves
- 1 bay leaf
- ¾ cup (175 ml/6 fl oz)
  white wine
- 2½ cups (500 g/1 lb 2 oz)
  long-grain rice
- ⅓ cup (80 g/3 oz) butter
- 2 tablespoons sunflower oil
- 2 tablespoons all-purpose
  (plain) flour
- 2 egg yolks, lightly beaten
- ¼ teaspoon meat extract
- 1 teaspoon chopped parsley
- salt
  Serves 6–8

Put the veal into a large pan, pour in enough water to cover and add a pinch of salt. Add the carrots, onion, bay leaf and white wine. Cover and bring to a boil, then lower the heat and simmer for 1½ hours, until the veal is tender. While the veal is cooking, skim off the froth that rises to the surface with a skimmer or slotted spoon.

Meanwhile, cook the rice in salted boiling water for 10–15 minutes, or until just tender, then rinse under cold running water. Drain well and set aside. Lift the veal out of the pan and carve the meat. Put the meat in a dish and ladle some of the stock over it to keep it warm. Strain and reserve the remaining stock.

To make the sauce, melt half with butter with the oil in a pan over medium heat and gradually stir in the flour, stirring constantly, for 2 minutes. Stir in 3 cups (750 ml/1¼ pints) of the reserved stock and cook, whisking constantly to prevent lumps forming. Gradually stir a little of the stock into the egg yolks in a bowl, taking care that the yolks do not curdle. Add to the sauce, together with the meat extract and the parsley. Season with salt if necessary. Add the veal meat and keep the sauce warm but do not allow it to cook any more. Melt the remaining butter in another pan. Add the rice, season with salt and heat through, stirring with a wooden spoon. Spoon the rice into a ring mold, then turn out onto a warmed serving dish. Spoon the veal into the center of the ring. Serve immediately with the sauce on the side.

LENTILS WITH BACON AND SAUSAGES

INGREDIENTS

- 1 small onion
- 2 cloves
- 2⅔ cups (600 g/1 lb 5 oz) Puy lentils
- 1 bay leaf
- 1 carrot, cut into 4 pieces
- 2 cloves garlic, unpeeled
- 9 oz (250 g) bacon in a single piece
- 12 small sausages
- generous 1 cup (275 ml/9 fl oz) olive oil
- salt

Serves 6

Stud the onion with the cloves. Put the lentils into a pan, add the onion, bay leaf, pieces of carrot, garlic cloves and bacon and pour in water to cover generously. Cover and bring to a boil, then lower the heat and simmer for 1–1½ hours, until the lentils are tender. Drain the lentils, reserving the cooking liquid. Remove the onion, bay leaf, garlic, carrot and bacon. Cut the bacon into small cubes and set aside.

Prick the sausages if they have artificial casings. Heat the oil in a skillet or frying pan. Add the sausages and cook, turning frequently, for about 5 minutes, until lightly browned and cooked through. Remove from the skillet and keep warm. Drain off about half the oil from the skillet and reheat. Add the cubes of bacon and cook, stirring, for about 3 minutes, then add the lentils. Stir well and season to taste with salt. Put the lentils into a warm serving dish, place the sausages on top and serve immediately.

Note: Some people prefer a little more liquid in the finished dish. If so, reserve and add some cooking liquid from the lentils to achieve the desired consistency. It is worth reserving the stock anyway in case there are lentils left over. They can be pureed them in a food processor and make a thick soup, garnishing it with croûtons or a little white rice.

PHOTOGRAPH PAGE 396

RICE WITH TOMATO, SAUSAGE, PEAS AND BELL PEPPERS

INGREDIENTS

- ⅔ cup (150 ml/¼ pint) sunflower oil
- 1 large onion, finely chopped
- 1 clove garlic
- 1 sprig parsley
- 4 fresh sausages, halved lengthways
- 2¾ cups (600 g/1 lb 5 oz) Calasparra rice, or other short-grain rice
- 1 chicken stock cube, crumbled
- 3½ oz (100 g) bottled roasted red bell pepper, drained and sliced
- ½ cup (75 g/2½ oz) canned or cooked fresh peas, drained and rinsed
- salt

Serves 6

Prepare a tomato sauce in advance, using 1 lb 10 oz (750 g) tomatoes (see page 181). Set aside.

Preheat the oven to 350°F (180°C/GAS MARK 4). Heat the oil in a paella pan or shallow flameproof heavy-base pan over low heat. Add the onion and pan-fry, stirring occasionally, for 6 minutes, or until softened but not colored. Crush the garlic in a mortar with the parsley and a little salt (to prevent the garlic slipping), then add it to the pan with the sausages and tomato sauce and let pan-fry a little. Next add the rice and stir for 3 or 4 minutes.

Dissolve the stock cube in 6⅓ cups (1.5 litres/2½ pints) boiling water. Pour into the pan with the bell peppers and season with salt, but take care as both the garlic and the stock cube will be salty. Cover the pan, put it in the oven and stir occasionally so that the rice stays loose. Add the peas toward the end of the cooking time. Cook for about 20 minutes until the rice is tender and all the liquid has been absorbed. Remove from the oven and let stand for 5 minutes, then serve.

PHOTOGRAPH PAGE 398

RICE WITH TOMATOES, BELL PEPPERS AND PORK LOIN

INGREDIENTS

- 4 tablespoons sunflower oil
- 1 lb 2 oz (500 g) boneless pork loin, diced
- 2 cloves garlic
- 1 sprig parsley
- 5 cups (1.2 litres/2 pints) stock, or water with a stock cube dissolved in it
- 6 tomatoes, peeled, seeded and chopped
- 3 bottled or canned roasted red bell peppers, drained and chopped
- 2½ cups (500 g/1 lb 2 oz) short-grain rice
- 1 pinch saffron threads
- salt

Serves 6

Heat the oil in a flameproof heavy-base pan over medium-high heat. Add the pork and pan-fry, stirring, until the pieces begin to brown. Remove from the pan and set aside. Reduce the heat to medium-low.

Crush the garlic in a mortar with the parsley and a little salt (to prevent the garlic slipping), then dilute it with a little of the stock and add it to the pan along with the tomatoes and bell peppers. Let cook for a few minutes, stirring occasionally, then add the rice and stir until the grains are well coated. Return the pieces of pork to the pan.

Dissolve the saffron threads in a little stock, then add the saffron mixture and the remaining stock to the pan. Season with salt – but take care because the garlic and the stock cube will be salty – and bring to a boil. Cover the pan, reduce the heat to low and let cook for 20 minutes, or until the rice is tender and the liquid absorbed. Let stand for 5 minutes before serving.

EMPANADA GALLEGA

GALICIAN EMPANADA

INGREDIENTS

- ¼ oz (10 g) dried yeast
- 3 eggs
- 3⅓ cups (400 g/14 oz) all-purpose (plain) flour, plus extra for dusting
- 1 tablespoon (15 g/½ oz) margarine, at room temperature
- 2 tablespoons sunflower oil, plus extra for brushing
- 14 oz (400 g) pork fillet or skinless, boneless chicken breasts, cut into strips
- 2 canned or bottled red bell peppers, or roasted red bell peppers, drained and cut into strips
- salt

FOR THE 'RUSTIDO':

- 2 tablespoons olive oil
- 3 onions, coarsely chopped
- 1 clove garlic, crushed
- 1 tablespoon chopped fresh parsley
- 1 chorizo sausage, sliced

Serves 6

Mix the yeast with a pinch of salt and ¾ cup (175 ml/6 fl oz) lukewarm water in a cup or a small bowl until smooth, then let stand for about 10 minutes, until the mixture is frothy. Beat 2 of the eggs in a bowl. Sift the flour with a pinch of salt onto a work surface. Make a well in the center and pour in the beaten egg and the yeast mixture. Gradually incorporate the flour into the liquid, then knead well on a lightly floured surface for 10 minutes. Add the margarine and knead for another 10 minutes. Add a little water to the dough if necessary. Once it is smooth and elastic, form it into a ball, place in a bowl and cover with a clean dish towel. Let rise in a warm place for 1–2 hours, until doubled in size.

Meanwhile, make the 'rustido'. Heat the olive oil in a skillet or frying pan. Add the onion and cook over low heat, stirring occasionally, for 10 minutes, until softened and translucent. Add the garlic and parsley and cook for another 5 minutes. Stir in the chorizo and cook for 2 minutes more. Remove the skillet from the heat and set aside. Heat the sunflower oil in a skillet. Add the strips of pork or chicken and cook over medium-low heat, stirring frequently, for about 8 minutes, until golden brown. Remove the chicken from the skillet with a slotted spoon and set aside.

Preheat the oven to 350°F (180°C/GAS MARK 4). Brush a 12-inch (30-cm) baking pan or ovenproof baking dish with oil. Divide the dough into 2 pieces, one slightly bigger than the other. Roll out the larger piece and use to line the pan or dish. Spread half the rustido over the dough, place the strips of meat on top and add the strips of bell pepper. Spoon the remaining rustido over the top. Roll out the remaining dough and use it to cover the mixture. Seal the edges of the dough carefully. Pinch the dough in the center of the pie with 2 fingers to create a chimney to allow the steam to escape. Beat the remaining egg and brush it over the dough to glaze. Bake for 45 minutes, until golden brown on top, increasing the oven temperature gradually if necessary. Serve hot or warm, straight from the dish if preferred.

PHOTOGRAPH PAGE 399

MEAT

COLD

Pork salad **369**

Spicy chorizo and gherkin pinchos **370**

Serrano ham with melon mousse **371**

Chicken and ham terrine **372**

Melon balls with ham **373**

Salami and cheese tapa **374**

Veal terrine with sherry **375**

HOT

Meatballs **376**

Chicken brochettes with spices and honey **377**

Rice with bacon, sausages and bonito **378**

Marinated meat pinchos **379**

Potatoes with chorizo **380**

Pork fillets in wine **381**

Fried date and bacon pinchos **382**

Bean stew **383**

Ham croquettes **384**

Rice with ham and chorizo **385**

Chicken livers with grapes **386**

Migas **387**

Pork and morcilla empanada **388**

Rice with morcilla **389**

Rice with chicken and green beans **390**

Picadillos **391**

Chicken with pine nuts, bell peppers and tomatoes **392**

Chicken and prune brochettes **393**

Chicken and bell pepper empanada **394**

Golden rice **395**

Lentils with bacon and sausages **396**

Calf's liver and bacon pinchos **397**

Rice with tomato, sausage, peas and bell peppers **398**

Galician empanada **399**

PORK SALAD
PAGE 326

SPICY CHORIZO AND
GHERKIN PINCHOS
PAGE 323

SERRANO HAM WITH
MELON MOUSSE
PAGE 325

CHICKEN AND
HAM TERRINE
PAGE 327

MELON BALLS
WITH HAM
PAGE 326

SALAMI AND
CHEESE TAPA
PAGE 329

VEAL TERRINE
WITH SHERRY
PAGE 329

MEATBALLS
PAGE 331

CHICKEN BROCHETTES
WITH SPICES AND HONEY
PAGE 333

RICE WITH BACON,
SAUSAGES AND BONITO
PAGE 335

MARINATED MEAT
PINCHOS
PAGE 337

POTATOES
WITH CHORIZO
PAGE 340

PORK FILLETS
IN WINE
PAGE 339

FRIED DATE AND
BACON PINCHOS
PAGE 343

BEAN STEW
PAGE 344

HAM CROQUETTES
PAGE 345

RICE WITH HAM
AND CHORIZO
PAGE 346

CHICKEN LIVERS
WITH GRAPES
PAGE 350

MIGAS
PAGE 348

PORK AND
MORCILLA
EMPANADA
PAGE 351

RICE WITH
MORCILLA
PAGE 352

RICE WITH CHICKEN
AND GREEN BEANS
PAGE 355

PICADILLOS
PAGE 354

CHICKEN WITH PINE
NUTS, BELL PEPPERS
AND TOMATOES
PAGE 358

CHICKEN AND PRUNE
BROCHETTES
PAGE 357

CHICKEN AND BELL
PEPPER EMPANADA
PAGE 352

GOLDEN RICE
PAGE 360

LENTILS WITH BACON
AND SAUSAGES

PAGE 364

CALF'S LIVER AND
BACON PINCHOS
PAGE 361

RICE WITH TOMATO,
SAUSAGE, PEAS AND
BELL PEPPERS
PAGE 365

GALICIAN EMPANADA
PAGE 367

GUEST CHEFS

Carles Abellan BARCELONA, SPAIN

Albert Adrià BARCELONA, SPAIN

José Andrés WASHINGTON, DC, USA

Frank Camorra MELBOURNE, AUSTRALIA

Sam and Sam Clark LONDON, UK

Alberto Herraíz PARIS, FRANCE

Alexandra Raij and Eder Montero NEW YORK CITY, USA

Seamus Mullen NEW YORK CITY, USA

José Pizarro LONDON, UK

Albert Raurich BARCELONA, SPAIN

The following pages contain a sampling of recipes from some of the world's
best chefs cooking Spanish or Spanish-influenced tapas.

CARLES ABELLAN

COMERÇ 24, BARCELONA, SPAIN
TAPAS 24, BARCELONA, SPAIN

Carles Abellan trained in Spain and worked at elBulli under Ferran Adrià for several years before opening Comerç 24 in the Born area of Barcelona in 2001. Six years later the restaurant was awarded a Michelin star. In 2006 he opened Tapas 24, inspired by the traditional tapas found in the local bars in Barcelona, where he produces tapas dishes at accessible prices, without compromising on creativity or raw materials.

ESQUEIXADA DE BACALÀ

SALT COD SALAD

INGREDIENTS
- 14 oz (400 g) salt cod, soaked in cold water for 12 hours, then cooked, drained and flaked
- 3 ripe tomatoes, grated
- ½ bunch scallions (spring onions), cut into julienne strips
- 1 green bell pepper
- 1 red bell pepper
- ½ bunch chives, finely chopped
- extra-virgin olive oil, for dressing
- salt

FOR THE BLACK OLIVE OIL:
- 3½ oz (100 g) pureed Kalamata olives
- 3½ tablespoons (50 ml/2 fl oz) extra-virgin olive oil

Taste the cod to check how salty it is. If it is too salty, soak it for a little longer. Cut it into small pieces. In a bowl, mix the tomato with oil and a little salt. Place the scallions in a bowl of lightly salted water.

To make the black olive oil, process the pureed olives and the oil in a blender.

Cut the bell peppers into thin julienne stips. Mix the peppers and the cod together in a bowl, then dress generously with olive oil. Spoon into a cylindrical mold and press down firmly. Add an even layer of the grated tomato mixture and sprinkle the chives over the top. Finally, layer a generous amount of the julienne strips of scallion over the top. Before serving, remove the mold and spoon the black olive oil around the edge of the plate.

COSTILLAS DE CONEJO

RABBIT RIBS

INGREDIENTS
- 14 oz (400 g) rabbit ribs
- 1 large egg
- 1 cup (50 g/2 oz) bread crumbs
- ¾ cup (200 ml/7 fl oz) sunflower oil

FOR THE DRY MARINADE:
- 1 oz (25 g) dried herbes de Provence
- ¼ oz (10 g) smoked Spanish paprika
- 2 teaspoons ground black pepper
- 1 teaspoon salt

FOR THE ALIOLI:
- 4 cloves garlic
- 1 egg
- 1½ teaspoons salt
- 4 cups (1 litre/1¾ pints) sunflower oil

To make the marinade, mix all the ingredients together in a bowl. Add the ribs, turn to coat thoroughly, then cover and leave to marinate in the refrigerator for 6 hours.

Next, make the garlic mayonnaise: bring a small pan of water to a boil. Add 3 of the garlic cloves and boil rapidly for 1 minute. Strain the garlic and place under cold running water to stop the cooking process. In a small bowl, crush the cooked garlic with the remaining raw garlic, the egg and the salt. Stir lightly with a whisk, then gradually whisk in the oil, 1–2 teaspoons at a time, until one-quarter has been added. Whisk in the remaining oil in a slow, steady stream. Set aside.

Beat the egg lightly and pour into a shallow dish. Spread the bread crumbs out on a plate. Heat the sunflower oil in a deep skillet or frying pan to 330°F (165°C). Coat the ribs in egg and then in bread crumbs, then carefully place them in the pan and fry until golden and cooked through. Using a slotted spoon, transfer the ribs to a plate lined with paper towel. To serve, place the ribs on a plate and serve the alioli separately in a bowl. Spread a little alioli on the ribs and then eat them with your fingers.

ALBERT ADRIÀ

Albert Adrià joined elBulli restaurant in 1985, first specializing in pastry, and then going on to run elBullitaller, the creative workshop where the dishes are developed, until he left elBulli in 2008. In 2006 he opened Inopia in central Barcelona, where he serves classic tapas made with impeccably sourced ingredients in a traditional Spanish tapas-bar setting.

BOQUERONES EN VINAGRE

ANCHOVIES IN VINEGAR

INGREDIENTS
- 21 fresh anchovies, cleaned
- about ¾ cup (200 ml/7 fl oz) good-quality extra-virgin olive oil
- 3 tablespoons finely chopped parsley
- 2 cloves garlic, peeled and finely chopped

FOR THE MARINADE:
- 4 cups (1 litre/1¾ pints) white-wine vinegar
- 1½ cups (360 ml/12½ fl oz) mineral water
- 1⅓ cups (330 ml/11 fl oz) white wine
- ¼ cup (50 g/2 oz) sea salt

Check the anchovies and discard any that are not in good condition. Open out, or "butterfly," the anchovies, then place them skin-side up and press along the backbones with your thumb. Turn over and lift out the bones, then cut each anchovy in half lengthwise along the back to make fillets. Plunge the anchovies quickly into a large bowl of of iced water. Let stand for 5 minutes, then drain.

Meanwhile, make the marinade by mixing together all the ingredients in a blender. Put the large fillets in one bowl and the small fillets in another bowl and cover each with the marinade. Refrigerate for 25 minutes. Check the condition of the anchovies after this time. If sufficiently marinated, remove from the refrigerator and drain, then spread them out on paper towels and pat dry. Drizzle 2 serving trays with enough olive oil to just cover the anchovies. Scatter the garlic evenly on the trays, add the anchovy fillets, then top with a sprinkling of parsley.

PINCHOS DE POLLO A L'AST

CHICKEN BROCHETTES

INGREDIENTS
- 3½ lb (1.5 kg) chicken thighs, boned
- toasted bread, to serve

FOR THE MARINADE:
- ⅔ cup (150 ml/¼ pint) white wine
- 5 tablespoons mild olive oil
- 2 teaspoons sea salt
- 1 tablespoon mixed dried rosemary, bay, thyme and black pepper

Mix the marinade ingredients together in a large bowl. Cut the chicken into very small cubes. Add the chicken to the marinade, turning to coat each piece thoroughly. Cover and transfer to the refrigerator.

When ready to cook, heat a ridged cast-iron skillet or frying pan or griddle over high heat until very hot. Thread the chicken pieces evenly onto 20–25 skewers. Brush the skillet with a little oil, then add the meat and cook, turning the skewers occasionally, until they are cooked to your liking. Serve with toasted bread.

TORRADA MALLORQUINA

MAJORCAN TOAST

INGREDIENTS
- 6¼ oz (180 g) tomatoes, peeled, seeded and finely diced
- 1¼ cups (300 ml/½ pint) Picual or other extra-virgin olive oil, plus extra for drizzling
- ⅓ cup (60 g/2¼ oz) sugar
- ½ oz (18 g) fresh oregano leaves
- 4 oz (120 g) black pig sobrasada, at room temperature
- 6 "air breads" (puces) or other rustic bread
- salt and pepper

Put the tomato in a large bowl. Season with salt and pepper and dress with the oil, sugar and oregano. Remove the skin from the sobrasada and cut it into pieces.

When you are ready to serve, heat the broiler (grill) to high. Lightly toast the bread on both sides. Spread a layer of the sobrasada over the crunchier side of piece of each bread and add a layer of the tomato mixture. Serve immediately, drizzled with a little olive oil.

JOSÉ
ANDRÉS

José Andrés began his career in Spain, including a period working under Ferran Adrià at elBulli restaurant, before moving to the USA and opening Jaleo, the first of several restaurants. At Jaleo he serves a wide-ranging tapas menu which reflects the rich regional diversity of Spanish food culture. Through many books and television appearances, Andrés is renowned as a leading expert on Spanish cuisine, and is often credited with introducing tapas to the USA.

SANDÍA CON TOMATE Y PISTACHIOS

WATERMELON WITH TOMATO AND PISTACHIO

INGREDIENTS

- ½ cup (120 ml/4 fl oz) Pedro Ximenez sherry vinegar
- 2 plum tomatoes, seeded and diced
- 1 quantity Sherry Dressing (see page 407)
- ½ small seedless watermelon, peeled and cut into four 2 x 4-inch (5 x 10-cm) blocks, approximately 1 inch (2.5 cm) thick
- 4 teaspoons chopped pistachios
- 6 oz (175 g) caña de cabra or other soft goat cheese
- 4 tablespoons microgreens
- 2 tablespoons fresh thyme
- 2 tablespoons Spanish extra-virgin olive oil
- sea salt

Bring the Pedro Ximenez sherry vinegar to a boil in a small pan. Lower the heat and cook until it reduces by more than half and turns to a syrupy consistency. Remove from the heat and let cool. Set aside.

In a large mixing bowl, toss the diced tomatoes with the sherry dressing. Slice the watermelon blocks into ¼-inch (5-mm) slices and fan the slices on the serving plate. Spoon the tomato mixture over the top of the watermelon. Sprinkle with the pistachios. Crumble the goat cheese over the top. Garnish with the microgreens and fresh thyme. Sprinkle with sea salt. Spoon a streak of Pedro Ximenez reduction down one side of the plate, and follow with olive oil. Repeat for the remaining servings and serve immediately.

Note: Microgreens are miniature salad leaves, herbs and cresses. Small leaves and herbs can be substituted.

ENDIBIAS CON NARANJA QUESO
DE CABRA Y ALMENDRAS

ENDIVE WITH ORANGES, GOAT CHEESE AND ALMONDS

INGREDIENTS

FOR THE SHERRY DRESSING:
- ½ tablespoon sherry vinegar
- 2 tablespoons Spanish extra-virgin olive oil
- sea salt, to taste

FOR THE SALAD:
- 3 oranges, peeled and cut into segments
- 3–4 Belgian endives (chicory)
- 4 oz (120 g) goat cheese
- 4 oz (120 g) sliced almonds
- chives, finely chopped, to serve
- sea salt

To make the sherry dressing, whisk together the sherry vinegar, olive oil and salt in a bowl. Set aside.

Trim the endives and separate out the leaves. Arrange the 20 largest leaves on a serving plate. Top each leaf with a few orange segments. Crumble a little goat cheese over the top and sprinkle with almond slices. Finally, drizzle with a little sherry dressing and sprinkle with chives.

GAMBAS AL AJILLO

GARLIC SHRIMP (PRAWNS)

INGREDIENTS
- 4 tablespoons Spanish extra-virgin olive oil
- 6 cloves garlic, thinly sliced
- 20 large shrimp (prawns), about 1 lb (450 g) in total
- 1 guindilla chili pepper (or any other dried chili pepper)
- 1 teaspoon brandy
- 1 teaspoon chopped parsley
- salt

In a medium skillet or frying pan, heat the oil over a medium-high heat. Add the garlic and cook for about 2 minutes, until browned. Add the shrimp and the chili pepper and cook without stirring for 2 minutes. Turn over the shrimp and cook for another 2 minutes. Pour in the brandy and cook for another minute. Sprinkle with the parsley and add salt to taste.

FRANK CAMORRA

Frank Camorra was born in Barcelona before emigrating to Australia as a young child with his family. Returning to Spain to travel extensively during 2000, he was inspired upon his return to Australia to recreate the flavors of his homeland. He opened MoVida restaurant in Melbourne, where he serves authentic Spanish tapas using the very best ingredients in a relaxed and energetic environment.

PINCHITOS MORUNOS

CHARGRILLED MOORISH LAMB SKEWERS

INGREDIENTS

- 1⅓ tablespoons sweet smoked Spanish paprika
- 1 teaspoon cayenne pepper
- ¾ cup (180 ml/6 fl oz) fino sherry
- 1 teaspoon ground nutmeg
- 2 tablespoons freshly roasted and ground cumin seeds
- 1 teaspoon turmeric
- 1 teaspoon fine sea salt
- 1 small handful parsley, chopped
- 2 cloves garlic, finely chopped
- 4 tablespoons olive oil
- 2¼ lb (1 kg) lamb leg meat, boned and all sinew removed
- ½ lemon

To make the marinade, mix together 1 tablespoon paprika, ½ teaspoon cayenne pepper and ½ cup (120 ml/4 fl oz) sherry with the nutmeg, cumin, turmeric, sea salt, parsley, garlic, and olive oil in a bowl. Cut the lamb into ½-inch (1-cm) cubes. Add the lamb to the marinade and mix well, ensuring all the pieces are coated. Cover, refrigerate and let marinate overnight, stirring 2 or 3 times.

Preheat a chargrill to medium-high, or, preferably, light the barbecue in order to broil (grill) the skewers over the embers. Thread the marinated lamb onto 12-inch (30-cm) metal skewers, making sure the meat is spread evenly along the skewers and is not bunched up too tightly. Thread any longer pieces lengthwise, which allows the meat to cook evenly. Make a basting liquid by mixing the remaining paprika, cayenne pepper and sherry. Place a fork in the curved side of the lemon half to make a fruity basting brush. Place the skewers on the grill and cook for 15–20 minutes, turning and basting each side several times. Remove from the heat and allow to rest briefly before serving.

LITTLE SHERRY PASTRIES FILLED WITH TUNA AND PIQUILLO PEPPERS

INGREDIENTS

- 5 oz (150 g) good-quality Spanish canned tuna, drained
- 5 oz (150 g) roasted or bottled piquillo peppers, drained and finely diced
- generous ⅓ cup (100 ml/ 3½ fl oz) garlic mayonnaise
- 1 pinch salt
- 1 pinch freshly cracked black pepper
- 1 egg, lightly beaten
- sunflower oil, for deep-frying

FOR THE PASTRY:

- 1 cup (120 g/4 oz) all-purpose (plain) flour
- 1 cup (120 g/4 oz) self-rising flour
- 1 pinch salt
- ½ cup (120 ml/4 fl oz) olive oil
- ⅔ cup (150 ml/¼ pint) dry fino sherry

To make the pastry dough, put all the dry ingredients in a large bowl and make a well in the center. Pour the oil and sherry into the well and mix together until a soft dough forms. Turn the dough out onto a lightly floured work surface and knead for a minute or so, being careful not to overwork the pastry. It should feel heavier and wetter than a regular pastry dough. If it seems a little dry, add a further splash of sherry. Cover the pastry and let rest in a cool place for 15 minutes.

Meanwhile, using your hands, flake the tuna into a large bowl. Add the piquillo peppers and garlic mayonnaise and mix well. Season to taste with salt and pepper. Cover and refrigerate.

Take a large handful of pastry dough and roll it out thinly on a cool, lightly floured surface. Using a 4-inch (10-cm) round cookie cutter, cut out rounds from the pastry. Place a tablespoon of tuna filling in the middle of each round. Brush each edge lightly with some of the egg, then fold over the pastry on itself to make a semi circle. Using a fork, press the edges of each empanadilla together to make sure it is sealed. Continue with the remaining pastry and filling.

To cook, heat the sunflower oil in a deep-fryer or pan to 350–375°F (180–190°C). Carefully add the empanadillas, in batches of 4 or 5, and cook until brown and crisp. Using a slotted spoon, remove and drain on paper towel. Season and serve still warm.

SAM AND SAM CLARK

Sam and Sam Clark, business partners as well as husband and wife, opened Moro restaurant in London in 1997. In doing so they were inspired by the robust style of Spanish cooking and the lighter, more exotic dishes of the Muslim Mediterranean. Their inspiration came from traveling through Spain, Morocco and the Sahara. They believe in simple, seasonal cooking and the importance of good ingredients.

ALMEJAS CON MANZANILLA

CLAMS WITH MANZANILLA

INGREDIENTS
- 2¼ lb (1 kg) small clams, such as venus clams or palourdes
- 4 tablespoons olive oil
- 2 cloves garlic, finely chopped
- ⅔ cup (150 ml/¼ pint) manzanilla sherry
- 1 large bunch parsley, roughly chopped
- 1 lemon, quartered, to serve
- bread or toast, to serve
- sea salt and black pepper

Scrub the clams under cold running water and discard any that are open or have broken shells, or that do not shut immediately when sharply tapped. In a large pan, heat the oil over medium heat. Add the garlic and cook for a few seconds until it begins to color. Add the clams and toss with the garlic and oil. Pour in the sherry and add half the parsley, shaking the pan as you go. Simmer for about 1 minute to burn off the alcohol in the sherry, then, when the clams are fully opened (throw away any that are still closed), taste for seasoning. The clams may not need any salt. Sprinkle the rest of the parsley over the top and serve with the lemon quarters and lots of bread or toast.

Note: In this recipe we use manzanilla sherry from Sanlúcar de Barrameda. It is a dry sherry with a slightly salty tang, and it goes perfectly with fish and shellfish.

PORK SKEWERS

INGREDIENTS

- 1 x 1 lb 2-oz (500-g) pork fillet, trimmed of fat and sinew
- sea salt and black pepper

FOR THE MARINADE:

- 1 generous pinch saffron
- generous ½ teaspoon coriander seeds, roughly ground
- generous ½ teaspoon cumin seeds, roughly ground
- generous ½ teaspoon fennel seeds, roughly ground
- 1 teaspoon sweet smoked Spanish paprika
- 2 cloves garlic, crushed to a paste with a little salt
- ½ small bunch fresh oregano, roughly chopped, or 1 teaspoon dried oregano
- 1 bay leaf, preferably fresh, crumbled or very finely chopped
- 2 teaspoons red-wine vinegar
- 2 teaspoons olive oil

As the name suggests, pinchitos morunos are skewers of meat (originally lamb, but nowadays mainly pork) marinated in a mixture of Moorish spices and grilled over charcoal. You will need 4 wooden or metal skewers about 10 inches (25 cm) long or 8 skewers 6 inches (15 cm) long.

Cut the pork fillet in half lengthwise and then into 1-inch (2.5-cm) cubes. Flatten the cubes slightly. Dissolve the saffron in 2 tablespoons boiling water. Place the pork in a large mixing bowl, add the saffron and the rest of the marinade ingredients except the oil and mix thoroughly. Then add the oil, toss again, cover and transfer to the refrigerator for 2 hours to allow the meat to marinate.

Grilling the pork over charcoal produces the best flavor, so light the barbecue a good half hour before cooking. Alternatively, heat a ridged cast-iron skillet or griddle over high heat until smoking hot. Thread the pork onto the skewers and cook over high heat for about 2 minutes each side, or until slightly charred on the outside but still juicy on the inside. Season with salt and pepper and serve immediately.

ALBERTO HERRAÍZ

Born into a family of Spanish cooks, Alberto Herraíz moved to France in 1997, where he opened Fogón restaurant in Paris, specializing in authentic paella and tapas dishes. Despite moving away from Spain, he maintains a deep and pure connection with his culinary heritage, and explores the full possibilities of traditional tapas by combining gastronomic traditions with contemporary cooking techniques to produce sophisticated and creative bite-size dishes.

SAINT JACQUES ET OURSIN DE MER

SCALLOPS AND SEA URCHINS

INGREDIENTS

- 1 tablespoon butter
- 2 tablespoons olive oil
- 1 onion, thinly sliced
- ½ leek, thinly sliced
- generous 3 tablespoons (50 ml/ 2 fl oz) dry white wine
- 9 oz (250 g) sea urchin meat
- 1 generous cup (250 ml/8 fl oz) sea urchin liquid
- 2 generous cups (500 ml/ 18 fl oz) cream
- 10 scallops, shucked and cleaned

Heat the butter and oil in a skillet or frying pan over low heat. Add the onion and leek and cook until soft. Add the white wine and cook for 1 minute. Add the sea urchin meat and its liquid, and the cream. Bring the mixture to a boil, then remove from the heat and set aside. When cool, transfer the mixture to a blender and puree to a liquid. Strain through a fine-mesh strainer into a bowl and season with salt and pepper. Put the sea urchin mousse mixture into a siphon and charge with 2 cartridges. Keep it warm in a bain marie. When ready to serve, place a little sea urchin mousse onto small serving plates and heat a ridged cast-iron skillet, frying pan or griddle to high. Cook the scallops on one side only, until just cooked through, then arrange them on top of the sea urchin mousse, and serve immediately.

CORNET DE FOIS GRAS ET JAMBON
IBÉRIQUE

IBERIAN HAM AND FOIE GRAS CONES

INGREDIENTS

- 10 x 5½-inch (14-cm) circular spring roll wrappers, cut in half
- 2 oz (50 g) mi-cuit foie gras
- 1 teaspoon Pedro Ximenez sherry
- 10 small slices Iberian ham
- melted butter, for brushing

Preheat the oven to 300°F (150°C/GAS MARK 2). Make cones with the spring roll wrappers by wrapping each semicircle around a large pastry (piping) bag tip (nozzle), and bringing the cut edges together. Brush the cut edges lightly with butter to help seal the join. It is best to use 2 layers of wrappers on each tip. Transfer the cones to a baking sheet and cook for 9 minutes. Set aside. In a blender, puree the foie gras with the sherry. Spoon the mixture into a pastry bag and transfer to the refrigerator to keep cool.

About 15 minutes before serving, remove the foie gras mixture from the refrigerator and allow to come back to room temperature. Pipe the mixture into the cones, and add a thin slice of ham before serving.

BOCADILLO DE SARDINE ET HUILE
DE SAUGE

SARDINE AND SAGE OIL BOCADILLO

INGREDIENTS

- 10 boned sardine fillets
- day-old French baguette, cut into ¾ inch (2 cm) thick slices
- 3 bunches sage
- 1¼ cups (300 ml/½ pint) olive oil
- Guérande salt, to serve

Place a sardine fillet on each slice of bread, and top with another slice of bread to make sandwiches. Bring a pan of salted water to a boil. Add the sage and blanch for 1 minute, then drain and place the sage under cold running water to stop the cooking process. Transfer the sage to a blender and puree to a liquid, then, with the motor running, gradually add the olive oil. Strain through a fine-mesh strainer into a bowl.

To serve, brown the sandwiches on a ridged cast-iron skillet or frying pan, barbecue or griddle and brush with sage oil. Sprinkle the Guérande salt over the top and serve immediately.

ALEXANDRA RAIJ
AND EDER MONTERO

Alexandra Raij and Eder Montero are the husband and wife chef team behind the Basque tapas restaurant Txikito in New York City. Montero was born in Bilbao, northern Spain, and cooked under chefs such as Carles Abellan and Xavi Sagristà before meeting Raij, who had found an affinity for Spanish techniques and flavors at Meigas restaurant in the USA. Together they opened Txikito, aiming to recreate the classic Basque simplicity and excellence in ingredients and techniques, from simple bar food to more sophisticated dishes.

ALBÓNDIGAS DE BONITO DEL NORTE Y ATÚN FRESCO

CRISPY TUNA AND BONITO
CAKES WITH MAYONNAISE

INGREDIENTS

- 12 oz (350 g) center-cut sushi-grade tuna
- 2 tablespoons parsley
- 2 tablespoons fresh marjoram
- 3 scallions (spring onions)
- 1 cup firmly packed canned bonito del Norte, drained
- ¼ cup finely chopped red onion
- ¾ cup (175 g/6 oz) mayonnaise, plus extra for serving
- 2½ cups (175 g/6 oz) panko bread crumbs
- ¼ teaspoon cayenne pepper
- 5 cups (1.2 litres/2 pints) canola oil, for frying
- salt

Remove all the connective tissue from the tuna and cut the flesh into chunks. Transfer to a blender and pulse 5 or 6 times. Roughly chop the parsley and marjoram, and finely chop the scallion. Mix the tuna, canned bonito, herbs, onions, and a little salt in a mixing bowl. Add the mayonnaise, bread crumbs and cayenne pepper and stir to combine. Adjust the seasoning to taste. Cover the bowl and let rest in the refrigerator for 20 minutes.

Roll the mixture firmly into 1½-inch (3.5-cm) balls. Meanwhile, heat the canola oil in a deep-fryer or deep pan to 350–375°F (180–190°C) or until a cube of bread browns in 30 seconds. Add the balls carefully, in batches, and cook until crisp and golden brown. Using a slotted spoon, carefully remove the balls from the hot oil and transfer to paper towel to drain. Serve immediately, with a little extra mayonnaise on the side.

MARINATED WHITE ANCHOVY AND EGGPLANT (AUBERGINE) PINTXO

INGREDIENTS

- 16 slices French baguette
- 16 boquerones (marinated white anchovies)
- 2 canned Piquillo peppers, sliced into thin ribbons 2 inches (5 cm) in length
- 2 hard-cooked eggs, halved and thinly sliced
- chopped parsley, to garnish
- olive oil, for drizzling

FOR THE EGGPLANT (AUBERGINE) PUREE:

- 1 medium eggplant (aubergine)
- 3 cloves garlic, peeled
- 2 tablespoons olive oil
- 2 tablespoons mayonnaise, preferably homemade
- 1½ teaspoons lemon juice
- salt

To make the eggplant puree, preheat the oven to 450°F (230°C/ GAS MARK 8). Make 3 slits in the eggplant and push a garlic clove into each. Set the eggplant on a 12-inch (30-cm) square of aluminum foil and drizzle with the oil. Season generously with salt, wrap tightly in the foil, transfer to the oven and roast for about 25 minutes, or until tender. Let cool, then peel the eggplant, discarding the skin, and puree the flesh and garlic cloves in a blender until smooth. With the motor still running, add the mayonnaise and lemon juice. Season to taste and chill before using.

To make the pintxo, lightly toast the bread on both sides. Spread a thin layer of eggplant puree over one side of each slice of toast and top with an open anchovy (skin-side up). Place a ribbon of piquillo pepper down the center of each pintxo. Top with a slice of egg and a pinch of parsley, and finish with a drizzle of olive oil.

Note: If boquerones are not available, substitute Italian marinated anchovies, or other marinated white anchovies. Piquillo peppers are widely available, but homemade roasted and skinned sweet red bell pepper can be substituted.

SEAMUS MULLEN

BOQUERIA, NEW YORK CITY, USA
BOQUERIA SOHO, NEW YORK CITY,
USA

Born and raised in Vermont, USA, Seamus Mullen spent several years studying in Spain, during which he developed a life-long love affair with Spanish food and culture. This was followed by stints at several restaurants, including Mugaritz in San Sebastián, northern Spain, and New York City's Brasserie 8½. Seeking to recreate the casual bars he had enjoyed while living in Spain, he opened Boqueria in New York City in 2006, where local ingredients are fully integrated with classic Spanish techniques and flavors. In 2008 he opened a second restaurant in SoHo.

MANCHEGO ADOBADO

MARINATED CHEESE

INGREDIENTS
– 1 lb (450 g) Manchego cheese, cut into ½-inch (1-cm) cubes
– generous 2 cups (500 ml/ 18 fl oz) Arbequina or other good-quality extra-virgin olive oil
– 1 sprig rosemary
– 1 sprig thyme
– 1 tablespoon whole black peppercorns
– 2 dried guindilla peppers, or 1 teaspoon red pepper flakes

Mix all the ingredients together in a bowl. Cover, transfer to the refrigerator and let marinate overnight. Serve with toothpicks (cocktail sticks).

COLES BE BRUSELAS Y CHORIZO

BRUSSELS SPROUTS WITH CHORIZO

INGREDIENTS

- 1 tablespoon extra-virgin olive oil
- 1 lb (450 g) Brussels sprouts, cut in half, with stems removed
- 8 oz (225 g) chorizo, diced
- 1 tablespoon butter
- 1 tablespoon lemon juice
- generous 2 cups (500 ml/ 18 fl oz) chicken stock
- salt and pepper

Heat the oil in a large pan over medium-high heat until the oil runs easily across the bottom. Add the sprouts cut-side down and cook, without stirring, until lightly browned. Add the chorizo and cook for about 2 minutes, until the fat is released, shaking the pan so the chorizo doesn't stick. Add the butter, lemon juice, chicken stock and season with salt and pepper to taste. Reduce the heat and simmer for about 5 minutes, or until the liquid is reduced and the sprouts are tender.

PINTXO DE GAMBA
AL AJILLO

SHRIMP (PRAWN) SKEWER WITH GARLIC AND GUINDILLA PEPPER

INGREDIENTS

- 3 oz (80 g) fresh rock shrimp (prawns)
- 2 dried guindilla peppers, or 1 teaspoon red pepper flakes
- 1 clove garlic, thinly sliced lengthwise
- 1 teaspoon chopped parsley
- ¼ cup (60 ml/2 fl oz) olive oil
- salt and pepper
- 4 x 6-inch (15-cm) bamboo skewers

Divide the shrimp between the bamboo skewers and place in a shallow dish. Mix the peppers, garlic, parsley and oil together in a bowl and pour over the top of the skewers, turning them to ensure they are completely coated. Cover the dish, transfer to the refrigerator and leave to marinate overnight.

Heat a ridged cast-iron skillet or frying pan or griddle over high heat. Season the skewers with salt and pepper, and cook for 2 minutes each side, or until the shrimp are cooked through. Serve immediately.

JOSÉ PIZARRO

José Pizarro has been the head chef and co-owner of Tapas Brindisa in London's Borough Market for more than five years. In 2009 he also opened Tierra Brindisa in Soho and Casa Brindisa in South Kensington. José trained as a chef in Cáceres in western Spain, before moving to Madrid to the award-winning Meson de Dona Filo where he began his love affair with fresh, brightly flavored dishes, before moving to London. His television appearances and cookbooks have brought his expertise in Spanish cuisine to a wide audience.

ARROZ CON LECHE

RICE PUDDING

INGREDIENTS

- 4 cups (1 litre/1¾ pints) milk
- 1 small cinnamon stick
- zest of ½ lemon, pith removed
- zest of ½ orange, pith removed
- generous ½ cup (125 g/4½ oz) Calasparra or other short-grain rice
- scant 1 cup (100 g/3½ oz) superfine (caster) sugar
- ½ teaspoon ground cinnamon

Put the milk, cinnamon stick, and lemon and orange zest in a pan, and bring to a boil. Remove the pan from the heat and leave the milk to infuse for 30 minutes. Discard the citrus zest and cinnamon stick.

Return the milk to the heat and bring to a simmer. Add the rice and cook, stirring constantly, over a low to medium heat for 10 minutes. Add the sugar, and continue to stir over a low heat for another 10 minutes. Remove the pan from the stove (hob) and leave the mixture to cool. Divide the rice between 4 small bowls and dust with the ground cinnamon before serving.

SALT COD WITH GARBANZO BEANS (CHICKPEAS) AND EGGS

INGREDIENTS

- 14 oz (400 g) salt cod fillets
- 4 cups (1 litre/1¾ pints) milk
- ½ small onion
- 1 bay leaf
- 3 cloves garlic
- 1 teaspoon black peppercorns
- 2 large free-range eggs,
  at room temperature
- 2 tablespoons extra-virgin
  olive oil
- ½ red onion, finely chopped
- 7 oz (200 g) garbanzo beans
  (chickpeas), canned or ready
  cooked
- 1 tablespoon lemon juice
- 1 tablespoon chopped parsley
- sea salt and black pepper

The day before you plan to serve the dish, put the salt cod fillets skin-side up in a large bowl and cover with plenty of cold water. Cover, put in the refrigerator and let soak for 24 hours, changing the water every 6 hours or so. To check if the cod is ready, take a little piece of flesh from the thickest part and taste it. It should still be a little bit salty, but not too much.

Put the milk, onion, bay leaf, 2 of the garlic cloves, the peppercorns and the cod in a pan. Bring to a boil and immediately turn off the heat, then leave the fish in the milk for another 5 minutes. Remove the fillet from the milk and, when cool enough to handle, carefully remove all the bones and skin with your fingers.

Meanwhile, bring some water to a boil in a clean pan. Add 1 teaspoon salt, lower the eggs into the water and boil for 6 minutes. Remove the eggs immediately and plunge them into iced water. This method should produce eggs with a runny yolk but a firm white. Shell the eggs. Finely chop the remaining garlic clove. Heat the olive oil in a wok or a skillet or frying pan. Add the chopped garlic and red onion and cook over medium heat for 5 minutes, or until golden. Add the garbanzo beans and the cod. Season with caution (remember the cod will still be salty), then add the lemon juice and chopped parsley and stir to combine.

Divide the mixture between 4 warmed plates. Cut the eggs in half and place yolk-side up on top of each serving.

ALBERT RAURICH

SALT-CRUSTED ORGANIC
...........AS THE EGG

DOS PALLILOS, BARCELONA, SPAIN

Born in Barcelona, Albert Raurich worked at several restaurants in Catalonia before joining elBulli in 1997, becoming head chef in 2001. While he was there, he created the concept of an Asian tapas bar with Ferran Adrià, and Dos Pallilos opened its doors in Barcelona in April 2008, serving Asian dim-sum-inspired dishes in a typical Spanish tapas setting.

OSTRA A LA PARILLA CON SAKE

GRILLED OYSTERS WITH SAKE

INGREDIENTS
- 10 oysters, 7 oz (200 g) each
- cooking salt, to serve
- 10 tablespoons sake mixed with 4 tablespoons reserved oyster juices

Open the oysters, keeping the bottom shell upright to avoid spilling the juices. Lift out the oysters and strain the juices through a muslin-lined sieve into a bowl, saving the bottom shell to serve them in. Cut the beard off the oysters and place them in the bowl with the juices. Cover and transfer to the refrigerator until ready to cook. Spread the cooking salt out on a serving plate. Heat a ridged cast-iron skillet, frying pan or griddle until hot. Place the oyster shells on the skillet or griddle, making sure they do not fall over. Divide the sake and oyster juices between the shells. When the liquid comes to a boil, place an oyster in each shell and immediately remove it from the skillet or griddle. Transfer the shells to the serving plate. Serve immediately, informing guests to eat the oyster quickly, then wait 25 seconds before drinking the sake, as the oyster shell will be very hot.

SEAWEED AND MOLLUSK SUNOMONO

INGREDIENTS
- ¼ oz (10 g) laurencia seaweed
- ¾ oz (18 g) codium seaweed

FOR THE COOKING LIQUID:
- ⅓ cup (80 g/2¾ oz) sugar
- ¾ cup (200 ml/7 fl oz) rice vinegar
- 4 cups (1 litre/1¾ pints) mineral water

FOR THE SUNOMONO VINAIGRETTE:
- ⅔ cup (130 g/4½ oz) sugar
- 2 teaspoons sea salt
- 1¼ cups (260 ml/9 fl oz) rice vinegar
- generous 2 cups (500 ml/18 fl oz) dashi stock
- 4 teaspoons yuzu juice

FOR THE SEAWEED:
- 1¼ oz (40 g) gigartina seaweed
- 2¾ oz (80 g) carrageen
- 3½ oz (100 g) green sea beans
- ¼ oz (10 g) sea lettuce

FOR THE MOLLUSKS:
- 1 lb 5 oz (600 g) cockles, cleaned
- 1 lb 10½ oz (750 g) cañaillas (a variety of mollusk similar to a large winkle), cleaned

To make the cooking liquid, mix the sugar, rice vinegar and mineral water in a pan. Heat to 175°F (80°C) over low heat, stirring well to dissolve the sugar. Remove from the heat and let cool. Next, make the sunomono vinaigrette: put the sugar, salt and rice vinegar in a bowl and stir thoroughly to dissolve the sugar. Add the dashi stock and the yuzu juice, stir again and set aside.

To cook the seaweed, bring half the cooking liquid to a boil in a pan and have a dish of iced water nearby. Add the gigartina seaweed to the pan and cook for 10 seconds, then remove with a slotted spoon and transfer to the iced water. Next, add the carrageen to the pan and cook for 14 seconds. Remove with a slotted spoon and transfer to the remaining (cool) half of the cooking liquid. Finally add the green sea beans to the pan and cook for 14 seconds. Remove and transfer to the bowl with the carrageen. Set the bowl aside but leave the pan on the heat. Cut the sea lettuce into pieces measuring 2⅓ x 2⅓ inches (6 x 6 cm). Place them in a sealed container, alternating them with sheets of nonstick paper to prevent them sticking. Pour in the hot liquid, leave for 1 second and then pour it out.

To cook the mollusks, heat a pan of salted water to 212°F (100°C). Add the cockles and cook for about 10 seconds, or until they open. Drain and set aside, reserving the liquid. Put the cañaillas into the pan, cover with water and a little salt and bring to a boil. Drain and set aside, reserving the liquid. When cool enough to handle, carefully remove the cañaillas from their shells, remove and reserve their intestines. Place the cañaillas and the intestines in a sealed container and add their reserved cooking liquid. Remove the cockles from their shells and transfer them to a separate sealed container, along with their reserved cooking liquid. One hour before serving, drain the seaweed and transfer to the bowl with the sunomono vinaigrette. Spoon a generous amount of seaweed onto 10 small plates, mixing the raw seaweed with the cooked. Alternate 4 cockles, 3 cañaillas and 2 cañailla intestines on top of each plate of seaweed. Dress with the sunomono vinaigrette.

DIRECTORY

The following stores stock high quality Spanish products such as chorizo, Serrano ham, olive oil, cheese and other items used in these recipes.

UNITED STATES
EAST COAST
Despaña
408 Broome Street
New York, NY 10013
+1 212 219 5050
www.despananyc.com

SOUTH EAST
A Southern Season
201 S. Estes Drive
University Mall
Chapel Hill, NC 27514
+1 800 253 3663
www.asouthernseason.com

La Tienda
1325 Jamestown Road
Williamsburg, VA 23185
+1 888 331 4362
www.latienda.com

MIDWEST
Zingerman's
422 Detroit Street
Ann Arbor, MI 48104
+1 734 663 3354
www.zingermans.com

WEST COAST
La Española Meats, Inc.
25020 Doble Avenue
Harbor City, CA 90710
+1 310 539 0455
www.laespanolameats.com

The Spanish Table (4 locations)
1426 Western Avenue
Seattle, WA 98101
+1 206 682 2827

1814 San Pablo Avenue
Berkeley, CA 94702
+1 510 548 1383

123 Strawberry Village
Mill Valley, CA 94941
+1 415 388 5043

109 N Guadalupe Street
Santa Fe, NM 87501
+1 505 986 0243
www.spanishtable.com

CANADA
Pasquale Bros. Downtown Ltd.
16 Goodrich Road
Etobicoke, Ontario
M8Z 4Z8
+1 416 364 7397
www.pasqualebros.com

UNITED KINGDOM
LONDON
Bayley & Sage
60 High Street
Wimbledon Village
London SW19 5EE
+44 (0)20 8946 9904

Brindisa
The Floral Hall
Borough Market, Stoney Street
London SE1 9AF
+44 (0)20 7407 1036
www.brindisa.com

East Dulwich Deli
15–17 Lordship Lane
London SE22 8EW
+44 (0)20 8693 2525
www.eastdulwichdeli.com

Iberica
195 Great Portland Street
London W1W 5PS
+44 (0)20 7636 8650

R Garcia & Sons
248–250 Portobello Road
London W11 1LL
+44 (0)20 7221 6119

Raoul's Deli
8–10 Clifton Road
London W9 1SS
+44 (0)20 7289 6649
www.raoulsgourmet.com

THE SOUTH
Williams & Brown
28a Harbour Street, Whitstable
Kent CT5 1AH
+44 (0)1227 274 507

Chandos Deli
6 Princess Victoria Street, Clifton
Bristol BS8 4BP
+44 (0)1179 743 275
www.chandosdeli.com

Effings
50 Fore Street, Totnes
Devon TQ9 5RP
+44 (0)1803 863435
www.effings.co.uk

THE NORTH
Appleyards
85 Wyle Cop, Shrewsbury
Shropshire SY1 1UT
+44 (0)1743 240 180

RECIPE NOTES

Define Food & Wine
Chester Road, Sandiway
Cheshire CW8 2NH
+44 (0)1606 882 101
www.definefoodandwine.com

Roberts & Speight
40 Norwood, Beverley
East Yorkshire HU17 9EY
+44 (0)1482 870 717
www.hamperbox.co.uk

AUSTRALIA
Delicado Foods
134 Blues Point Road
McMahons Point
Sydney NSW 2060
+61 2 9955 9399
www.delicadofoods.com.au

Casa Iberica
25 Johnston Street
Fitzroy
Melbourne VIC 3065
+61 3 9417 7106

Alimento Deli
99 Smith Street
Summer Hill
Sydney NSW 2130
+61 2 9797 2484
www.alimentodeli.com.au

El Mercado
72 Tennyson Road
Mortlake
Sydney NSW 2137
+61 2 8757 3700

Unless otherwise stated, milk is assumed to be whole.

Unless otherwise stated, eggs are assumed to be large and individual vegetables and fruits, such as onions and apples, are assumed to be medium.

Unless otherwise stated, all herbs are fresh, and parsley is flat-leaf parsley.

Unless otherwise stated, pepper is freshly ground black pepper. Some recipes call for fresh yeast. If unavailable, substitute 1 teaspoon instant dry yeast for ¼ oz (10 g) fresh yeast.

Cooking times are for guidance only, as individual ovens and stoves vary. If using a fan oven, follow the manufacturer's instructions concerning oven temperatures.

To test whether your deep-frying oil is hot enough, add a cube of stale bread. If it browns in 30 seconds, the temperature is 350–375°F (180–190°C), about right for most frying. Exercise caution when deep frying. Wear long sleeves and never leave the pan unattended.

Some recipes include raw or very lightly cooked eggs. These should be avoided by the elderly, infants, pregnant women, convalescents and anyone with an impaired immune system.

Cup, metric and imperial measures are given throughout, and UK equivalents are given in brackets. Follow one set of measurements, not a mixture, as they are not interchangeable.

All cup and spoon measurements are level.
1 cup = 8 fl oz; 1 teaspoon = 5 ml; 1 tablespoon = 15 ml. Australian standard tablespoons are 20 ml, so Australian readers are advised to use 3 teaspoons in place of 1 tablespoon when measuring small quantities.

Note that the number of servings yielded is based on serving several dishes at once, tapas-style.

Inés Ortega would like to dedicate the book to her
son, José, who inspired her, and who tasted many
of the recipes.

Phaidon Press Inc.
180 Varick Street
New York, NY 10014

Phaidon Press Limited
Regent's Wharf
All Saints Street
London N1 9PA

www.phaidon.com

First published 2010
© 2010 Phaidon Press Limited
ISBN 978 0 7148 5613 1

A CIP catalogue record for this book is available from
the British Library.

Translated by Equipo de Edición and Angela Bradford
Designed by Pablo Martín (Grafica)
Photographs by Mauricio Salinas
Printed in China